W9-COF-906

faith is a star

faith is a star

WRITTEN AND EDITED BY

ROLAND GAMMON

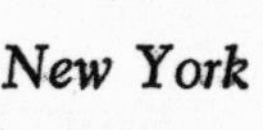

New York *E. P. Dutton & Co., Inc.*
1963

 * First Edition.

Published simultaneously in Canada by Clarke, Irwin & Company Limited, Toronto and Vancouver

Library of Congress Catalog Card Number: 62-14730

Paul De Kruif. From "Research for a Prayer," *Guideposts,* August 1954

Catherine Marshall. From "How You Can Find God's Guidance," *Guideposts,* July 1954

James A. Pike. From *Doing the Truth,* Doubleday & Company, Inc., New York, © 1955

Bobby Richardson. From a leaflet published by the American Tract Society, Oradell, New Jersey

Carlos P. Romulo. From *I Walked with Heroes,* Holt, Rinehart and Winston, Inc., New York, © 1961

Warner Sallman. From "The Story Behind a Picture," *Guideposts,* February 1962

Edward Durell Stone. From *The Evolution of an Architect,* Horizon Press, Inc., New York, © 1962

Lowell Thomas. From an article in *Christian Herald,* June 1961

Paul Tillich. From *Dynamics of Faith,* Harper & Row, Publishers, Inc., New York, © 1957

Elton Trueblood. From *The Life We Prize,* Harper & Row, Publishers, Inc., New York, © 1951

The beliefs and opinions expressed by the individuals writing for this collection of interviews are not necessarily those of the Radio–Television Commission which commissioned this book. Neither does the individual who appears on "*Master Control*" radio nor the thoughts he or she expresses in this book necessarily indicate any connection with the Southern Baptist Convention.

Introductory Chapter

"Religion," wrote that sublime Scotsman Thomas Carlyle, "is the chief fact with regard to a man." By religion Carlyle did not mean a man's church creed or profession of faith, but "the thing a man does practically believe, the thing a man does practically lay to his heart and knows for certain concerning his vital relations to this mysterious universe, and his duty and destiny here . . . and I say, if you tell me what that is, you tell me to a very great extent what the man is, what the kind of things he will do is. Of a man or of a nation we inquire, therefore, first of all, what religion they had."

This book is such an inquiry. It tells the story of the daily practical religion of a variety of American leaders. It represents three years of determined, delighted entry into the councils of the great and the company of the holy to ask: "What is your faith and what part has it played in your life achievement?" Their diverse yet spiritually affirmative answers confirm in an age of doubt and dread that religion is still the "chief fact" in the lives of heroic men and women.

But books, unlike "Beauty old yet ever new," do not spring full blown from the brow of Zeus. Before they can become even leaky skiffs sailing the seas of wisdom they must be planned, blueprinted, built, and finally launched. So this one. It all began in 1960 when, lunching with Ware Lynch, a New York friend and public relations executive, and Dr. Paul Stevens, director of the Radio and Television Commission of the Southern Baptist Convention, I learned that *Master Control*, the Convention's network radio show, featured religious interviews with distinguished Americans. Here, we agreed, was the stuff of a book—so I set to work in the mood of *Heroes and Hero Worship*.

The three-year passage, now ending, has been an adventurous one. Working closely with the Commission, using recorded material from *Master Control*, talking directly with the divines, statesmen, scholars, physicists, artists, authors, athletes, actors, soldiers, missionaries, movie stars, opera singers, homemakers, empire builders—and occasionally those lesser-known yet equally worthy Christians and Jews for whom also "Faith Is a Star"—has been an enriching experience. Now I can only hope that their collective witness of God's eternal voice and inward word will mean as much to the reader as it has to me. For here, indeed, is God's plenty; here is the place the Light shines through.

To the author, their revelation of truth is deep. To the reader, he that seeketh, findeth. To all who pursue a better way and a truer understanding, their testimony touches where God and man meet, where the mystery of life lightens, where self-knowledge becomes self-mastery. Herein the blessed truths of the omnipresence of God, the comfort of Christ, the dignity of man, the reality of brotherhood, the joys of the spirit, the miracle of love, the gift of grace, the overcoming of sin, the power of prayer—"The eternal God is thy dwelling place and underneath are the everlasting arms"—all are freshly reaffirmed and reaffirmed in a personal, persuasive, *yea*-saying way that provides new inspiration for us all.

I cannot close without gratefully acknowledging the professional help and ready cooperation of Dr. Stevens and his assistant, Clarence Duncan; of my researcher, Lenore Fleming, and secretaries Muriel Knapp and Ruth Atkinson. When this book's inevitable sequel begins its "collection of the seeds of light," I am determined to assemble this superb team again.

ROLAND GAMMON

New York, N.Y.
Summer 1963

Contents

Contents

faith is a star

GEORGE ROMNEY

"The glory of God and Man is intelligence."

* * *

A phenomenal success story in American business in the 1950's, George Romney catapulted into the national political scene in the 1960's when he became Republican Governor of Michigan. As the dynamic president of American Motors Corporation, he launched his single-minded crusade in 1954 against Detroit's "frozen big-car mentality" and introduced the Rambler, America's first economical compact car, into the huge automotive market. As the business phenomenon of American Motors' fantastic commercial comeback (its seventy-million-dollar indebtedness was paid off in four years, and the company rose from twelfth to sixth in national sales), he moved as a political independent in 1962 to win the State's Republican nomination and defeated Democratic incumbent John Swainson for the governorship.

The missionary zeal that has characterized George Romney's business and political careers comes naturally to a man whose forebears were Mormon pioneers. Brought up in Salt Lake City, educated at the University of Utah, and successively a deacon, teacher, elder, and missionary in the Mormon Church, he later headed the Automobile Manufacturers Association, served as working chairman of the Detroit Citizens Advisory Committee on School Needs, and helped organize a non-partisan Citizens for Michigan Committee. Until elected Governor of Michigan, he served as president of the Detroit Stake of the Church of Jesus Christ of Latter-day Saints.

* * *

A Yardstick to Measure Life's Values

MY RELIGION IS MY MOST PRECIOUS POSSESSION. IT TEACHES ME THE purpose of life and answers life's greatest questions: where we come from, why we are here, and where we are going. It provides me with yardsticks for life based on eternal values.

Some of these values are:

The end of all learning is to know God and, knowing Him, to love Him and strive to be like Him.

The greatest power on earth is that portion of God's power which He has delegated to men.

The glory of God and the glory of man is intelligence—knowledge used correctly.

When we serve our fellowmen, we serve our God.

Every person has a gift or gifts, and developing them and helping others to do so through self-expression is one of life's greatest achievements, the best example of which is parenthood.

There is no end to personality, character, or progress.

Our physical body is the temple of our eternal spirit.

The Holy Bible contains so many eternal truths, it is difficult to say which one is most important. However, the one expressed in the first chapter, fifth verse of James probably has had the greatest impact on my life. It contains a glorious promise and an infallible rule for resolving our uncertainties of fears arising from lack of knowledge or understanding. It reads:

"If any of you lack wisdom, let him ask of God, who giveth to all men liberally, and upbraideth not; and it shall be given him. But let him ask in faith, nothing doubting, for he that doubteth is like the surge of the sea driven by the wind and tossed."

Acting on this principle I have gained a priceless possession—a knowledge that God, our Father in Heaven, lives; that Jesus is the Christ, having been His only earthly son. Also, I have found this wisdom formula useful in resolving many perplexing problems in my own life.

Life today is far more complex and baffling than it has ever been. The expansion of man's knowledge has surpassed his ability to comprehend more than a fraction of what is known. Then too, everything we know on earth exists in an imperfect form. Thus the need for Divine guidance is understandable. As a former businessman and now a public official, I am aware of the need for wisdom in dealing with complex matters that involve the lives of others. Decisions affecting their material and social welfare must be made that require more knowledge than anyone can obtain in a lifetime.

Because of my religion, I have used this wisdom formula when making some personal decisions. It has worked, not immediately in some cases but with such certainty that I have known its fulfillment. I know it will work for anyone, regardless of his religion, race, or status, because its conditions can be met by anyone.

To me, it is as natural to use this formula in seeking economic, social, and political guidance as in matters of faith and worship. In my opinion those individuals and institutions reflecting the greatest degree of spiritual and moral truth are eventually the most successful. I agree with Thomas Carlyle who said, "It is the spiritual always that determines the material."

The most obvious proof of this is our own country. Its political institutions were founded on certain basic spiritual and moral truths.

They have helped shape our economic and social institutions which, while far from perfect, have given us the greatest material abundance in history. In the long run, spiritual progress and material and social progress go hand in hand.

However, even America has realized only a few of its potentialities. Furthermore, our superior material abundance is threatening to destroy the very spiritual foundation on which it rests. Either we go forward in applying spiritual and moral truths to our lives and institutions, or we fall back and lose the greatest opportunity any people ever had.

We face constant change. The tensions and uncertainties that result can be replaced with confident serenity by truths God has revealed to guide His children, and by asking Him for wisdom where additional personal guidance is needed.

Considering the extent to which our actions fall short of the guidance God gives, I am comforted by two thoughts:

A poet encouragingly wrote, "I aspired, and though I achieved not, I was satisfied."

The late and great William S. Knudsen said to me, "No man ever stumbles sitting down. When we stumble, we are at least trying."

WALT DISNEY

"Children are our most precious product."

*   *   *

Walt Disney, Hollywood producer and showman, became world famous in the 1920's with the creation of a comic cartoon character—Mickey Mouse. Since then, he has added, among others, such lovable personalities as Snow White, Bambi, Dopey, and Donald Duck to the Disney cast, and has produced hundreds of animated shorts and fifty-seven full-length motion pictures. In the process he has captured twenty-nine Academy Awards and has been honored with more than seven hundred others from around the world. In 1955 he built Disneyland Park near Los Angeles, which rapidly attracted children of all ages from the ends of the earth, including such notable ones as President Eisenhower and Prime Minister Nehru of India.

Walt Disney was born in Chicago in 1901 of parents of Canadian–Irish–German descent. Later, while growing up on a Missouri farm and going to high school in Kansas City, he attended the Congregational Church and Sunday school. Like any other enterprising American, Walt's first business venture was a newspaper route at age nine. His first art job was at a Kansas City advertising agency where for fifty dollars a month he drew such inspiring objects as salt blocks, egg-laying mash, and contented cows. In 1923 he went to Hollywood and with his brother Roy began producing films in the rear of a garage.

The Disney Studio today covers fifty-one acres in Burbank, with four sound-stages, a theater that seats five hundred and fifty persons, and the most modern animation and live-action facilities in the industry.

Still winning Academy Awards, university honorary degrees, magazine, club, and film festival citations by the dozen, Disney is busier than ever with a full schedule of both cartoon and "live" films. In addition, he produces the popular weekly TV program, "The Wonderful World of Color," over the NBC Network. To Walt Disney, his work has barely begun, for he sees "the cartoon industry as our greatest medium of fantasy . . . whose possibilities are absolutely unlimited."

*   *   *

Deeds Rather Than Words

In these days of world tensions, when the faith of men is being tested as never before, I am personally thankful that my parents taught me at a very early age to have a strong personal belief and reliance in the power of prayer for Divine inspiration. My people were members of the Congregational Church in our home town of Marceline, Missouri. It was there where I was first taught the efficacy of religion . . . how it helps us immeasurably to meet the trial and stress of life and keeps us attuned to the Divine inspiration. Later in De Molay, I learned to believe in the basic principle of the right of man to exercise his faith and thoughts as he chooses. In De Molay, we believe in a supreme being, in the fellowship of man, and the sanctity of the home. De Molay stands for all that is good for the family and for our country.

Every person has his own ideas of the act of praying for God's guidance, tolerance, and mercy to fulfill his duties and responsibilities. My own concept of prayer is not as a plea for special favors nor as a quick palliation for wrongs knowingly committed. A prayer, it seems to me, implies a promise as well as a request; at the highest level, prayer not only is a supplication for strength and guidance, but also becomes an affirmation of life and thus a reverent praise of God.

Deeds rather than words express my concept of the part religion should play in everyday life. I have watched constantly that in our movie work the highest moral and spiritual standards are upheld, whether it deals with fable or with stories of living action. This religious concern for the form and content of our films goes back forty years to the rugged financial period in Kansas City when I was struggling to establish a film company and produce animated fairy tales. Many times during those difficult years, even as we turned out "Alice in Cartoonland" and later in Hollywood the first "Mickey Mouse," we were under pressure to sell out or debase the subject matter or go "commercial" in one way or another. But we stuck it out—my brother Roy and other loyal associates—until the success of "Mickey Mouse" and "Silly Symphonies" finally put us in the black. Similarly, when war came to the United States in 1941, we turned from profitable popular movie-making to military production for Uncle Sam. Ninety-four per cent of the Disney facilities in Hollywood became engaged in special Government work, while the remainder was devoted to the creation of morale-building comedy, short subjects.

Both my study of Scripture and my career in entertaining children have taught me to cherish them. But I don't believe in playing down to children, either in life or in motion pictures. I didn't treat my own youngsters like fragile flowers, and I think no parent should.

Children are people, and they should have to reach to learn about things, to understand things, just as adults have to reach if they want to grow in mental stature. Life is composed of lights and shadows, and we would be untruthful, insincere, and saccharine if we tried to pretend there were no shadows. Most things are good, and they are the strongest things; but there are evil things too, and you are not doing a child a favor by trying to shield him from reality. The important thing is to teach a child that good can always triumph over evil, and that is what our pictures attempt to do.

The American child is a highly intelligent human being—characteristically sensitive, humorous, open-minded, eager to learn, and has a strong sense of excitement, energy, and healthy curiosity about the world in which he lives. Lucky indeed is the grown-up who manages to carry these same characteristics into adult life. It usually makes for a happy and successful individual. In our full-length cartoon features, as well as in our live-action productions, we have tried to convey in story and song those virtues that make both children and adults attractive. I have long felt that the way to keep children out of trouble is to keep them interested in things. Lecturing to children is no answer to delinquency. Preaching won't keep youngsters out of trouble, but keeping their minds occupied will.

Thus, whatever success I have had in bringing clean, informative entertainment to people of all ages, I attribute in great part to my Congregational upbringing and my lifelong habit of prayer. To me, today, at age sixty-one, all prayer, by the humble or highly placed, has one thing in common: supplication for strength and inspiration to carry on the best human impulses which should bind us together for a better world. Without such inspiration, we would rapidly deteriorate and finally perish. But in our troubled time, the right of men to think and worship as their conscience dictates is being sorely pressed. We can retain these privileges only by being constantly on guard and fighting off any encroachment on these precepts. To retreat from any of the principles handed down by our forefathers, who shed their blood for the ideals we still embrace, would be a complete victory for those who would destroy liberty and justice for the individual.

ADLAI E. STEVENSON

"Where there is no vision the people perish."

* * *

Adlai E. Stevenson, twice the Democratic nominee for President of the United States, today leads the U. S. Delegation to the United Nations. The grandson of Adlai Ewing Stevenson, Vice President of the United States during the second term of President Grover Cleveland, he has served his country in various state, national, and international capacities for thirty years.

After graduation from Choate School and from Princeton University in 1922, he studied law at Harvard and Northwestern universities. Mr. Stevenson began his long, illustrious governmental service in 1933 when he worked in the Agricultural Adjustment Administration; and in 1944 he became special assistant to Secretary of the Navy, Frank Knox. In 1943, at the direction of President Roosevelt, he headed a mission to Italy to plan the economic revival of that war-ravaged country; in 1944 he toured the European theater of war as part of an Air Force survey mission; in 1945 he became special counsel to Secretary of State Stettinius in the preparation of the United Nations organization.

Entering active politics in 1948, Mr. Stevenson was elected Governor of Illinois by the largest plurality in the history of the State. In 1952 and 1956 he was nominated by the Democratic National Convention to run for President against General Eisenhower. Mr. Stevenson was appointed to his present United Nations role by President Kennedy in 1961.

* * *

Religion—the Strength of the Republic

I BELIEVE THE CHRISTAN FAITH HAS BEEN THE MOST SIGNIFICANT single element in our history and our tradition. From the beginning, it has been the most powerful influence in our national life. It has inspired our highest achievements.

Religious faith remains, in my opinion, our greatest national resource. It animates the great majority of our adult people. It expresses itself in many ways, although there are many who find it difficult to give formal expression to that faith.

Yet it is a very real thing to most of us. We believe that there is a Creator who has given us life and the capacity and obligation to distinguish good from evil, to serve the good and oppose the evil. We feel under a constant obligation to measure up to the highest moral purposes we know, and that in the long run the good will prove to be the wise and practical and the lasting.

We think that in the tasks of government, as in all other aspects of life, it is incumbent upon us not only to serve righteousness—the good, the ideal—but at times to take risks for it.

Gilbert Chesterton once said: "If our statesmen were visionaries, something practical might be done." In our American vocabulary, we are afraid of that word "visionary." But in the sense that Chesterton used it, in the sense of vision to see the wise course and to follow it, we pray that our leaders shall be blessed with it, because we know that "where there is no vision the people perish."

There is one thing of incalculable worth which this religious outlook has given us as a nation. It is our protection against the moral confusion, which is too often the moral nihilism, of this age. The blight of moral relativism has not fallen destructively upon us. We talk of the difficulties of charting a moral course; we acknowledge that there are all too many who confuse mere legality with morality; but the mass of our people expect of their public servants probity and decisive distinction between right and wrong in the discharge of their public responsibilities.

Here is the ultimate foundation beneath the strength and security of the Republic. Not in our wealth, not in our productive ingenuity, not in our arms, but here in the religious convictions of our people is our stability for the present and our confidence for the future.

In my public life I have tried always to follow the rule laid down twenty-five hundred years ago by the Prophet Micah: "To do justly, to love mercy, and to walk humbly with my God."

WILLIAM ERNEST HOCKING

"All of us are constant seekers for our own meaning. No one can be unaware of the touch of admonition or of summons, in which—whether or not he uses the word God—he finds his lonely lifeline taking on the added dimension of Companionship, of Duty, of Destiny."

* * *

The "dean" of contemporary American philosophers, William Ernest Hocking, was born in Cleveland, Ohio, in 1873. A graduate of Harvard, he obtained his Ph.D. from that university in 1904 and did postgraduate work at Göttingen, Berlin, and Heidelberg. For nearly half a century, he has been a "breakthrough" thinker in the developing synthesis of traditional truth and modern scientific discovery.

Dr. Hocking, who is a Congregationalist, was instructor in the history and philosophy of religion at Andover Theological Seminary, and has held professorships in philosophy at the University of California and Yale University. From 1914 to 1943 he was professor of philosophy at Harvard and has been a guest lecturer at Leiden, Glasgow, Oxford, and Cambridge universities. Married in 1905 and the father of three children, Dr. Hocking has written twenty-two books, including, The Meaning of God in Human Experience, Living Religions and a World Faith, Science and the Idea of God, The Coming World Civilization, *and* Freedom of the Press.

Dr. Hocking is a member of the American Philosophical Society, the History of Science Society, the British Institute of Philosophy, the International Institute of Arts and Letters, and the Society of Dutch Letters. He has traveled widely in Europe and the Orient in the interest of positive and liberal religious thought. Harvard's ninety-year-old Philosopher Emeritus now makes his home in Madison, New Hampshire.

* * *

A Philosophy of Faith

One distinctive note of the modern world is human self-reliance. In a world in which men are willing and able to do the hard thinking and observing essential to scientific mastery, God has in practical matters nothing specific to do. This applies first of all to the physical sciences and then extends to all the rest; each tends to become a "closed science." Even in the sciences of man and society, God has too often become the permanently irrelevant consideration.

We must be wholly in accord with the positive loyalty of the modern world to the scientific method, which has been the source of its power. But on what this modern spirit denies, we have two comments to make:

1. The "religion" it rightly denounces is *not religion;*
2. The "God" it gets along without is *not God.*

The charge of irrelevance is reversed.

Consider a man like Albert Schweitzer, who brings to Lambaréné the full equipment of scientific medicine: how absurd to suppose that he is obliged to limit his religion because of science, or his science because of his religion! It is his religion that demands the science. Or a man like Mahatma Gandhi: his sense of God can have been in no straits because of his veterinary work at Sabarmati or his non-violence crusade to establish Indian independence. Whatever God means to such men, He is not a substitute for science and the arts of modernity.

The wide modern drift toward an implicit atheism under various names is based on a valid denial, not of God, but of a false idea of God. It is a nominal atheism that leaves God's actual role in the world untouched. In fact, it is a positive service to religion if the modern spirit clears the atmosphere of notions of God built on scientific patterns, and so essentially superstitious. Wherever the science and technology of the modern world penetrate, the baser forms of magic and medicine fade away.

God is not an object among objects, nor a power among powers, nor a cause among causes. He does not figure as a factor in the field of any of the closed sciences. But if God is not an object, what is God? We may remind ourselves that this self of ours is not and cannot be an object. It cannot be put at arm's length and observed as a thing: it cannot be severed from its feelings and purposes—its subjectivity—and remain itself. If God shares in the quality of selfhood, God too cannot be an object.

Nature, as the totality with which science deals, appears to the closed natural sciences as a self-continuing process without evident beginning or ending in either space or time, and answering no questions as to how just this particular cosmos, and no other, happened to be. We may fairly say that for science Nature contains no mysteries, but is a total mystery, if one persists in the irrelevant question of total origin. Mankind tends to persist, and to confront mystery. In my judgment, there is no escape from the element of mystery in man's attitude to the cosmos; but the mystery invites approach. For there is mystery in all life, in all selfhood, in all creativity.

The great mystics are right in refusing to identify God with any perceptible being. And if it is true that every descriptive implies a limitation, we face the uncomfortable paradox that it is just the most real of which the least, or nothing, can be said. Must we then fall back on the Mahayana "Void" or the Chinese "Tao" unnamable and non-assertive: "the name that can be named is not the eternal Name. The Nameless is of heaven and earth the mother"?

A practical application of the same paradox was made by a hard-headed American businessman who said that in dealing with men he divided them into two classes—those who had faith and those who did not have faith: the important thing was to have faith, period. What men believed in might vary widely: it is the faith–attitude, he thought, that matters. A scrupulous faith, drawn to extreme reticence, may reach the point of declining to specify what it believes in, without losing the substance. The presence or absence of the faith–disposition today marks the essential distinction between the man capable of purpose and the drifter, the beatnik, the nihilist.

Under the circumstances of our time the elemental issues in human mentality present themselves in the raw state. What we see in humanity adrift is a self-steering apparatus without a chart, a latency open to direction. In that emptiness, any directive indication for me would come with *authoritative force, as from a Mind other than oneself*. The drifter lives not guideless but in a shifting polytheism. We have a suggestion that this role of direction-giving is the role of God in the normal mind—not as an "object" but as a pointing.

Following the indication that God, while not an object, is a source of direction, let us look closely into ourselves, toward the central region of selfhood where the need of direction is most immediately felt. For it is through intimate experience that we have our direct feeling of reality, an insight which some modern psychologists share with Mohammed of old—"God is nearer to you than the great vein in your neck." Turning toward this inner self of ours—the kernel or nucleus of experience, which, I believe, has pent-up energies comparable with those of the physical atom—let us inquire whether we find ourselves aware of any directive impulse. I suggest that we do find ourselves summoned to reject a passive immersion in sensation, to live thoughtfully in a world of things, events, laws, common to all selves. We are stirred to take our private experience as universal, so that it may enter the fabric we call Truth—valid for all. *In brief, we are called to think.*

And if this is the case, is not that summons to objective living—in which science itself first becomes possible—is not that the call of reality? Mahatma Gandhi speaks of a law which can be "felt," both in the physical order of the world and in the moral order; but to be aware of a moral law is to feel duty in the world-atmosphere, an expectancy which cannot be inanimate. Hence Gandhi's dictum: "Law and the Lawgiver are one." There is an indefinable *mysterious power*, he believed, that pervades everything and everyone; that pervading power, source of the law of truth and love, is God.

We find in our own experience a sense of direction having a certain authority, as if to say, "This way lies your road to fulfillment." Instincts and drives are not enough to shape a human life. There is, indeed, for the chart of our total voyage a blank left for our own free designing. Sartre is so far right—it is we who must make ourselves, not nature, not heredity, not society, not God. But also not without direction; and not in complete solitude. As all of us are constant seekers for our own meaning, no one can be unaware of the touch of admonition, or of summons, in which—whether or not he uses the word God—he finds his lonely lifeline taking on the added dimensions of companionship, of duty, of destiny.

We here touch the germ of "religion"—the sense of participation in a purposive world-trend. This awareness of direction-giving, quite literally the redemption of solitude, is the specific antidote to aimlessness, and the solution of solipsism. Indeed, it is only through the awareness of the Direction-Giver that our life becomes fully human. For God is most immediately felt as that Other-selfhood that silently pervades our private experience, giving it universality; He is the pervasive Thou-art, whereby what we experience is not "my world" but "our world." He is not an object, but the demand for objectivity: it is not science that confirms God—it is God that begets science.

This felt summons to think, to live outward and not solely inward, is a call not only to duty, but also to fulfillment; "This way lies my Destiny"—a union of requirement and promise. It becomes clear that there can be no genuine humanism without God.

DAVID SARNOFF

"Whatever man conceives in his heart and mind can become a reality."

* * *

Brigadier General David Sarnoff, chairman of the board of the Radio Corporation of America, is recognized throughout the world as a pioneer in the development of radio, television, and the electronic industry. Inventor, educator, executive, organizer of the National Broadcasting Company, General Sarnoff long ago earned the broadcasting industry's tribute as "Father of American Television."

Under his unswervering leadership in championing both black and white and color TV, RCA introduced the first postwar receiver in 1946 and to date has manufactured eleven million home sets. Against sturdy odds, he also championed all-electronic, fully compatible color television to the end that color programming is now filling more and more network hours. The result: millions of Americans today share his great dream of mass communication.

Born in 1891 near Minsk, Russia, young Sarnoff was brought to this country in 1900 by his parents. Fascinated as a youth by the new means of communication, "wireless," he landed his first job as a junior operator with the Marconi Wireless Telegraph Company. In 1919 when the Radio Corporation of America was formed at the request of the Government, it acquired the Marconi Company, and Sarnoff became commercial manager. In 1926 he organized NBC "to provide the best radio programs available for broadcasting in the United States." In addition to his scientific and industrial activities, General Sarnoff has achieved international recognition for his efforts in military communications, especially during World War II. As government consultant and Cold War strategist, he has served on three special Presidential commissions. General and Mrs. Sarnoff, who live in New York City, have three sons and eight grandchildren.

* * *

Invisible to Infinite

It was my good fortune to have been born about the same time the electron was discovered, shortly before the turn of the century. By a similar and equally happy accident of fate, at age fifteen I was drawn into the newly emerging art, science and industry of radio, where I have found active occupation ever since. Thus, for the past fifty-seven years, the electron has been my constant—and constantly challenging—companion.

In the course of my more than a half-century's relationship with electronics, I have seen it exchange the telegraph key for satellite television, and watched it grow from a means primarily of communications for ships at sea to a mighty influence over the destinies of mankind.

Through electronics, we can range from invisible to infinite; probe the inner secrets of the living cell, or those of Venus. We can, with the swiftness of light, transmit voice and images high in space above the Atlantic and cause them to reappear on the television screens of an opposite continent. Space television reports the world's weather, and so helps predict it and perhaps ultimately control it.

Electronic "sentries" guard the nation's security in the Far North. Electronic "eyes" supervise operations too remote, inaccessible or dangerous for human eyes to view. Electronic "brains" perform in minutes and in volumes calculations that normally would take man years to complete. Electronic "hands" out-race and out-pace the finest human efforts, relieving much of mechanization's tedium. The electron has become the most versatile instrument ever placed in the hands of man, and the uses of this atomic sub-particle, the smallest bit of matter known to nature, have barely begun to be explored.

Having been so closely associated with the development and growth of electronics for more than half a century, it would be untrue to deny a deep sense of pride at man's accomplishments, and the vaulting progress of his sciences. Nevertheless, there also is a feeling of awe and humbleness, springing from a lifetime's association with science, at the awareness of powers beyond the capacities of mind or science even to comprehend.

Everywhere in science we can behold the handiwork of a Supreme Architect of the Universe. The myriad suns of which our own resembles one grain in the Sahara sands, the majestic cycles of the celestial movements, the precise operations of natural laws —these cannot be regarded as mere accidents.

Nor can the harmony of their relationships and their effects upon life on this planet be measured by the human mentality. An intuition beyond reason informs us that these are the revelations of a Divine Intelligence.

It was Hans Christian Oersted, the Danish scientist who discovered the relationship between electricity and magnetism, who correctly said: "The Universe is a manifestation of an infinite reason, and the laws of nature are the thoughts of God."

Thus, as the horizons of science advance, and as our knowledge expands, we become more and not less humble, more reverent, not less. For science is presenting us with questions of ever greater profundity to which it does not possess the answers.

To provide fulfillment on this earth for humanity, science alone is not enough. Man's yearning reaches past mere comfort or knowledge or power to seek dignity, beauty, truth and purpose in life. For these, there are no substitutes to take the place of our Judeo-Christian precepts. If the role of science is to pave a path of progress for mankind, the role of religion is to guide it along true lines of morality and principle.

Today, science and religion meet on common ground, in a common effort to achieve a common need of world understanding, peace and harmony. Never were science and religion more compatible.

At a time of almost unlimited capacity for human advancement —or human destruction—it is perhaps our high destiny to rekindle an awareness of the divine attributes with which we are endowed, and to rededicate our responsibility for giving them expression.

We may yet be a generation which, hopefully, by taming its fears, its hungers and its terrible weapons, may serve to usher in an age of universal understanding and peace.

JOHN H. GLENN, JR.

"If we let Christ's principles guide us, we will see the results in our own lives."

* * *

As America's first man-in-orbit, Colonel John H. Glenn, Jr., of New Concord, Ohio, became her greatest public hero since Lindbergh. Already famed as a Marine test pilot, combat flier in World War II and the Korean War, recipient of five Distinguished Flying Crosses, Colonel Glenn flew into immortality and the admiration of the entire free world when on February 20, 1962, he piloted the space capsule Friendship 7 *three times around the globe. With this one brave blast-off into the sunlit void, astronaut Glenn provided one hundred million Americans with their sharpest thrill and strongest moral tonic since World War II.*

A lifelong Presbyterian and regular churchgoer, Glenn attended Muskingum College in New Concord where he was active in Christian Endeavor and the YMCA. He learned to fly in a Navy program for civilians and married his high school sweetheart, Annie Castor, in 1943 before flying off to combat duty in the Pacific's Marshall Islands. In 1951, at the controls of an F-8U, he set a new cross-country speed record of 3 hours, 23 minutes. Today, returned to Project Mercury astronaut duty after triumphant welcomes in New York and Washington, "Bud" Glenn is stationed near Houston, where, with his wife and children, he is a member of the Presbyterian Church in Seabrook, Texas.

* * *

Why I Know There Is a God

"WHY DO YOU WASTE YOUR TIME GOING TO CHURCH?"

I was asked this question by a fellow pilot in a Marine fighter squadron on Guam. This fellow's name was Sam, and Sam made no bones about the fact that he had been in church exactly twice in his life. One time was when he was baptized, and the other time was when his wife insisted on being married in church.

Well, by various devious means we got Sam into church for the third time on Guam. I'm sorry to say this doesn't have a happy ending as far as Sam's becoming a practicing Christian. But the question posed by Sam—why do we waste our time by going to church?—might be one for all of us to answer once in a while.

Another way of asking the same question is probably to say, "Why do we believe in God?" I think it follows that if we believe in God, we probably will wind up in church. Is there a power greater than we are? Is there really a God that we worship, or are we just wasting our time? Have you ever doubted there really is a God?

I certainly have many times, and I admit it freely. I think perhaps this is part of our growth pattern in Christian life—that we do doubt sometimes. We may doubt that there is a God, and we search our minds for signs that we really believe and should believe in him. Through such questioning of ourselves I think we may be better Christians.

When I was selected for the U. S. Space Program, one of the first things given to me was a space handbook put out by the Government Printing Office. It contains one paragraph about the hugeness of the universe which impressed me very much: "When we recall that our galaxy is some 100,000 light years in diameter, the sun being an insignificant star some 30,000 light years from the galactic center, circling in an orbit of its own every 200 million years as the galaxy rotates, we realize that even trying to visualize the tremendous scale of the universe beyond the solar system is difficult, let alone trying to attempt physical exploration and communications. Nor is the interstellar space of the galaxy the end, for beyond are the millions of other galaxies, all apparently rushing from one another at fantastic speeds. The limits of the telescopically observable universe extend at least two billion light years from us in all directions."

Now what is the point I am making? It is the orderliness of the whole universe about us, from the smallest atomic structure to the greatest thing we can visualize: galaxies, millions of light years across, all traveling in exact prescribed orbits in relation to one another.

Could this all have just happened? Was it an accident that someone tossed up a bunch of flotsam and jetsam which suddenly started making these orbits all of its own accord? I can't believe that is really true. I think this was a definite plan. This is one big thing in space that shows me there is a God, some Power that put all this into orbit and keeps it there. It wasn't just an accident.

Let us go on to compare some of our Project Mercury speeds to some of these things we've been talking about. We get to thinking sometimes that we're pretty good in this project and that we're really going out with some tremendous speeds. But when you think about the tremendous areas of space and speed, our efforts from Earth here really are pretty puny. We will get up to about eighteen thousand miles an hour in orbit, which is about five miles per second. This is pretty fast by our earthly standards. We'll be at an altitude of a little over a hundred miles. But in terms of what's already going on in space, this is really a pretty puny human effort.

We are used to dealing in scientific terms in all the measurements that are taken in science. But you can't reach out and say, "I would like to be a 110-volt Christian, and I am only a 5-volt Christian this morning. I'll have to go get pumped up some place."

You can't measure God in that way. We can't see, feel, smell, or touch our religious power. It's an intangible something.

The same thing is true of the Christian principles in our lives. If we let them guide us, our senses don't have to pick them up. We see the results of God's power in our lives and in the lives of other people. So we know it is there. We see the results of it. We're going to believe in God and the teachings of Christ. But what was this man Christ like whom we're going to follow?

He is revealed to us in the Bible. As far as physical characteristics go, we don't know too much about Him. My impression of Christ physically is that He was a real man's man. I think He is someone we'd all be proud to follow. I read in an article that the Bible says Christ led His disciples from one spot to another spot in a day's time. This distance was measured, and it turned out to be some thirty-two miles. How many of us could walk thirty-two miles by tomorrow morning, leading a group of men? I doubt if I could do it. I think Christ was a real man's man.

The important thing, of course, is not the physical strength of Jesus. The important thing is that Jesus had His beliefs, and He had the courage of His convictions to act upon them, to live by them. He believed, and He acted. These guide lines guided Christ in His everyday life when He was here on earth. The guide lines

He used are available to us today, and they are just as timeless today as they were in Jesus' time.

These guide lines apply just as much to one business as they do to another. But the choice is ours. We are the ones who have to make the choice. God hasn't said, "You *will* do this." We have been placed here as free agents to decide whether we will or will not live by these guide lines. The choice is ours.

JAMES A. PIKE

"Vocation is the absolute claim of God upon the whole of life."

* * *

James A. Pike, Bishop of California, is an eloquent and courageous spokesman for the Episcopal Church in the United States as well as for the progressive wing of the entire Protestant movement. From 1952 to 1958 he served as Dean of the Cathedral Church of St. John the Divine in New York City, the largest church in the country. In 1958 he was consecrated Bishop at Grace Cathedral in San Francisco. Since he left first the Roman Catholic Church, then agnosticism, to become an Episcopalian, he has been an ardent advocate of liberal Christian crusades inside and outside the church.

Bishop Pike was born in 1913 in Oklahoma City, where, after his father's death, his mother supported the family by teaching in high schools there and in California. After a parochial and public school education, he graduated in arts and law at the University of Southern California and after his admission to the California bar he earned a doctorate in the Science of Law at Yale in 1937. As a lawyer, he joined the Securities and Exchange Commission's legal staff in Washington, D.C., taught at George Washington University Law School, and became a member of the bar of the United States Supreme Court. During World War II James Pike served in the Navy, and in 1944, while still in uniform, he was ordained.

Dean Pike took his theological training at Virginia, General, and Union Theological seminaries, graduating from the latter magna cum laude. After serving at St. John's in Washington, D.C., and at Christ Church in Poughkeepsie, New York, he served as chaplain of Columbia University and head of its Department of Religion. For years Bishop Pike's numerous "extracurricular" activities have included such posts as president of the New York Chapter, American-Israel Society, chairman of the Housing Committee of the Urban League, and membership on the Board of the Red Cross and the U. S. Food for Peace Council. He is currently chairman of the California Advisory Committee of the U. S. Civil Rights Commission. A widely quoted author and television personality, he has written Beyond Anxiety, Doing the Truth, If You Marry Outside Your Faith, The Next Day, *and* Beyond the Law. *He is a leader of the movement for the union of the churches. Bishop Pike is married and the father of four children: Catherine, twenty, James, Jr., seventeen, Constance, fourteen, and Christopher, thirteen.*

* * *

A Christian Vocation

IN MY HALF-CENTURY OF CONSCIOUS SPIRITUAL EXPERIENCE, MY LIFE has reflected the religious changes and conflicts known to many Americans—childhood confidence in the family religion, adolescent rebellion, young adult indifference to the church, and finally a rewarding faith. After attending parochial and public schools, I attended Hollywood High School where I still passionately believed that the Roman Catholic Church was the only true church. Entering a Jesuit institution, Santa Clara University, with the same zeal, in the second year I found I could not accept the Church's position on birth control and papal infallibility. By the time I reached twenty-five and graduated from the University of Southern California Law School, I was a confirmed agnostic.

Prophetically enough, in view of the journey I was to take, my first doubts concerning the Roman Catholic faith concurred with the first serious intimations of my vocation to the priesthood. What seemed a painful paradox at the time now seems to me to have been a difficult lock opening out to a fulfillment. God's intentions for us cannot be reached by simple decisions made easily by men confused by Original Sin. As I grew older I realized that temptation itself is usually an attraction to oversimplification, blinding us to the many-sided figure of the true Christian life.

In addition to my reluctance to accept papal infallibility, I had intellectual difficulties with scholastic philosophy and the dogmatism of my highly qualified instructors led me back to the secular life. I abandoned my Christian faith (I "threw out the baby with the bath water") and sought the meaning for my life in a law career and a zest for social reform. I had yet to learn that one can be a Christian and still have uncertainties about many religious questions without departing from essential doctrine.

It was while working as a government lawyer in Washington that the inadequacy of these secular aims as a total meaning for life increasingly dawned on me. Especially during my Navy service in World War II and especially during a period of serious personal crisis, I began searching for the religious cornerstone: the fact that *God is* makes all the difference in regard to the moral choices and decisions we must make in this existence. In 1942, out of an explicitly felt need for a more meaningful basis for our personal lives, for our marriage, and for our social concerns, my wife and I decided to give serious intellectual consideration to religion.

Once again I found myself struggling with the issue of Vocation. I had simply postponed facing up to the *absolute claim of God upon the whole of life*. Along with every other human being who has ever lived, we both were forced to ask ourselves, "Why are we here?" "What is the purpose of life?" Reinhold Niebuhr, Paul Tillich, C. S. Lewis, B. I. Bell, William Temple, and many others helped us to see that when a person enters a church, he needn't be asked to park his education outside. They influenced our decision for Christianity and its understanding of man's nature and destiny in God's world.

God made us for a purpose. The basis for our dignity is that He cares that we fulfill the purpose for which He made us. This is why the basic law of life in both Old Testament religion and New Testament religion—expressed in the Shema of Israel and the "two great commandments"—is the summation of our Vocation, the purpose of our life: "Hear, O Israel, the Lord thy God is is one God. And thou shalt love the Lord thy God with all thy heart, and with all thy soul, and with all thy mind, and with all thy strength. This is the first and great commandment. And the second is like unto it, thou shalt love thy neighbor as thyself. On these two commandments hang all the law and the prophets."

God so loves us that He made us in His image as He has revealed Himself to us. Hence, He means us to correspond to His Nature in the Holy Trinity as Creator, Redeemer, and Holy Spirit. Our creative role gives us the great privilege and prestige of containing rivers by the building of dams, of the sowing and reaping of wheat, of directing businesses and raising families, of making fine wine out of grapes, of designing precision instruments and rockets for the moon, and in the millions of other tasks He has left to us in the finishing of His universe.

God means us to be redemptive in our personal relationships; to love our neighbors in their faults as well as in their virtues. He reveals the Redeemer in Jesus Christ, through whom He has translated Himself into the language of human life. Jesus Christ is the supreme image of how God always has been and always will be toward the sons of men. God relates Himself to us in our limitations and sins, and we in His image are capable of so relating ourselves to others. Indeed, this particular type of relationship is the most distinctive expression of our Christian vocation. "God has so loved us; we ought also to love one another."

As God the Holy Spirit works through the life of the group, "the blessed company of all faithful people," we too are meant to live and work in community. Thus the effectiveness of our creativity and of our redemptiveness is magnified. But community is not only means, it is end. In the Kingdom of God the interrelations of our lives and our talents are to be expressed to the limit of our capacities. And it is not just something that is waited for; the Kingdom has already come to the extent that creativity expresses itself redemptively in fellowship.

I believe that all baptized Christians belong to the one true church. However, when I returned to Christianity, I chose the Episcopal Church for reasons which slowly revealed themselves to me. In fact, the process of clarification and deepening in the faith, both intellectually and personally, did not rest there—nor has it yet. But I would like to try to summarize some of the reasons for my choice. I believe that the Anglican Communion can justly make the very large claim that it is more Catholic, more Protestant, and more Liberal than any other church in Christendom.

We are more Catholic in that we hold entire "the Faith once for all delivered to the Saints" in unbroken continuity with the early Church. We returned, through a series of reformations, to an older, purer form of Catholicism and continue to cleave to the *earlier* ways, such as episcopal government, public confession and voluntary private confession, vernacular liturgy, and the doctrine of the real Presence. We are "old-fashioned Catholics."

"Protestant" means recognition of the principle that the Church is under continuous judgment of Christ Himself, and that the visible Church thus always needs reformation. But the churches of the Reformation adopted confessions of faith, detailed doctrines which were thereafter looked upon as final tests of orthodoxy. And so, in a sense, they had had their reformation. But the reformation in Anglicanism has been a gradual thing. Because we date ourselves from no one great Reformer, and because at no point did we adopt such a confession of faith, we have been freer to receive new applications of the Protestant principle. We are, therefore, more Protestant than the classical Reformation churches: we are a Church *in reformation* all through.

Our Church is more liberal than other liberals, because it is free from the absolutizing of any system of doctrines and yet free to utilize their insights in its task of understanding and communicating the Gospel. Our loyalty is not to the particular formulations of past centuries, but rather to the truth they are seeking to express. This is not merely intellectual or artistic borrowing; it is the natural expression of our feeling for the communion of saints. We are free to be helped by all the witnesses to the Faith, and yet bear final allegiance only to Him who is the author and finisher of our faith. And our obligation to think as Christians does not require us to close our minds to secular analysis of the human task.

Any one teaching, attitude, or emphasis of Anglicanism can be found elsewhere in Christendom (and often better implemented), but not so many true, good, and beautiful things can be found together. We cannot claim that ours is the "true Church," but I am convinced that it is the truest. In humble awareness of the gap between our potentiality and our actuality, I pray as an Episcopalian that we become dedicated instruments for what is most surely the mind of Christ, the restoration of the visible unity of His Church.

BOBBY RICHARDSON

"My purpose in life is to please God—to know and to love Him—I am not ashamed of this."

* * *

Star second baseman of the World Champion New York "Yankees," Bobby Richardson enjoyed the greatest season of his career in 1962—being voted the American League's second most valuable player behind magnificent Mickey Mantle. He led the League in at bats (692), in hits (209), and in longest hitting streak (17 games). Again in 1959—the year the "Yankees" lost the Pennant—Richardson was the team's best hitter with a .301 average.

Usually referred to as "little Bobby Richardson" (he's 5'8", 165 pounds), his play in American Legion ball first excited scouts from several major-league clubs. He signed with the Yankees in 1954 and spent four years with such minor-league teams as Norfolk, Olean, Binghamton, and Denver. Born in Sumter, South Carolina, in 1935, Bobby is as fine a young hitter as the major leagues have seen—and a respected Christian gentleman on and off the playing field.

* * *

The Yankees—and Jesus Christ

CHRISTIANITY FIRST STARTED TO MEAN SOMETHING TO ME WHEN I broke into baseball in 1952. We were in spring training in Class A baseball in Virginia, and most of the fellows more or less thought that they had their positions won. Then, one day, word came that there was a talented player coming down from a higher classification club. Immediately I noticed there was an unusual amount of talk about this player and I wondered why. As I got to know him, I found out why: he was a dedicated Christian who devoted his life to God. Some of the things he stood for, important things to him, others on the team resented; perhaps it was because of the way they wanted to live their lives. That is, *outwardly* they resented him. But I noticed they soon developed respect and admiration for him too. *Inwardly*, he drew them closer to God, as he did me.

Whether we realize it or not, there is somebody, a neighbor across the street, a friend, or maybe our own son, who is looking up to us. I believe our example to these people can become our most powerful effort in life. Influence is not only something we all hear and think about; its effect on those we meet daily, or perhaps only *once* in our lifetime, may make a difference that shapes our whole lives.

This is my seventh year with the New York Yankees and my tenth in organized baseball. I'm often asked if a pro's life isn't pretty rough in the Big Leagues. But I rather think baseball, like a lot of other professions, is tough because it is hard to take a stand. There is one verse of Holy Scripture, for instance, that has strengthened me a lot: "I am not ashamed of the gospel of Christ, for it is the power of God unto salvation to everyone that believeth." I find, when you so take your stand, you've got the respect of those around you.

When I graduated from high school I had an opportunity to fulfill an ambition of many young fellows—to enter professional baseball! I signed with the New York Yankees and reported to their farm club in Norfolk. I will never forget it! This was my first time away from home in a big city. The fact that I knew no one, nor even to whom I should report, was discouraging and made me downhearted and lonely. About this time I received a letter from a former coach in which he quoted Matthew 6:33, "Seek ye first the kingdom of God, and his righteousness; and all these things shall be added unto you." This renewed my faith, brought me closer to God, and things went well.

Wearing a Yankee uniform has meant something special to me, and it still does. But in making the grade into the Yankees, I owe a lot to others; all the way from my dad, who used to practice with me every day, to former Yankee stars, Jerry Coleman and Frank Crosetti, who helped me with my quick double-play throw from second to first base. And Casey Stengel, that really remarkable man, who managed the Yankees for so long. He knows his baseball and he's a good leader whom all the baseball players respect. As a matter of record, it was Casey Stengel who gave me my greatest thrill in baseball. In 1957 he picked me for the American League All-Star team—my first year up in the majors; in 1959 he kept me in the lineup, "the year the Yankees lost the Pennant," until I ended the season with a .301 batting average—the dream of every young player!

We must have a purpose in life, and that purpose should be to please God—to know Him, to love Him, to walk with Him in our daily lives.

Baseball is a profession full of temptation, just as other professions, and it is a challenge to lead the Christian life. Another verse that has strengthened and challenged me, because I know to claim it means a completely surrendered life, is Galatians 2:20: "I am crucified with Christ: nevertheless I live; yet not I, but Christ liveth in me: and the life which I now live in the flesh I live by the faith of the Son of God, who loved me, and gave himself for me."

I realize simply that it is God who has given me the ability, the opportunity, and certainly any supposed earthly glory that might come through playing ball. I enjoy the sport I am in, but only because I feel that this is where God would have me serve Him.

Twelve years ago when I accepted Jesus Christ as my Saviour, I took John 3:16 at its word: "For God so loved the world, that he gave his only begotten Son, that whosoever believeth in him should not perish, but have everlasting life." It was a wonderful day that I made this decision, and I am thankful that He sent His Son to die on the cross for me, that I, through His grace, might have everlasting life by simply trusting in His completed work of salvation at Calvary.

"I am not ashamed of the gospel of Christ: for it is the power of God unto salvation to every one that believeth" (Romans 1:16). As we count up we find

> Only one life,
> 'Twill soon be past.
> Only what's done for Christ
> Will last.

It matters not our profession or our field; the thing that counts for eternity is our personal relationship with the Lord Jesus Christ.

MARY G. ROEBLING

"To serve God and my church and to love all human beings is my creed."

* * *

Mary G. Roebling, president of the Trenton Trust Company, occupies a prestige position as America's leading woman banker. Prominent in business, philanthropy and various international goodwill societies, Mrs. Roebling served as the first woman member of the Board of Governors, American Stock Exchange, and was appointed economic ambassador of New Jersey by Governor Meyner. She is also on the National Committee for Economic Development, the Committee for International Economic Growth and the Committee for National Trade policy.

Educated at the University of Pennsylvania and New York University, Mary Roebling is the widow of Siegfried Roebling, late vice president of John A. Roebling's Sons Co. In addition to her own extensive banking and business enterprises, she is a director of several corporations. A notable patron and participant in New York–New Jersey cultural and charity events, she supports the Metropolitan Museum of Art, the National Conference of Christians and Jews, all patriotic organizations from Mayflower Society to the D. A. R., the Order of Lafayette and the International Rescue Committee.

Mrs. Roebling was chairman of women's activities at the 1959 World Congress of the International Chamber of Commerce in Washington, D.C. and that same year was a delegate to the Atlantic Congress of NATO in London. Among her many public activities are Trustee, U. S. Council, International Chamber of Commerce; National Board, Women's Medical College of Pennsylvania; National Council, Metropolitan Opera Association; Trustee, Ithaca College; Member of Boards, Statue of Liberty Society; National Society for Crippled Children and Adults; Founders, Salk Institute for Biological Studies; George C. Marshall Research Foundation; National U. S. O. and National Travelers Aid Association; Vice President and life member, National Defense Transportation Association; Member, New York World's Fair Corporation; National Consultant, Women's Archives, Radcliffe College.

In recent years Mrs. Roebling has been given the Mary Bailey Foundation Award for Achievement; New Jersey Conference of

Christians and Jews Brotherhood Award; Trenton's "Woman of the Year" Medal; Eisenhower Prayer Award; Gold Key Award, N. Y. Federation of Jewish Philanthropies; National Association of Insurance Women Award; Philadelphia Ad Women "Distinguished Daughter of New Jersey." A member of St. Mary's Episcopal Church and honorary member of the Women's Guild, Mrs. Roebling is an untiring supporter of inter-faith activities at home and abroad. She is the mother of two children, Mrs. Betty Dutch of Trenton and the stage and screen actor, Paul Roebling of New York.

* * *

My Creed

EACH DAY I SEEK . . .

To preserve my physical health, to grow in mental strength.

To allocate my time wisely to most important things.

To serve God and my church.

To love all human beings, whatever their needs; wherever they may be.

To take pride in my homeland and my community, and work for their best interests.

To be a dutiful daughter, a wise parent, a kind sister, a good neighbor and a more generous, more ideal American woman. . . .

The above statement is my Christian Creed, the principles of mind, heart, and body by which I have tried to live my life. After testing them for two generations in all the surge and joyful sweep of girlhood, college, marriage, motherhood, widowhood, and now a far-ranging business career, I am convinced that these principles are the essence of religion, the stuff of Scripture, and the beacon lights desperately needed by a bewildered humanity.

That this Biblical wisdom was taught to me from childhood only reflects the good luck I had in picking my parents! They were the dearest, most dedicated folks more than fifty years ago in Haddonfield, New Jersey—and God be praised for His blessings—they still are today at age eighty-six in Trenton! Ours was an intense Methodist household in which God's Word was preached and practiced.

Mother, who was a professional pianist and concert singer, always said Grace at every meal, always read aloud from the Bible every night. It was my devoted mother who inspired me to read and memorize the Psalms by the time I entered high school. Daddy, a retired telephone company executive, and lay preacher, was a deacon in the Haddonfield church and taught the Sunday Bible class there. Methodist missionaries were such regular and eloquent visitors to our house that at one time I felt God-inspired to become a missionary to China.

Thus was my youth and younger years cast and colored in a way that was never to change, only to deepen and intensify. Today, as an adult, religion and especially the Christian faith is the most precious part of my life. Although business is a challenge, I believe we earn money only to use it for good. Although society offers gracious fellowship, I believe we enter it only to help as many people as we can. Although praise and rewards come to us all if we do our work well, I believe the first thing and the last thing of life is to find God and be found by Him. As William Barrow has written, "Religion is equally the basis of private virtue and public faith; of the happiness of the individual and the prosperity of the nation."

DREW PEARSON

"It is hard to measure the most important thing in the world—the change in men's hearts."

* * *

Judged Washington's top reporter by many of his colleagues, Drew Pearson has a reputation for getting stories others can't get and for printing or broadcasting what others will hush up. His syndicated column, "Washington-Merry-Go-Round," recently earned him The Saturday Review's *praise as America's most influential columnist. A hard worker who enjoys operating under pressure, this world-renowned Washingtonian is nevertheless a quiet, retiring man who shows strong traces of his Quaker ancestry.*

Born in Evanston, Illinois, Pearson spent his boyhood in Swarthmore, Pennsylvania, where his father was professor of speech at Swarthmore College. He later graduated from Swarthmore himself where he made Phi Beta Kappa. The journalist, who was to start the Friendship Train rolling more than a quarter of a century later with much-needed food for the victims of World War II, went overseas in 1919 on a similar mission. He supervised the relief program of the American Friends Service Committee in devastated Balkan villages.

Drew Pearson's first book, Washington Merry-Go-Round, *written with Robert S. Allen, was a best-selling exposé of personalities in the nation's capital. Never a man to flinch from a fight, Pearson regards the job of a Washington reporter as being that of "Watch-dog of the people." He has taken on a variety of opponents, including the Ku Klux Klan, the Federal Communications Commission, Senator Joseph R. McCarthy, and a long line of White House residents. On the international scene, he has been a vigorous fighter against both Fascism and Communism. Drew Pearson has been given France's Legion of Honor and Italy's First Order Star of Solidarity, but derived even greater satisfaction from another award he received in 1948—"Father of the Year."*

* * *

The Way to His Goal

The goal was set for all of us nearly two thousand years ago by the Son of Man who came into the world to give His life for the cause of peace on earth, good will to men. Today, when I read the newspaper headlines I sometimes feel that we have taken several steps backward from the day He sacrificed Himself for us. But I have learned that from one's lowest moments the best things come. That can be true of persons; and it can be true of the world.

I remember the lonesomest Christmas of my life. It was in Marseilles, France, in 1947. My wife was sick. The children seemed very far away. I sat in an overcoat trying to keep warm and to write a column which would be of interest to people four thousand miles away. I felt so blue myself that I didn't see how I could possibly interest anyone. I wished that I had never thought of the Friendship Train, which had brought me to France. I wished I had never come to Europe, and vowed that if I ever got home I would never leave.

The streets of Marseilles were bleak and dismal. Frenchmen, unable to afford much of a Christmas, were celebrating in their homes. Not even the French Cable Company wanted to open up to send the day's column. In the afternoon, however, the sun tried to shine a little, my wife slept, and I went to an old cathedral overlooking the city with a young priest from Philadelphia. We had two things in common: we once lived in the same city, and we were terribly homesick.

But the Friendship Train succeeded. It rolled across our country and gathered forty million dollars' worth of food from the heart of America. Seven hundred carloads were distributed to the poor and hungry survivors of World War II in France and Italy. And a year later the French people sent the Gratitude Train to the United States. It carried all sorts of precious gifts—battle-torn flags, silks, lacework, woodcarvings, priceless paintings by French masters—all given in the spirit of "Merci America."

From such experiences I have learned that people want to work for peace, democracy, and Christian charity. They are not content to leave these matters in the hands of their governments. They want to do things themselves. They want to make their own contributions—even though small—to building neighbors. They want to do this not only here at home, between neighbors around the corner, but also abroad, between neighbors who speak foreign languages.

Since that bleak Christmas of 1947 people have made countless efforts in the spirit of the Friendship Train. Millions have given personal gifts to CARE to provide for others; student exchanges have been followed up by the hard work of idealistic young Americans in the Peace Corps; whole American towns have adopted and provided for needy communities in foreign lands; hundreds of thousands of Pen Pals have helped spread understanding among people of good will; all church groups have collected food and clothing; and American business and labor have contributed urgently needed medical supplies to ease suffering throughout the world.

The list of people, clubs, and organizations who want to help other people is so long it would be impossible to print. Despite the cynics and the pessimists, this great urge exists. It is the most heartening light on the horizon, and it springs directly from the Man who gave us first the Sermon on the Mount and then, finally, Himself. He set the example, and the goal.

There is still great want and hunger in the underdeveloped nations, but Europe, at least, has returned to full prosperity. Her recovery was due in large part to the help that was given her people. Thus, we have tried to imitate Christ in the giving of material aid, which we can measure in dollars and cents. But how far have we progressed toward His goal of peace set two thousand years ago? This progress has been less perceptible, because the path of peace lies in the hearts of men. It is hard to measure the most important thing in the world—the change in men's hearts.

Perhaps the greatest gift given us by Jesus of Nazareth was the vision of what man could become—the dignity and divine worth of man. We still have a long way to go in achieving the goal Christ set for us. And yet, looking back over the years that have passed, I am convinced that we in the United States have made gains. Not enough gains perhaps, but some. For example, as a nation we were at times taken up on the mountain top and shown temptations that were ours for the taking . . . by force. But we resisted. Our respect for the dignity of small countries and our encouragement of young, weak nations have made a profound impression on the world. It is one step that we have taken toward fulfillment of the Sermon on the Mount.

Hitler's greatest mistake was that he denied the dignity of nations . . . and of man. Christ taught that man was the son of God—the fallen son, and therefore capable of doing evil but still the son of God. Hitler assumed that man was no more than a beast, and treated him as such. He operated on the premise that, as in the jungle, might makes right, that it is the function of the strong to use the weak in any way they see fit. This was probably the biggest reason why the world turned against Hitler. It is also the biggest reason why a good part of the world has turned against Soviet Russia, and will continue to do so. For despite all the propaganda that the Soviet system is created for the benefit of man, that system fails to recognize man's dignity. His body may be fed, but not his soul.

It may seem slight solace to moralize about our country's milestones of accomplishment in the two-thousand-year struggle upward toward the Sermon on the Mount. But we have made progress. We are more moral than we used to be. The problem now is integration, not lynching. The general rule now is not to stuff a ballot box but to encourage people to get out and vote. We try to provide for the old and the sick and the unemployed, and we no longer shoot down striking men on picket lines.

And while we still have a long way to go in our personal faith and in our national ethics, it is only by reviewing the travail and pain of the past that we can measure the way to His goal.

CARLOS P. ROMULO

"For freedom, for myself and others, I have always been willing to fight and at times to die."

* * *

General Carlos P. Romulo, "a small man from a small country," as he describes himself, has for thirty years helped lead the Philippines' struggle for freedom, represented his country in Washington and the UN, and became a heroic symbol of the worldwide revolt against injustice and inequality. An energetic editor, teacher, and fervent patriot before World War II, he served as General MacArthur's aide-de-camp on Bataan, Corregidor. Later he accompanied General MacArthur and the liberating Allies in the invasion of Leyte and the recapture of Manila.

General Romulo, recipient of the Philippine Congressional Medal of Honor, headed his nation's delegation to the UN conference in San Francisco in 1945 and took part in subsequent General Assemblies in London, Paris, and New York. He was appointed Filipino Ambassador to the United States in 1952. The recipient of forty-two gold medal awards of merit and forty-nine honorary college degrees, General Romulo won the Pulitzer Prize in journalism for a series of articles on the Far East. In the fall of 1962 he became president of the University of the Philippines.

* * *

A Walk with Heroes

I HAVE ALWAYS BELIEVED IN CHRISTIANITY AND THE CHURCH. THEREFORE I have also always believed in prayer. From my earliest recollection as a boy in the tiny Filipino town of Camiling, I was taught the enduring values of history, patriotism, and religion. In our home, by speech, manner, and heritage we were Spanish and Catholic; we were an affectionate family and into it came priests from the church, nuns from the convent, and farmers from the hills, all of whom became my friends. The dark, richly carved furniture, the family altar with its tall image of the Virgin holding her Son, and the many religious paintings dominated by a large reproduction of Da Vinci's *The Last Supper*—all left a lasting impression upon me of parental authority and divine love.

That love—and my formal faith in it—has been put to many tests during my ever-changing career as a teacher, soldier, journalist, author, and diplomat. But if I were forced to name the severest test of my Christian creed, I would sum it up in one word—Bataan. As a colonel on General MacArthur's staff, I had fled with him to Corregidor when the Japanese overran the Philippines. For four months under your stalwart, indomitable MacArthur and our frail, indomitable President Quezon, I had broadcast daily to my captive countrymen behind the Japanese lines. My wife and children were lost, my country and all I cherished were in ruins. Americans and Filipinos, fighting and dying together, could not check the advance of General Homma's Japanese hordes, and at last in April, 1942, with the increasing daily threat of hunger, gangrene, and death, came orders to abandon the "Rock."

General MacArthur had been flown out of Corregidor to Melbourne in order to direct Pacific war strategy from Australia; for of what use is a captured commander? President Quezon, his family, and staff had escaped by submarine to set up our Government-in-exile in America. Now, broadcasting over the Voice of Freedom with General Wainwright in command and hoping against hope that help would arrive, I knew the end had come for bomb-blasted Bataan. Finally on April 9th, on the eve of our formal surrender, I was ordered by Wainwright to leave the Rock. For several days ground crewmen had been working to repair a war-wrecked German bomber for the hour of escape. Just at dawn on the day Bataan fell, our pilot, Lieut. Roland Barnick of Boise, Idaho, sent our patched-up aircraft hurtling down the bomb-riddled runway into a hail of Japanese fire from across Manila Bay. For the next three hours we skimmed the waves, dodging bullets from sea and sky, until finally we crash-landed on an Iloilo beach . . . safe as "the last man off Bataan" and eager to join MacArthur in Australia.

From the time I crept out of our filthy tunnel that fateful dawn, I had prayed incessantly for the safety of my brave companions and myself. That day, as they had been before and since, my prayers were answered.

It is this practical kind of Christianity that has been my mainstay in my thirty years of public life. So, by keeping and living this faith, a small boy from a small country has been able to work with heroes, become the Philippine Ambassador to the United States, and finally even president of the United Nations General Assembly. So, under the layers of ego-built armor, I am today what I was in my earliest days as a teacher and editor in prewar Manila with all the flaws and weaknesses and ideals peculiar to man. If certain emotions seem stronger in me than in the average man, it is because I have not lived an average life. Within, I tremble against injustice and with a passion for freedom. I felt those emotions first as a young child; they have never left me. For freedom, for myself or others, I have always been willing to fight and at times to die.

Fortunately today, since the brave flights of Gagarin, Titov, Glenn, and Cooper, this same faith enables me and other thoughtful humans to identify ourselves vicariously with man in space. The view of Earth's peoples is beginning to change for the better: when we see the Earth from another star, then the races and religions do not seem very far apart. We see ourselves increasingly as a single interdependent community. We realize in this nuclear-energy age that we all have common dangers, common aspirations, a common destiny.

World tensions will always characterize our social environment. Hard times lie ahead, with tough encounters, but hard times can be made good times. The U. S. educator Henry M. Wriston recently wrote in *Foreign Affairs:* "There never was a golden age when men lived happily, securely, without tensions." We may fix firmly in our consciousness that there never will be. If we will but remember the counsel by Thomas Jefferson, "The tree of liberty must be refreshed from time to time with the blood of patriots and tyrants," this, then, is my warning: expect struggle, sacrifice, hardship, danger; yes, and "sweat, blood and tears." We need not despair because of tensions, threats, and new alarms in the Cold War.

At the same time, I have great long-term hopes. I describe them as long-term hopes, because patience and endurance over many years will be necessary.

1. I believe that dictatorship is a dying institution. Tyranny will diminish and pass away as universal literacy, economic im-

provement, and an educated political maturity provide the checks and balances of the democratic process. My corollary here is that power always tends to corrupt, and therefore every republic must be vigilant for its natural rights.

2. I believe that the central idea of the American Revolution, the declaration that all men have rights, will be accepted universally. My corollary here is that the right to differ with America, and with every other country, is part of the right to be free.

3. I believe that the struggle between the Free-choice West and Communism will not culminate in a catastrophic war. As Hinduism and Buddhism, Judaism and Christianity, Christianity and Islam settled down eventually, without succeeding in one replacing the other, so modern capitalism and socialism will learn to adjust without a nuclear holocaust. My corollary here is that private ownership and individual enterprise will gain adherents, even while welfare legislation for basic needs of health, education, and care of the aged will be increasingly assured by state governments.

4. I believe that disarmament will come, irrespective of the results from ongoing discussions in Washington, Geneva, and other world capitals. All nations really want to get out from under the crushing burden of arms. And they will! My corollary here is that as disarmament comes—step by step—the nations of the world will devote their saved capital to their own growth and to the development of nations that want to overcome their poverty.

5. I believe that the United Nations Organization will grow in strength so that it may legislate rules by which an international community may operate, and become authorized to judge international disputes in court and to police world law. My corollary is that knowledge, love, imagination, and faith in a Divine Power are as necessary for nations as for individuals in building the world brotherhood essential to human survival and development.

NORMAN VINCENT PEALE

"If thou canst believe, all things are possible to him that believeth." There is the crux of it. "If thou canst believe. . . ."

*　　　*　　　*

To millions of people the ministry of Dr. Norman Vincent Peale summarizes the spiritual awakening that has swept over the United States since World War II. Thousands crowd New York's Marble Collegiate Church every Sunday to hear him preach; his printed sermons are read monthly by three hundred and fifty thousand people; his books and TV programs reach millions more. His world-renowned best seller, The Power of Positive Thinking, *which has been translated into thirty languages, epitomizes Dr. Peale's vitally direct approach to Christianity and his untiring efforts to change men's hearts and minds for the better.*

Norman Vincent Peale, who was born and raised in Ohio, attended Ohio Wesleyan University, earned both Master of Arts and Bachelor of Sacred Theology degrees from Boston University. After serving as minister in Brooklyn and Syracuse, New York, he was called to Marble Collegiate Church in 1932. His supercharged New York life includes membership in the Rotary Club, the Union League Club, and the Metropolitan Club. He also is a Thirty-third Degree Mason, former Grand Chaplain of the Grand Lodge of New York, and a Past Imperial Chaplain of the Shrine.

In addition to his inspirational books and articles, Dr. Peale serves as editor-in-chief of Guideposts, *a popular religious magazine with a million subscribers, writes a weekly column, "Confident Living," appearing in two hundred newspapers, and lectures frequently in leading United States cities. A motion picture, "Look to the Stars," based on Dr. Peale's life and produced by Frank Ross, is being released by United Artists early in 1964. He also is the founder–president of The American Foundation of Religion and Psychiatry. Among his many honorary degrees and medals are the Horatio Alger Award, the American Education Award, the Ohio Governor's Award, and the Tau Kappa Epsilon Award. Dr. and Mrs. Peale have three children of whom their only son, John, has chosen to follow his father's footsteps in the ministry.*

*　　　*　　　*

The Challenge of Christian Change

CHRISTIANITY DEALS WITH VAST REALITIES, BUT IT DOES SO IN AN uncomplicated way. Read and reread the Gospels and the letters of St. Paul. There is where you find what Christianity really is. Don't think you get it out of the councils of the churches or out of the publications of the various church bodies. Go back to the sources—the Gospels and St. Paul. They teach righteousness, truth, life, and love. Those are the four words that give the essence of what Jesus taught.

The question is—can we in this very sophisticated American civilization get back to these essential teachings again?

Christianity teaches the facts about God and it teaches the facts about man. What does it say about God? That He is a spirit and that they that worship Him must worship Him in spirit and in truth. Because God is so vast that our minds can't comprehend Him, He encompassed Himself for us in the form of a man. Therefore Jesus said, "He that hath seen me hath seen the Father." Christianity says to the world, "You want to know what God is like? He's like Jesus." And that means He's full of truth and righteousness and love and goodness.

And what does Christianity tell us about man? It says men are created in the image of God. It says, "And ye shall know the truth, and the truth shall make you free." The New Testament pictures man as a great soul who is a sovereign entity in himself. The great fundamental Christian teachings about man are that man can come to know the truth and that thereby man can change. That is the glorious message of Christianity—you don't need to remain as you are! You cannot change by your own unaided power, but you can be changed by God. The Bible shows an enormous respect for the potential of the human being.

A person who has recently achieved some wonderful changes in his life wrote to me describing the experience like this: "I realized that I was living on a minimum level. I was just getting by and that was all. So I decided to change. I prayed to God for help and guidance. I filled my mind with great ideas from the Bible, developed new approaches to my problems. My life began to change. Now I am a scorner of minimum living. I wonder why I lived on a minimum level for so long."

The secret of that man's release was that he became a real believer. Christianity in its deepest power will never open up to any of us until we become real believers.

"If thou canst believe," Jesus said, "all things are possible to him that believeth." There is the crux of it: "If thou canst believe." You have to learn to believe that which is hard to believe. There is power in this. You can rationalize it away if you wish—but you do so to your own great loss. To have great faith you have to struggle for it. And when you achieve faith, what do you do? You throw back the barriers of defeat, frustration, hate, and conflict.

Belief is after all a form of thought. All the believing you ever do will be done in your mind. You can either disbelieve yourself into a frustrated life or believe yourself into a great life. It is up to you. We do not half realize the power of thought to destroy or to create. Thoughts actually are forces. You can't see them, but they have substance nevertheless. They are dynamic forces.

If you constantly think negative thoughts, you thereby activate negative forces around you and draw back upon yourself negative results. This is on the basis of the law that like attracts like. Send out hate, and what do you get back? Hate. Send out fear, and what do you get back? Nothing but fear. Send out defeat, and what do you get back? Nothing but defeat.

All destructiveness originates in thought! And by the same token, all creative, powerful, majestic living originates in thought. Get a good thought, build it up, nurse it. Get a faith thought, make it grow. Don't let it stop on a minimum level. Make a giant of it. Take the New Testament as it is. Fill your mind with it. Saturate your soul with it. "Nothing is impossible to him that believeth." Remember that our God is a Creator and a Recreator.

This doesn't mean you can avoid having trouble in life. You are bound to suffer pain, frustration, hardship, and injustice. But that is only half the story. The rest of the story is that you can rise above these things. How much faith have you?

Christianity teaches that God is a God of love. It teaches that He is a God of righteousness. It teaches that man gets full of sin, but that Jesus died on the cross for his redemption. It teaches that the Holy Spirit abides to live with him. It teaches the transformation of human life for time and eternity. This is the essence.

Most of us merely play with these great Christian teachings. We believe them and yet we don't really believe them. Just how truly and how deeply do we accept and live by the words of Jesus Christ?

What do you want from life? Minimum level or the maximum? The difference between the two is in the depth, vitality, and power of your belief. "If thou canst believe, all things are possible to him that believeth." Let us become believers, delving deeply into the power of faith until we come up with changed lives, lives of such vitality that they will flow out to change the life of the world.

Thank God that we do not have to depend on our own strength alone. We can pray for help to believe and defeat our doubts. We can pray that our belief may grow until we are true believers and the great things of life become possible to us, through Jesus Christ our Lord.

WALTER H. JUDD

"He that would be the greatest among you, let him be the servant of all."

* * *

Dr. Walter H. Judd served ten terms in the U. S. Congress as a Representative from Minnesota. A former medical missionary in China and an expert in Far Eastern affairs, he especially made his influence felt in Congress as a member of the Foreign Affairs Committee for sixteen years; in the House of Representatives from 1943 to 1963, he played an increasingly significant role in establishing our relief, recovery, rearmament, and economic rehabilitation programs in Europe and Asia. Dr. Judd served as an American delegate to the United Nations in 1957 and to the World Health Organization in 1950 and 1958

Born in Rising City, Nebraska, in 1898, Walter Judd worked his way through the University of Nebraska Medical School by tackling an assortment of jobs which included dish-washing, school-teaching, cafeteria-cooking, and playing in a band on the Chautauqua Circuit! During World War I he enlisted as a private in the U. S. Army and was discharged a lieutenant in the Field Artillery. In 1925, as a medical missionary of the Congregational Church he made his first tour of bandit- and malaria-ridden South China. After six years of dangerous service to the Chinese people, he returned to warn the United States of the rising menace of Russian Communism and Japanese militarism; in 1934 he returned to Asia to set up a 125-bed hospital in North China which for four years he directed through revolution and invasion.

Dr. Judd helped organize the Council of Europe in 1951, and became a delegate to its first Consultative Assembly in Strasbourg, France. In the U. S. House of Representatives, where in 1962 his colleagues voted him one of its five most influential members, he authored such laudable legislation as Technical Aid to Underdeveloped Nations, Pacific Defense Pact (SEATO), and the International Children's Emergency Fund. In recognition for his achievements as a Christian statesman and missionary, twenty universities and colleges have conferred upon him honorary doctorate degrees.

* * *

The Christian Business of Changing Men

IT IS THE RESPONSIBILITY OF EVERY CHRISTIAN TO TRY TO BUILD God's kingdom on earth. That is, we must try to create a society whose motives and actions are based on belief in a just and loving God as revealed in Scriptures and in the moral order of the universe. Our job today is to be more Christian in our personal and public life here at home and in our relations with people abroad. This is our responsibility to all the people in the world. Jesus said, "He that would be greatest among you, let him be the servant of all." And, with Christ, "all" means *all*—here and around the world.

The world crisis we are in is not so much a test of our power as a nation as it is a test of our character, our steadfastness, and our faith. If anything alarms me, it is not the dedication of our enemies to their faith; it is the failure of so many of us to have faith in our own faith. Do we really believe, as we say, that it is possible to change the world by changing men—by the leaven process? Are we willing to work, work, *work* for our Christian faith?

No one will deny that the world is in the midst of one of the most critical periods in all its history. We are living in a sort of twilight zone between the end of one era of life on this planet and the beginning of another. What kind of era is the new one to be?

That will depend on the outcome of the fierce warfare that is going on all around the globe. It is a conflict that we did not choose and do not like, but which we cannot escape nor wish away.

It is a conflict of arms. Because of atomic weapons, the military threat is the gravest in our history.

It is also a conflict of economic systems. Which will crack up first under the strain?

It is also a conflict of educational systems. Which will produce not only the smartest, but the toughest minds?

It is a conflict of wills. Which will work the hardest?

It is a conflict of philosophies of life, two totally different ways of looking at things.

Most basically of all, it is a conflict of religious faiths. One teaches men to love God; and out of that comes, little by little, love for men. The other teaches men to hate God; and inevitably that leads to hatred of men.

It is plain that this world conflict is moving to a climax. Wars, including cold wars, do not go on forever.

That is why, in the end, the struggle will turn on the strength of our individual faith and how effectively it moves us to treat all men as brothers. For many reasons in our foreign-aid programs we haven't emphasized the things of the spirit, because we have not identified that as the heart of the task. Yet, putting first things —the kingdom of heaven on earth—first in our own lives and in our dealings with others now is a necessity for survival.

In aiding our Allies in the Cold War, some have imagined that if we made people richer and fatter that would satisfy them. No, man desires more than material aid. That is the law of history; that is the faith of Scriptures.

What I am saying is only what the wisest of men said so simply and so profoundly long, long ago: "Man does not live by bread alone"—or by guns, or dollars, or dams, or roads, or schools, or hospitals. Man can't live well without them. But he can't live by them alone. They do not feed his spirit.

Jesus gave the best demonstration of this that I know. He was sitting by a well waiting for his disciples when a woman came out to draw water. She was a bad woman, and he might truly have said to her, "Lady, I haven't seen anyone in a long time in quite such desperate need of a Point Four Program as you. Now I know exactly what you should do. I have all the answers for you. If you will just do as I tell you, everything will be all fixed up." She would have turned from him in resentment and scorn.

Instead, what did He do? He asked her to help him: "Please, may I trouble you to give me a cup of water to drink?" His first words called attention, not to how He could help her; but to how she could help Him. She was important and needed. And, of course, she responded by opening her heart so that He was able in the next few minutes to reveal to her some of the most profound things He said in His whole ministry. But He began by paying attention to her deepest needs to be recognized and respected as a person.

We understand that people want to be free; and we are trying to help them become free. But that isn't all they want; that's only the first step. As soon as they are free they want to be together! They want to belong, to be a part of, to be important. They want to be useful, they want to count for something.

You and I are never again going to be able to relax until the Communist conspiracy fades or changes, gives up its program of world conquest. It can never do that until it ceases to be Communist. And it cannot cease to be Communist until those who belong to it cease to be Communists. *The way to change Communism is to change Communists—that is, to change men; and that is the business of the Christian religion.*

The more desperate the need, the more are men driven back to the One whose "arm is not foreshortened." We can win, not by ducking the difficulties, or by denying the forces of evil; but rather by facing them, knowing that God is still stronger. In short, our greatest need is to recapture a faith in our own Christian faith, at least equal to the faith the Communists have in their Communist faith.

Man, today, controls almost all of nature except his own nature. For that he must have a Saviour. Christ still changes the human heart. He brings together God with His law and His love, and man with all his needs.

Surely God has a right to expect the people of America, whom He has blessed beyond almost any in history, to turn again to His Son and to serve Him and work with Him. If we in our strength and comfort will not rise to this challenge—will not accept this world task—God will not be destroyed. He will not even be mocked. He will find some other land, some other people, to do His will. And our civilization will go to its doom as have some twenty civilizations before it. It is amid the secular aspects of our own life in America and then out around the world that you and I must bear our Christian witness.

J. EDGAR HOOVER

"To trust in the Lord with all thine heart is the only path to happiness, success, and true fulfillment."

* * *

J. Edgar Hoover, Director of the Federal Bureau of Investigation since 1924, has what his minister, the Rev. Dr. Edward Elson, calls "an unfailing zeal for righteousness." This same Christian consecration has been his since his youthful Bible-reading Sundays in the Hoover home in Washington, D.C., his Sunday-school teaching in the Capital's First Presbyterian Church, his unflagging church attendance no matter where his FBI work may take him. Today, as a crusader for American democracy and head of an organization of 14,000 employees, including 6,000 Special Agents, he exercises that same moral influence on millions of American youngsters to whom he is almost an idol.

A vigorous champion of the philosophy that "Democracy cannot survive without the constant influence of the Christian faith," Mr. Hoover has applied the same high principles to the U. S. Justice Department. A member of many national and statewide law enforcement associations, he also is a member of the Board of Directors of the Boys' Clubs of America; a trustee of The George Washington University, and a member of the National Presbyterian Church. He is a Mason, Shriner, and honorary National Councilman, Boy Scouts of America. Among the many awards that Mr. Hoover has received are the U. S. Medal of Merit, the President's Award for Distinguished Federal Civilian Service, the Cardinal Gibbons Medal, the Jewish War Veterans' Gold Medal of Merit, and Freedoms Foundation's George Washington Honor Medal.

* * *

The Path to True Fulfillment

THE MODERN AGE HAS ACHIEVED MIRACLES—JET PLANES THUNDER through the sky at hundreds of miles an hour, rockets are probing the outer recesses of space, and the energy of the atom is being harnessed by the human hand. Twentieth-century man is the beneficiary of a world so marvelous, staggering, and overwhelming that it would have been unbelievable even fifty years ago.

This is the heritage of man's victory over his physical world. He has conquered space, built gigantic structures of steel and concrete, and invented countless items of personal convenience. His mind is ever at work attempting to conceive new devices which will lessen human pain and provide greater material comfort.

If man's needs could be measured in terms of physical well-being alone, modern-day American civilization might be characterized as highly successful. Unfortunately this is not true. Man does not live by bread alone. He has much deeper needs. He is more than a physical creature, with bones and flesh; he has spiritual needs that must be filled.

A spiritual underpinning of life—this is today the crying need of society. Everywhere, in all walks of life, we see giant fissures of immorality, criminal deeds, and evil temptations. Men are committing acts that are wrong, bringing shame upon themselves, their families, and their friends. These are men of little faith—men who trust their own abilities, not the guidance of a Supreme Being.

Time after time, in my thirty-nine years as Director of the Federal Bureau of Investigation, I have seen men and women disregard law and order. They sought, through force and violence, to create their own empires. Murder, kidnaping, extortion, and burglary—these were their weapons of attack; the gun, blackjack, and knife, their tools of operation. They were thinking only of themselves, how they could, at least temporarily, satisfy their own physical desires. They gave not a single thought for the other fellow, not even a pause to consider the consequences of their criminal act. The glorification of the "selfish I"—this is the motivating philosophy of the criminal mind.

Too often in this age of hurry and bustle, we all are inclined to press forward the "selfish I." . . . The vast, over-all panorama of society, of God's great creation, becomes distorted. We become, as it were, tiny islands, thinking—far too exclusively—of our own tasks, needs, and ambitions. . . .

This represents, all too tragically, a perversion of the teachings of Jesus of Nazareth, who said, "I am the way." Modern man, in many instances, has attempted to push God aside, to ignore and even scorn Him, and to usurp His authority. This is the tragedy of modern civilization: the principles of religion, the teachings of the Holy Bible, and the supremacy of God have been disregarded. Our job as dedicated citizens is to return to God, to pay homage to Him, and underpin our great civilization with spiritual strength.

Through many years of active life and the observation of many kinds of people, I have found that the strongest, wisest, most competent, and reliable man is also the first to admit his inadequacy. Contradictory though it may sound, he is strong because he is humble—and remembers always that man is the creation of God. No rule of life is more basic.

When man "leans on his own understanding" . . . when he lives by his own strength . . . when he boasts of probing the mysteries of the atom, the depths of the sea, or the secrets of outer space—he forgets God and claims he is his own master. The result is untold suffering.

Even though one's position is maintained, even though material wealth increases, success quickly turns to failure when God has been forgotten. There is no peace of mind, no personal satisfaction, no personal experience of inward joy.

To "trust in the Lord with all thine heart" is a mark of strength. And it is the only path to happiness, success, and true fulfillment.

RALPH W. SOCKMAN

"We choose the living Christ as we choose a life partner—on faith."

* * *

Dr. Ralph W. Sockman, whom a parishioner once described as "looking like Adolphe Menjou and acting like John Wesley," is minister emeritus of Christ Church Methodist, New York City, and director of the Hall of Fame for Great Americans. As pastor of the 2,000-member Park Avenue parish for forty-four years and as network minister of NBC's "National Radio Pulpit" for thirty-four years, Ohio-born Ralph Sockman has become one of America's best-known, best-loved Protestant divines. Today he also rates as a popular and perapatetic lecturer in demand from coast to coast.

Born in Mt. Vernon, Ohio, and graduated from Ohio Wesleyan University, young Sockman was attending Columbia University when he became inspired to enter the ministry. He joined the Madison Avenue Methodist Episcopal Church (now Christ Church Methodist) as a student. After completing his course at Union Theological Seminary and receiving his Ph.D. degree at Columbia, he was called to the pulpit of that church in 1917. Retiring last year to devote more time to writing and lecturing, he continues as president of the Council on Religion and International Affairs. During 1963–1964, Dr. Sockman is Harry Emerson Fosdick Professor at Union Theological Seminary.

A literary and clerical long-distance champion, Dr. Sockman at seventy-four has written twenty books, hundreds of syndicated columns and articles, and more than two thousand sermons. His best-selling books include The Higher Happiness, The Whole Armor of God, *and* How to Believe. *A trustee of four universities and the recipient of twenty-one honorary degrees, he has been an active member of the World Council of Churches, the Methodist General Conference, and the Union Theological Faculty. Of debonair, indefatigable Ralph Sockman, the Dean of Drew Theological Seminary once remarked, "More than any other man, he makes religion real and he makes it relevant."*

* * *

The Whole Armor of God

Once I was in a bath club in Honolulu, changing my clothes for a dip in the ocean, when I overheard two men at an adjoining locker. One said, "That radio preacher—Stackman or Sackman—is in Hawaii at present."

"Oh, Dr. Sockman, I guess you mean. I heard him the other night at the University of Hawaii."

"Indeed," the first fellow replied, "is he worth hearing?"

"Well," said the second voice, "I guess he's on vacation!"

In our restless search for new scenes, new interests, new excitement, perhaps during that Hawaiian "vacation" I had succumbed to the familiar habit of receiving mental impressions so fast that I was not digesting them spiritually. Perhaps I had not been selective enough in my travel experiences so that I could still preach with power and zest. Perhaps, through overstressing mere activity rather than contemplation and disciplined thinking I had slipped into the sin of shallowness. In any event, the humorous comment of my unseen friends served to underscore one of life's profoundest principles: we must be earnest to seek the truth, responsible in living it to the full, honest to follow where it leads.

Having been brought up on an Ohio farm and in the evangelical Methodist Church of the 1890's, I early learned a rigorous respect for hard work, devotion to duty, and a personal experience of the Christian Gospel. Long ago, then, I learned that faith at its finest is developed by faithfulness in action rather than force of argument, by commitment to Christ in thought and deed rather than a casual indulgence of life as it passes by. I learned too the heart-warming, life-changing witness of the Spirit, and, like John Wesley nearly two hundred years before, "felt my heart strangely warmed, felt I did trust in Christ alone for salvation." Today that dutiful Christian training still manifests itself in what I try to practice as a personal creed: *Give the best you have to the highest you know—and do it now.*

The most penetrating test of a Christian life or of great living is perhaps this: does it get better the farther on we go? Great Christian living must come by growth. Many of us may have grown up in godly homes and find it difficult to date the precise moment of our decision for Christ. Yet however gradual our growth in the Christian life, there must be a definite commitment of the will. As the late Halford Luccock said, "We cannot just ooze our way into the Kingdom of Heaven."

Our relationship to God in Christ is personal. We learn to know persons in a way different from that by which we learn to know facts. If we wish to know the truth about a non-personal subject, we assemble the data and then make up our minds. But in dealing with persons we reach a point where we must make a decision and then let the future reveal more facts. We choose the living Christ as we choose a life partner—on faith. Furthermore, Jesus Christ is not a mere historic figure whom we can study without commitment. He said: "He who is not with me is against me, and he who does not gather with me scatters." (Matthew 12:30) Jesus Christ so embodies the gathering forces of love that we cannot be neutral toward him. We either gather with him in the spirit of love, or scatter the anti-Christ in the spirit of fear and hate. This element of decision is tragically minimized in the modern conventional church.

Commitment of the will must be followed by cultivation of the whole nature. It is possible that all of us may have committed ourselves to Christ. But it is safe to say that not all of us are converted to Christ. We may be converted in our personal morality but not in our political views, in our sexual control but not in our social concern, in our family relationship but not in our economic practices. Christian conversion is a progressively pervasive process. A person does not enjoy the new life in Christ until he has learned to like what Jesus liked. Nor will he enjoy the life hereafter. Christ's promise is: "I go to prepare a place and when I go and prepare a place for you, I will come again and will take you to myself, that where I am you may be also." (John 14:2–3) To be where Christ is without having learned to like what he liked will not be heaven, but quite the opposite. The difference between heaven and hell is a matter of taste more than of temperature.

Words without works are as "sounding brass or a tinkling cymbal." But works without words may soon lack the music of their doing. This is true in family love. It is equally true in our relation with God. The psalmist saw the need of voicing our feelings when he prayed, "O Lord, open thou my lips and my mouth shall show forth thy praise." The Methodist movement owes almost as much to Charles Wesley for his hymns as to John Wesley for his organizing genius. Theology without hymnology would create a cold and sterile church.

Evelyn Underhill once asserted that in the long run we come closer to God through common worship than through closet worship. When we join with fellow worshipers before the eternal symbols of our faith, our awareness of God's past mercies gives us confidence in the future and we sing:

"O God, our help in ages past,
Our hope for years to come."

When we behold the Son of God entering the world in the beauty of Bethlehem and growing up to be the unmatched miracle of the ages, we are moved to sing, "O come let us adore him, Christ the Lord." When we see the gentleness of Jesus blended with such gianthood of strength that the longer we behold him the more we come under the spell of his power, our convictions find voice in the words, "Lead on, O King Eternal."

When we behold Christ on the Cross, praying for his crucifiers, we hear love's last and highest word and we cry with Isaac Watts:

"Were the whole realm of nature mine,
That were a present far too small;
Love so amazing, so divine,
Demands my soul, my life, my all."

Today Christ is going on in the world. We are called to be witnesses to a winning Christ now.

HUNTINGTON HARTFORD

"The difference between the holy man and the artist perhaps is chiefly one of degree: the emphasis in the one case being on goodness and truth, in the other on beauty."

* * *

Huntington Hartford combines a socially alert command of wealth with an unflagging enthusiasm for people, places, and projects of cultural import. As such, he is both financier and art patron—a kind of modern Medici who believes the beautiful can be as important as the useful. Moreover, in his intensive crusade to raise America's artistic and cultural standards he also has demonstrated a Renaissance versatility as author, editor, publisher, builder, philanthropist, businessman, art critic, and scientific investigator.

"Hunt" Hartford, grandson of George Huntington Hartford, founder of the Great Atlantic and Pacific Tea Company, was born in New York City and educated at St. Paul's and Harvard. Before resolving what he calls "the struggle to find your true place in life," he did dutiful turns as an A & P office worker, PM newspaper reporter, and Coast Guard officer in the Pacific in World War II. Gradually, after his return to civilian life, he sensed his mission as a cultural entrepreneur and launched the first of a score of enterprises dedicated to the Seven Lively Arts. In 1949 he established the Huntington Hartford Foundation, a mountain retreat for writers, painters, and composers, at Pacific Palisades, California.

Today, Hartford's multifarious activities mount their zenith from New York to London to Nassau where he is developing Paradise Island as a twenty-million-dollar cultural resort. He serves as board chairman of the Oil Shale Corporation, Speed Park Automatic Garages, and the Handwriting Institute, Inc. He publishes Show, *the monthly magazine of the arts. Strengthening his campaign against modern decadents and their "incomprehensible art," Hartford built the recently completed, white-marble Gallery of Modern Art in New York. He was married recently to Diane Brown. His own book,* Art without Culture, *will be published in the spring of 1964 by the Bobbs-Merrill Company.*

* * *

Has God Been Insulted Here?

ALAN SEEGER, THE POET, HAS "A RENDEZVOUS WITH DEATH," AND death, to paraphrase his famous words, took his hand and led him into his dark land. John McCrae had a rendezvous, too, near Flanders fields where "poppies blow between the crosses, row on row." And how many unknown poets, with time for only one great contribution, their lives, like those boys in Elizabeth Barrett's poem for whom

> "the guns of Cavalli with final retort
> Have cut the game short. . . ."

Such tragedies were accidents of fate, as were Keats' tuberculosis, Shelley's drowning, Scott's insanity, Lautrec's broken legs. Mere man could not prevent them.

But what about the tragedies that might have been prevented, what about the lives that might have been turned to happier channels? What of the "mute inglorious Miltons" who were often mute and inglorious, according to the famous *Elegy*, because of poverty or a lack of an opportunity for education? Must flowers described in the eighteenth century as "born to blush unseen" waste their sweetness on nothing but desert air—even Mojave—in the twentieth? Must the Franz Schubert of our day, if he exists, die at thirty-one from penury, as Gray called it, or another Chatterton or Vachel Lindsay take poison because he faces starvation?

It has been my practical working religion for two decades now to try to insure that these questions are never answered in the affirmative. For artists, writers, composers—all the music-makers and dreamers of dreams—are not only a nation's most precious product, but in Shelley's phrase, "the unacknowledged legislators of the world."

In my view, the great artist, in spite of all his eccentricities, is the truest Christian. I say this for two reasons: 1) a real artist gives us more love in his work than all the do-gooders the world applauds, and 2) his highest work, as Ruskin suggests, is the expression of his delight in God's work, not his own. Thus, in our own century of unfaith and therefore uninspired art I have concluded that the greatest art is the most religious and that the greatest artist is a devout, if not orthodox man.

In the Golden Age of Pericles, it was the highest distinction of the Greeks that they recognized the indissoluble connection between beauty and goodness. In the radiant age of Raphael, Titian, and Leonardo da Vinci, the humblest apprentice knew that inspiration is the perpetual breathing of God's spirit working in us, speaking to us, sending forth his light for the redemption of mankind. Today, to its detriment and decadence, contemporary art knows little of these insights and is, therefore, more and more concerned in its own self-conscious trivia; institutionalized religion too suffers from this same loss of spirit, and despite a brave show of statistics has forfeited its central place in our culture. In short, modern man has been falling apart for half a century and his decadent art and externalized religion show it.

The aura of morality and even of religion, which we sense in great works of art but are never quite able to put our finger on, exists in a kind of mystical trinity composed of the artist, his fellow man, and the catalyst of nature. Whether the artist is creating primarily for the benefit of himself or for others is a moot question. But as the philosopher John Dewey says, there is no doubt that the function and consequence of the artist's work are to effect communication which by its intimate association with others takes on a definitely religious and moral quality. The visible sign of this morality is the artist's subject matter as demonstrated on canvas; it is an indication that the artist is giving himself to the world, that he cares enough about it to become deeply involved in it. Its symbol might well be the drawing of a teacher on a blackboard, for the work of the artist is the highest form of teaching—that which reaches the heart. Indeed, the religious leaders of history—Moses, Jesus, Confucius, St. Augustine, Luther—also were teachers in the noblest sense of the word. The difference between the holy man and the artist perhaps is chiefly one of degree: the emphasis in the case of the one being on goodness and truth, of the other on beauty.

Thus, the ultimate purpose of great art, in my opinion, is a moral one; one would be at a loss otherwise to explain the tremendous veneration in which art and artists have been held even to the irreverent present. There are many great paintings, and perhaps it would be difficult for even the hairsplitter in esthetics to find a moral in all of them. If a painter tells a story, as in the case of "The Last Supper" or the "Descent from the Cross," even the most literal person will have no difficulty in understanding what the artist is trying to say. But in the large majority of paintings the moral is sublimated by the nature of the subject matter. What lesson can one draw, for example, from looking at a landscape of Inness or a seascape by Homer? The fact that the lesson is not easily expressed in words, however, is no indication of its absence; the teaching is simply taking place without the knowledge of the pupil. It is the old lesson which Beauty has taught for so many years without material compensation, the lesson of goodness and kindness and strength which has caused poets to identify it with the word "truth." But in cases where such beauty is indeed absent, particularly if it happens to be replaced on the canvas by ugliness, there is little doubt of the alacrity with which the average observer will recognize the loss.

More than one hundred years ago the eminent Leo Tolstoi had a great deal to say regarding the interrelation of art and religion and the decline of both in nineteenth-century Europe. "The only significance of life," he wrote, "consists in helping to establish the kingdom of God; and this can be done only by means of the acknowledgment and profession of truth by each one of us. . . . Art is the human activity having for its purpose the transmission to others of the highest truth and best feelings to which men have risen." Today, the Frankenstein of unbelief and scientific materialism walking the world only points up how far we fall short of Tolstoi's noble mark. Ours is a time of big business, big labor, big science, and often the twin domination of state and church. Science seeks to reduce everything to mathematics, business to dollars and cents; our art veers between the extreme abstract and the photographic, our psychology between Freud at one end of the scale and the mental gymnastics of IQ tests at the other. Ours is a century of dogma in which the searching, discursive spirit of art, democracy, and true religion is often deemed outmoded.

As a friend of artists, as I hope I am, I have always hated the goose step whether of the mind or body. I hated it at prep school where I was forced to go to church in a blue suit and stiff collar on Sundays when I would have preferred to play football. Later in college I tried to avoid the mechanics and math courses where mundane and heartless logic prevailed. During the war I joined the Coast Guard, because I had a vague feeling that it might be less regimented than some of the other branches of the service. And in recent years I have been fighting the philosophical battle to restore a creative middle ground to the world between the subjective miasmas of Stravinsky, De Kooning, and T. S. Eliot on the one hand and the objective clichés of Dale Carnegie, Norman Vincent Peale, and Bishop Sheen on the other.

So, in art as in life, I take my stand *against* contemporary extremes of abstract expressionism and the exponents of obscurity, confusion, immorality, and violence who practice it. So, believing with John Sloan that art should bring life to life, I take my stand *for* art that cherishes human values and communicates a vision of spiritual truth. Today, for those of us who demand content as well as form in art, and who ask that the artist show us something of life's super truth, the great French sculptor Auguste Rodin perhaps said it best: "Art is contemplation. Art is the most sublime mission of man since it is the expression of thought seeking to understand the world and to make it understood."

RAFER L. JOHNSON

"Win or lose, I am a member of the greatest team that was ever formed, the winning team coached by Jesus Christ."

* * *

Rafer L. Johnson wears the proud title, "World's Greatest Athlete." He earned this high honor by setting both world and Olympic decathlon records in the Olympic Tryouts and Olympic Games in 1960. Now West Coast director of People-to-People, Inc., and assistant track coach at the University of California at Los Angeles, he has also toured for the Peace Corps and State Department in diplomatic goodwill missions.

Born in Texas and brought up in California's San Joaquin Valley, Rafer Johnson starred in major sports in high school and at UCLA. During his college years he served as student body president of UCLA and had the privilege of running on track teams that won the NCAA Championship, the highest honor that can come to a college track team. In 1960, after amassing a record of 8,683 points in the decathlon, Johnson was awarded the James E. Sullivan Amateur Union Memorial Trophy, and was named "Male Athlete of the Year" in the annual Associated Press poll of 256 sports writers. He was also named "One of Ten Outstanding Young Men of the Nation for 1960" by the U.S. Junior Chamber of Commerce.

A well-proportioned 6'3", 200-pound stalwart, Johnson now lives in Los Angeles where he is a member of the Bel Air Presbyterian Church.

* * *

Winning for the Glory of God

The greatest thrill of my life, you ask? Who can doubt that it was becoming world decathlon champion in Rome where I captained the U.S. Olympic team in 1960. Competing for two days in the events that make up the Olympic Decathlon, meeting and making friends with the finest athletes from all over the world, finally defeating Russia's track-and-field star, Vasily Kuznetsov—all this excited me with a boundless gratitude that I had represented my country and college well, but it was not the greatest experience of my life.

On October 29, 1953, when I was still a junior in high school, I accepted the Lord Jesus Christ as my personal Saviour. Although fortunately mine had been a warm Christian home and I had long been active in my church and Sunday school, I knew that something was missing until I asked God to take over my life and to guide me in my day-to-day living. At first, accepting Christ was not the tremendous emotional experience I had expected. But gradually, as I realized how He was always present in my sports, studies, and everyday life, the tears often flowed and I thanked God for the many gifts He was bestowing upon me. As St. Paul wrote to the Philippians: "But whatever gain I had, I counted as loss for the sake of Christ. Indeed, I count everything as loss because of the surpassing worth of knowing Christ Jesus my Lord."

Since that significant year, I have loved Jesus Christ with all my heart. He is the leader of my life. He gave me good health, an athletic body, and the desire to compete, and without His help I would never have had the pleasure of being on many championship teams in high school, college, and the Olympic Games of 1956 and 1960. That is why today, whether on or off the field of competition, I fully agree with Philippians 4:13 which says: "I can do all things through Christ which strengtheneth me."

Several years ago my track coach at UCLA, "Ducky" Drake, told me, "When an athlete goes in seriously for the decathlon, it is not just a matter of physical conditioning—it's a whole way of life!" This I have discovered to be true, completely true, and now specifically I have discovered three things that are absolutely essential both in athletics and in life. One is being physically ready for competition. Athletes who expect to win have to be at their peak; they have to be at the top level of their conditioning.

The second point is the mental attitude of the competitor. This is just as important to him as the physical aspect. If you think you will lose, you have already lost. Mental training has become a tremendous part of an athlete's conditioning. Records are broken because athletes think they can do it.

But without the Lord's help, without his guidance through each event, even though I am physically and mentally ready for competition, I would not perform up to my capabilities. That is why

I consider it so important to be spiritually ready, spiritually sharp. Here is something we can keep with us and be a part of as long as we live; something we can give to others, not just in athletics, but in any phase of life. In the long run this third aspect, spiritual conditioning, is the most important.

I will soon be forgotten as a world record holder and Olympic Games champion, because in a few years we will have more champions. But I will always be able to look back to the days of competition and see the golden thread of the Lord Jesus' leadership. Win or lose, I am a member of the greatest team that was ever formed, the winning team coached by Jesus Christ.

STEVE ALLEN

"Injustice will not be overcome by injustice, atomic bomb by atomic bomb or total war by total war."

* * *

Steve Allen, one of America's few intellectual comedians, emerged in the past decade as a top TV personality and an ardent crusader for such causes as desegregation, disarmament, prison reform, abolition of capital punishment, and a "sane" nuclear policy. His ever widening success in the seldom related fields of show business and social welfare has brought him fame and fortune, a network television show, and the unjustified tag of "controversial" personality.

Born in New York City and brought up in Chicago and Phoenix, Steve Allen turned up as a radio announcer at station KOV in Phoenix in 1941. Subsequently his career as disk jockey, radio funnyman, and creative showman took him to Los Angeles and Chicago before the Columbia Broadcasting System shifted him to New York for the "Steve Allen Show." In 1957 Allen became the whimsical, witty star of NBC-TV's "Tonight" show, and almost overnight became a national celebrity.

Parallel with his emergence as a TV star, Allen also began to write, and among his serious books are The Funny Man, Fourteen for Tonight, *and his autobiography,* Mark It and Strike It. *He also has appeared in a Broadway show, starred in two movies, recorded twenty-five musical albums, composed some hundred popular songs. Recently Allen returned to big-time television with his own program, produced by the Westinghouse Broadcasting Company and broadcast every evening over nearly fifty stations. He is married to actress Jayne Meadows, and they have a young son, William Christopher Allen.*

* * *

The Precariousness of the Human Condition

THAT OUR NATION IS IN THE THROES OF A MORAL COLLAPSE OF SERIous dimensions is, apparently, no longer a debatable conclusion. Liberal and conservative spokesmen vie to see who shall express the conviction most vigorously. Churchmen and secularists, too, agree that we have fallen upon evil days. Their various groups naturally differ as to the reasons for the situation, but that it exists no one seems prepared to deny.

The dreary litany of specifics is by now all too familiar:

The corruption of labor;

The corruption of big business;

The ever growing power of organized crime which, having taken its initial strength from the traffic in illegal alcohol, narcotics, gambling, and prostitution, now reaches into the garment industry, boxing, the restaurant and nightclub field, transport, and a host of other legitimate business areas;

The corruption that has long been characteristic of big-city politics;

The recurring waves of scandals involving cheating in school examinations and "throwing" of athletic contests;

The moral cancer implicit in racial segregation;

The increase in crimes of violence;

The recent television and radio scandals;

And so on, God help us, ad infinitum.

Such examples come to mind readily. Others, no less harmful, are somewhat less obvious. A television program dramatically reveals the sorrowful plight of the nation's migrant farm workers, in itself a situation deplorable morally as well as economically. But the reaction of some Americans (insinuating that the program was "Communistic" rather than expressing the slightest charitable interest in the unfortunate condition of the thousands of citizens involved) was as depressing, judged morally, as was the callousness of the robber barons of an earlier generation.

One's daily newspaper is the source for more additional evidence than one can countenance without literally wincing:

Two-thirds of the world goes hungry while we stockpile food till it decays.

Five hundred thousand men, women, and children in the United States rot their lives away in mental hospitals, some of which would have been a disgrace in the nineteenth century.

Our prisons are full to overflowing, while our society continues to ignore the question as to what turns innocent children into criminals.

When it appears that a notorious offender might not be killed by the state, a governor receives thousands of letters of protest, most of them deeply shocking in their naked, savage cruelty.

Certain Indian tribes in our western states live in squalor and poverty that, while it may be casually dismissed from American minds, serves as handy fuel for the lighting of Communist fires in other parts of the world.

But above and beyond all of these, there is an example of our moral insensitivity that cries out for attention, the same sort of attention that the world all too belatedly gave to the Nazis' extermination of millions of Jews. The sin of which I speak is not, to be sure, the exclusive property of Americans. The Russian Communists are as guilty as we are—probably more so—though only God is qualified to judge. But their participation, morally speaking, is utterly irrelevant. Evil may sometimes be a social business, but one is called to account for it individually nevertheless.

Today the people of the United States are quite prepared, if provoked, to actually burn alive hundreds of millions of innocent men and women, young and old. I deliberately put the matter in such blunt terms, because it is long past time to do so and because there is apparently no other way to start people thinking of the moral questions raised by nuclear weapons.

To those of my readers who are usually described by the term "professional patriot" (true patriots will have no trouble understanding me), I wish at once to make clear that I share their horror of Communist tyranny and would hope that each and every one of them shares my opinion of Fascist tyranny. Some of them say "better dead than Red." I say "better neither dead nor Red," nor have I the slightest interest in "appeasing" the Russians. I happen to agree with Presidents Eisenhower and Kennedy that the nuclear arms race must somehow be stopped and our present direction reversed. But concerning disarmament, arms control, unilateral initiatives, and related questions, let's ask: Are there any moral restrictions whatsoever upon the use of H-bombs? If so, what are they? Have the churches spoken of the issue? Did they speak loudly enough to be heard?

C. Wright Mills, in his "Pagan Sermon to the Christian Clergy," has clearly stated the challenge: "The verbal Christian belief in the sanctity of human life has not been affected by the impersonal barbarism of twentieth-century war. But this belief does not itself enter decisively into the plans now being readied for World War III. . . . Total war ought indeed be difficult for the Christian conscience to confront, but the Christian way out makes it easy; war is defended morally and Christians easily fall into line—as they are led to justify it—in each nation in terms of Christian faith itself. . . . To ministers of God we must now say . . . if you do not alarm anyone morally, you will yourself remain morally asleep. If you do not embody controversy, what you say will inevitably be an acceptance of the drift of the coming human hell. . . . Yet who among you has come out clearly and unambiguously on the issues of internecine war and the real problems of peace? Who among you is considering what it means for Christians to kill men and women and children in ever more efficient and impersonal ways?"

"The task facing us," Father Theodore M. Hesburgh, C.S.C., president of the University of Notre Dame, has said, "will not be done if our philosophers and theologians continue to live among, work with, and speak to people of problems long since dead and buried. . . . Here is an age crying for the light and guidance of Christian wisdom. What must future judges think of us if we live in the most exciting age of science ever known to mankind and philosophize mainly about Aristotle's physics? We live today in the threatening shadow of cosmic thermonuclear destruction and often theologize about the morality of war as though the spear had not been superseded by the I.C.B.M."

Obviously, churchmen have expressed convictions about this complex matter; they can scarcely be expected to give approval to the mass incineration of innocent civilian populations. Pope Pius XII has referred to the nuclear arms race as "homicidal, suicidal madness," although in so doing he was not speaking morally, merely indulging in common sense. But theological commentary on the morality of nuclear war, for all practical purposes, has made no impression whatsoever upon the national conscience!

There has been only one similar instance of such widespread moral blindness in our century. The German people somehow never got around to really hearing the moral criticism of nazism that was voiced here and there, now and then, by German clergymen. Professor Gordon Zahn of Chicago's Loyola University has explained that a fierce nationalistic spirit, a surge of patriotism of the most unthinking sort, simply encapsulated the German conscience so that any crime, no matter how horrible, came to be tolerated, if not brazenly approved, so long as it was in the supposed interest of the Fatherland.

If such a thing was wrong in Germany, it is wrong anywhere, though I am certainly suggesting no point-by-point analogy between the German situation and our own. I merely ask: is it possible that America's conscience at the present moment of history is becoming similarly callous? Is it conceivable that our minds, so heated at contact with evil in early times, have become accustomed to it in this century?

As an entertainer and socially aware writer, I have become increasingly concerned about all these critical matters. I hope, as fellow Americans, that you are too . . . or time is running out for all of us. As a rabbi friend of mine recently said, "The present crisis must awaken us to the terrible relevancy of war's inner life to our outer situation. Either we transform our inner life, or we perish."

FRANK C. LAUBACH

"Lead America! Save your country and your souls by saving others. Win the world for liberty and Christ."

* * *

Forty years ago, the Rev. Frank C. Laubach went among the primitive Moro tribe in the Philippine Islands as a Christian missionary. Soon, in addition to setting up a mission station, he reduced their Moro language to writing, and then worked out the prototype of his now world-famous Each-One-Teach-One picture-word literacy system. He performed this same miracle with twenty other Filipino languages and dialects. Swiftly the news went around the world: Frank Laubach had cut the Gordian knot of illiteracy!

Since that time as apostle to the illiterates, Dr. Laubach has taught an estimated seventy-five to one hundred million adults to read and write. Called by Lowell Thomas, "the foremost teacher of our times," and by Norman Vincent Peale, "a real flesh-and-blood saint," this seventy-eight-year-old missionary educator today directs a worldwide literacy program that operates in 311 different languages in 103 countries. Traveling to remote places of the world, working directly with heads of state as well as with the diseased and destitute of the earth, Frank Laubach insists that Americans awake, intervene to save the hungry hordes of Asia and Africa, seize the fast-vanishing opportunity to stem the moving tide of Communism.

Dr. Laubach is the author of a score of books including Wake Up or Blow Up, The Silent Billion Speak, *and* Letters by a Modern Mystic. *With Mrs. Laubach he makes his home in New York City, where he is president of the Laubach Literacy Fund, and where he is trying to arouse all America to* "AWAKE"—Wage a War of Amazing Kindness Everywhere.

* * *

An Army of Compassion

A gigantic revival is sweeping across the United States. People by the millions are being converted. It is not a religious revival. It is a new attitude toward our underprivileged fellowmen on the other side of the world. We have been shocked awake. We are discovering that this is a terribly small and sick world needing our immediate assistance—fast and vast—and on a tremendous scale. If we do not hurry, we shall perish together.

We are having a conversion from isolationism to internationalism. This conversion may not have struck you yet, but it will. It may hit you in the next few minutes. It has hit our government. Recently I attended a meeting called by the United States government in Washington, D.C., about world literacy—the first of its kind ever held. The entire emphasis in that meeting was worry, because we are too slow. We are losing the world; we must do far more to help educate the illiterate hungry half of the world. We must hurry.

Time is running out—that's why I'm in a hurry! America stands at the bar of humanity and justice—that's why God is in a hurry! With the world situation growing more and more terrifying and with millions of hungry people in Asia, Africa, and Latin America defecting to Communism, we *all* ought to be in a hurry! Before it is too late we must lift the world, or lose it. Before it is too late, we must organize a vast Army of Compassion, a Christ-like army of technical missionaries and teachers, to help the downtrodden "silent billion" lift themselves up, to teach them to read and write, to bring them our know-how in agriculture, education, medicine, and home crafts.

America today must have a cause, a cause expressed by Jesus in the Lord's Prayer: "Thy kingdom come. Thy will be done on earth as it is in heaven. . . ." The kingdom of God—the greatest cause the world has ever known—that should be our cause!

What can we as Christians do about the world crisis? What can we do about the billion hungry, landless, illiterate, destitute people who are the object of the Communist onslaught in Asia, Africa, and South America? There is only one thing we can do: that is to send enough Christ-like, warmly human American technical experts to show these needy people how we made our own tremendous progress. It would be folly to leave it all to the government, for as much as government can do, it will never be enough. Similarly, it will be folly to leave it all to guns, missiles, bombs, and the Pentagon, for guns are ineffective against the revolt of the hungry half of the world; only compassion can stop their hunger. Jesus himself warned us that they who take up the sword will perish by the sword. No, we must stop this fatal drift toward doom by putting the program of Jesus Christ into operation; you and I and all earnest Americans must help these needy millions to live, to learn, to read, to plant, to build, to lift themselves out of ignorance and disease.

If we help these hungry masses of people now, we can have them as our friends. If we do not help them soon, they will hate us and go Communist. Yet for them and for us, the New Testament is full of hope. "The spirit of the Lord is upon me because he hath appointed me to preach the Gospel to the poor: he hath sent me to heal the broken-hearted, to preach deliverance to the captives, to set at liberty them that are bruised, to preach the acceptable year of the Lord." If we sit on our hands another five or six years we shall have passed the point of no return. The world will cave in our America.

Ever since my Methodist upbringing in Benton, Pennsylvania, I have felt sure that Christ's Gospel of love and compassion provided the best answer for men and nations. Ever since my wife Effa and I went to the Philippines in 1912 to work as missionaries and God led me to begin the "Each-One-Teach-One" literacy program among the savage Moros, I have been convinced that we must first teach our illiterate brothers and sisters to read—and then follow with the Bible, democracy, education, sanitation, modern agriculture, and other technical skills. The task is colossal. We must teach a billion people to read and so enable them to rise out of their dreadful poverty. That is why we must train our Army of Compassion now, an army, not armed with bombs and bullets, but carrying books and plows, knowledge and know-how for a desperate one and a half billion people the world over.

Who will send out this great Army of Compassion? Our government and many other governments will sponsor them; mission boards will; universities will; a wide variety of private agencies will send them. All these are now sending a mere trickle, which must become a mighty river. We have the money; we have the people; we have the channels; we have an open door; we have the mandate of God to help these helpless people. In fact, we have every advantage over the Communists if we go out to save the world with love in action. The only reason we have been losing the world is because we didn't care. It would be so easy if we tried.

I am speaking for a billion illiterates who need your help, and need to know your Christ. But I also feel above and around me an invisible host. Heaven trembles lest you and I may prove too small and too late, lest we may be bound by our weak habits when God summons us to great deeds.

I am not afraid of the Communists. I'm afraid of some Americans who have neither fire nor vision—men who begin to see why this might be hard or premature or too informal or too big. The put-on-the-brake type, the go-slow type, the do-nothing type—enough of them can ruin God's program! I tell you what we need to fear—fear the way we are now, for we aren't good enough, daring enough, far visioned enough for this splendid hour. We aren't good enough for God.

But will the American people respond? Yes, I have talked about this Army of Compassion in a hundred cities, and I know our people are eager. They are eager for something Christian they can do for the world besides wringing their hands in helpless frustration. I believe that Americans will lift this old world far above the distress and fury and fear and hate which breed Communism. This is the Christian answer. It is the will of God.

PITIRIM A. SOROKIN

"God Himself does not know *what* He is because God is not *what*."

* * *

Pitirim A. Sorokin, born and educated in Russia, is the founder and director of the National Research Society for Creative Altruism in Boston. Prominent sociologist and professor at Harvard University, Dr. Sorokin has published some thirty books since his arrival in the United States in 1923. All in all, his published works have been translated into forty-two foreign languages.

Reared among the Ugro–Finnish people in northern Russia and baptized a Christian in the Russian Orthodox Church, he was educated at the University of St. Petersburg where he later became a teacher of sociology. As early as 1906, he was arrested and imprisoned because of his political activities. He was a leader in the founding of the Soviet Republic, and from the beginning of the Revolution vigorously fought Lenin, Trotsky, Kamenev, and other Communist conspirators. In 1922 he was arrested, condemned to death, and finally banished by the Soviet Government.

In the United States, Sorokin taught at the University of Minnesota before becoming chairman of the sociology department at Harvard. In 1949 a grant from the Lilly Endowment enabled him to establish the Harvard Research Center in Creative Altruism. His books include The Crisis of Our Age, The Ways and Power of Love, *and* Social and Cultural Dynamics.

* * *

Creative Altruism

EVENTFULNESS HAS BEEN THE MOST SIGNIFICANT FEATURE OF MY life adventure. In a span of seventy-five years I have passed through several cultural atmospheres: pastoral hunter's culture of the Komi; agricultural, and then urban culture of Russia and Europe; and, finally, the megalopolitan technological culture of the United States. Starting my life as a son of a poor itinerant artisan and peasant mother, subsequently I have been a farmhand, itinerant artisan, factory worker, clerk, teacher, conductor of a choir, revolutionary, political prisoner, journalist, student, editor of a metropolitan paper, member of Kerensky's Cabinet, an exile, professor at Russian, Czech, and American universities, and a scholar of international reputation.

No less eventful has been the range of my life-experience: besides events of joy and sorrow, the successes and failures of normal human life, I fully tasted six imprisonments—three under the Czarist regime and three under the Communist; the unforgettable experience of a man condemned to death and daily, during six weeks, expecting his execution by the Communist firing squad. I know what it means to be damned and praised; to be banished or to lose one's brothers and friends in a political struggle. And yet, in a modest degree, I have experienced also the blissful grace of creative work and mystical religion.

These life-experiences have taught me more than the innumerable books I have read and the lectures to which I have listened. Especially, as a non-dogmatic believer in the Judaic-Christian tradition, I have come to appreciate and try to experience three profound truths: 1) the existence of God or the highest creative Reality as a *summum bonum* and supreme mode of being; 2) living in truth, love, and beauty; 3) the need for the practice of creative unselfish love.

I agree with the mystics and great logicians of all great cultures that our language cannot define God or the ultimate Reality of the universe. In this sense, the ultimate Reality-value is the *mysterium tremendum et fascinosum*, transcending all our concepts, categories, and logical laws. Only symbolically can this unutterable Reality be designated by a name or word like God, Tao, Chit, Brahman, Atman, Nirvana, the Oversoul, the Cosmic Mind, the True Self, the Creator, the Supraessence, and so on. These names and the visible symbols of the invisible ultimate Reality are but a mere "finger pointing at it" and in no way identical with it. As J. S. Erigena has written, "God Himself does not know *what* He is because God is not *what*."

Fortunately, these limitations in our comprehension of the *mysterium tremendum* are greatly overcome by the fuller, more frequent supraconscious enlightenment expressed by a few "chosen and anointed"—by the great religious leaders, by the true seers, sages, and prophets on the one hand, and by the creative geniuses in all fields of culture on the other; by great scientists, philosophers, artists, poets, musicians, and other creators of the greatest masterpieces or values of the human universe. Creative giants, who are examples of these chosen and anointed, include Jesus, Moses, Buddha, Confucius, Lao-Tze and Mohammed; Plato, Aristotle, Shankara, Plotinus, St. Thomas Aquinas, Kant, St. Francis, and Gandhi; Galileo, Newton, Bach, Beethoven, Homer, Shakespeare, Raphael, and Michelangelo. Graced and moved by the highest suprarational genius, they reveal to us by their discoveries and creations aspects of the ultimate Reality-value which otherwise would remain hidden from us. Through their revelations, we come to know with Jesus "the Way, the Truth, and the Life."

When our limited minds try to understand the supreme modes of the cosmic Creativity, we grasp at least its true main differentiations: creative truth, creative love, and creative beauty. Like the Christian Trinity of God-Father, God-Son, and Holy Ghost, each of these aspects of the supreme forms of the ultimate Reality is distinctly different from the other two; at the same time, like the Trinity, each of these aspects is inseparable from, and transformable into, one another. Genuine truth is always good and beautiful; real goodness—love—is always true and beautiful; and true beauty is always true and good.

On the human level, the supreme form of being of a person or a group also expresses itself in the form of living in and creating an ever fuller truth, ever nobler love, and an ever sublimer beauty in the human universe. Humanity's lower forms of being consist in living in uncreative ignorance, in destroying truth, in doing evil, and in cultivating ugliness in the human universe. Thus, the paramount task of Christianity and other genuine religions today is the mental, moral, and behavioral transfiguration of human beings and groups, in making them more aware spiritually of the *mysterium tremendum*, more intelligent mentally, nobler morally, purer aesthetically, and more creative in their total life. This transformation must be total—not the performance of a prescribed ritual or the "conversion to Jesus" after an eloquent sermon—and the transfigured individuals must practice the noble precepts and verities they preach.

In my integral religion, man is seen as having three interrelated forms of being: 1) the unconscious (reflex-mechanism of body); 2) the conscious (rational mind); and 3) the supraconscious creator (Nous, Pneuma, Spirit, Soul). In my view of the emerging new world culture, the highest formulae of democracy are given in the Sermon on the Mount and in the Beatitudes. In our age of hate and hypocrisy, living and practicing sublime unselfish love, so beautifully defined by Jesus and taught by the ethics of all the world religions, becomes the paramount need of humanity. Only a notable altruization of persons and groups along the precepts of the Sermon on the Mount can save mankind from the pending catastrophes. Only the growth of unselfish and creative love can decrease the raging interhuman strife and help in establishing a lasting peace in the human universe. Such are the main tasks of Christianity and the other world religions at the present time.

DON J. ODLE

" 'I am made all things to all men, that I might by all means save some.' The objective of Venture for Victory is no less—that people might come to a knowledge of the wonderful love of our Lord Jesus Christ."

* * *

Widely admired for his international "basketball evangelism" program, "Venture for Victory," Don J. Odle is in his sixteenth year as athletic director and basketball coach at Taylor University in Upland, Indiana. His teams have won three Hoosier Conference championships and finished second three times. The author of three books, he was selected the "Outstanding Young Man of the Year" in 1954 by the Indiana Junior Chamber of Commerce, "Alumnus of the Year" by Taylor University, and recently received the "Service to Mankind" award from Indiana's Sertoma Club.

For the past twelve years under the "Venture for Victory" program, Don Odle has taken a group of college stars to the Orient and South America on tours that combine basketball and Christian evangelism. This unprecedented achievement earned him citations from Freedoms Foundation and Look *magazine, and in February, 1958, "Venture for Victory" was acclaimed in the U. S. Congress. To date, his "Victory" all-stars, playing in nineteen countries, have compiled a record of 610 wins against 20 losses.*

At the request of the Formosa Chinese Government, Odle coached the Nationalist basketball team in the 1960 Olympics, and for two years he was chairman of the basketball committee for the National Association of Intercollegiate Athletics. Past president of the Hoosier Conference, he is a member of the People-to-People Sports Committee created by former President Eisenhower to promote art, entertainment, business, and sports in foreign countries. Mr. and Mrs. Odle live in Upland, Indiana, where they are members of the Methodist Church.

* * *

Venture for Victory

It was in 1952 that the Lord showed me how He could make use of a basketball coach. I was sleeping soundly that morning—as you sometimes are when suddenly awakened by the Lord—when the phone rang. It was an overseas call from my friend Dick Hillis, Director of Orient Christian Crusades. He was speaking from Taipei, Formosa. I was very glad to hear from Dick but surprised by his sudden call. I was even more stunned when I learned the reason for his calling halfway around the world: President and Madame Chiang Kai-shek were concerned about the spiritual welfare of the people on Formosa. On their behalf, he asked me to bring over a team of Christian athletes for a campaign of basketball evangelism.

Now I had never considered myself an evangelist, and I had no idea how such a program would work. I had no idea how I could make it work. Yet I had to give Dick my answer. In those few moments of an overseas phone call I made the most far-reaching decision of my career. Out of habit I tried to put my trust in the Lord and let the Spirit lead me. I told Dick, "Yes, I'll do it."

That early morning call sparked the beginning of the Venture for Victory basketball team. All this suddenly happened to a man who fifteen years before had arrived at Taylor University with little Christian training and less interest. Fortunately I found the Lord waiting for me on campus—at a fall revival worship service. Where I had come to college to study business, He directed my life into athletics. When the phone rang that morning in my Upland, Indiana, home, I was beginning my tenth year of coaching at Taylor University.

But why basketball evangelism? Dick Hillis explained to me what President and Madame Chiang Kai-shek had said. A Protestant missionary holding a meeting in one of their cities would draw a crowd of six hundred or seven hundred, while right across the street seven thousand people would gather for a basketball game. This was the kind of crowd—from seven thousand to ten thousand spectators—that they wanted to hear the Christian

Word. We agreed to help evangelize the Chinese and Filipino peoples with a team of Christian all-stars.

That first year abroad I learned that the people of the Orient love athletics. There are a thousand teams on the island of Formosa and most of them play all year around. People will walk for miles, sleep on the ground in the rain, and battle for a chance to see the games! And the story is the same in the Philippines, where basketball is the number one sport and twenty-nine thousand at a time crowd into a stadium to see a game. Similarly, sports fans go wild about basketball in Korea, Malaya, Indonesia, Thailand, Vietnam, and all over the Far East. More important, we found that our Venture for Victory teams could be the key to places formerly forbidden to Christian missionaries. One year the government of Kuala Lumpur, Malaya, waived a law banning public preaching just to make it possible for us to play; as we told them, Venture teams never schedule a game unless the boys are permitted to make their plea for men's souls.

Starting with that 1952 team, our young college players are chosen annually for their athletic skill, talent, and Christian devotion. They come to us from all over the country—Christian lads who love the Lord and are willing to share their faith in Christ with others. They are willing to travel into primitive jungles and play in mountainous regions; sometimes we dribble uphill the first half and dribble downhill the second half; always between halves each boy gives his Christian witness. Yet how shocking it is in these isolated places to find soft drink signs but no Bibles! Sometimes it seems that Americans are readier to commercialize than to share the thing that made America great, our faith in God.

But thanks to the Lord, the boys of Venture for Victory present a different picture. Wherever they go, they impress people the right way—these tall, athletic, clean-looking American youths. The full spiritual impact of their ministry cannot be told in words. Playing from seventy to eighty games in a dozen countries, they reap a harvest of souls after every contest. And they do this while adjusting to constant travel, strange food, difficult sleeping conditions, and the driving play of eager, experienced opponents. Very often, in both Asia and South America, the words, "hot, hungry, and homesick," just about summed up our feelings.

But there are often fascinating adventures to take our minds off our troubles. Once when we were playing the Seven Tigers, a famous team in the Orient, the immense crowd overpowered the guards and a riot started between the people on the ground and those in the stands. Although we managed to escape without getting clobbered, we told the Commanding General we needed protection during the games; at our next playing field we were met by two hundred soldiers with fixed bayonets and twenty-five machine guns. Lucky, too, for the game was a "real barn-burner," which we won by one point! When the game was finally over and the boys had given their testimonies for Christ, you could see how thrilled and pleased everybody was. Then, during the Decision for Christ meeting, imagine our surprise when the members of the Chinese team, including the coach, came forward and enrolled in the Bible correspondence school!

Interest in the game waned once while we were playing at a Formosan naval base. The reason? The game occurred in 1958 during the intense shelling of Quemoy and Matsu by the Chinese Communists. After the game the men were to put to sea and face death. For once our audience wasn't very concerned with basketball. At half-time, however, when we talked about Christ and eternal life, there was breathless attention. Afterward, when we came to the Decision meeting, no one left; those brave young sailors stayed there listening as long as possible.

These stirring experiences have made a great spiritual impression on our Venture players. All but one member of the first Venture team have entered the ministry or the mission field. Seven of our young men have dropped their secular careers and returned to the Orient as full-time missionaries. The common testimony of all is, "My life can never be the same." Basketball might seem a strange way of winning souls. But St. Paul once said: "I am made all things to all men, that I might by all means save some." The objective of Venture for Victory is no less—that people might come to a knowledge of the wonderful love of our Lord and Saviour Jesus Christ.

JEROME HINES

"Christ is the Morning Star of my life. Any philosophy that leaves out the living Christ is totally inadequate."

* * *

That rare American, a native of Hollywood, Jerome Hines has been called by the New York press "the best basso at the Met." Now in his seventeenth season as a Metropolitan Opera star, his record and wide recognition tend to bear this out. Since 1946, when he made his New York debut in Boris Godunov, *he has appeared at the Metropolitan in more than thirty leading basso roles. Among them are the title roles in* Boris Godunov *and* Don Giovanni, *King Marke in* Tristan und Isolde, *Ramfis in* Aïda, *Mephistopheles in* Faust, *Woton in* Die Walküre, *and King Henry in* Lohengrin. *He was the first native-born American ever to sing Boris at the Met.*

Born in the movie capital where his father was an associate producer, Mr. Hines attended UCLA and made his professional debut with the Los Angeles Civic Light Opera Company in Pinafore. *Later, upon graduation, he sang with the San Francisco Opera, the New Orleans Opera, and the Hollywood Bowl Orchestra; and in 1949, winning the Cornelius Bliss Scholarship awarded by the Metropolitan, he sang at the Goethe Festival in Aspen, Colorado. In 1953, after the regular Metropolitan season, Hines made his first RCA Victor records with Maestro Toscanini and the NBC Symphony, and gave a series of performances at the Edinburgh Festival.*

More recently Mr. Hines won acclaim for his singing in Parsifal, Tristan, *and* The Ring *at the world-renowned Wagner Festival in Bayreuth, Germany. He also made his debut at such famous opera houses as Milan's La Scala and, Buenos Aires' teatro Colón, and at the Munich Opera Festival. The handsome, 6′6″ artist sang in the White House last year at the invitation of President and Mrs. Kennedy, and is also a composer who has written, produced, and starred in operatic dramatizations from the Life of Christ. He is married to the Italian soprano, Lucia Evangelista, and they are the parents of three sons. The family lives in South Orange, New Jersey, where they are members of the Christian and Missionary Alliance Church.*

* * *

The Spiritual Battlefield of Life

DURING MY CONCERT TOUR OF THE SOVIET UNION IN 1962, I HAD two unusual opportunities to carry God's Word to godless Russia. The first occurred in Leningrad where I sang the Mephistopheles role in *Faust*. As the curtain came down and I walked off-stage into the wings, the male and female chorus began to applaud and shout the Russian equivalent of "Bravo, comrade!" I stopped, feeling somewhat embarrassed before this palm-pounding praise, and raised my hand to say in full operatic voice: "Thank you, but praise Almighty God, not me."

The second such incident came at the climax of the tour in Moscow when I sang the title role of *Boris Godunov* before a Bolshoi Theatre audience that included Premier Khrushchev. At the end of the opera, Boris exclaims, "Forgive me, forgive me" —and falls dead. But suddenly I decided to do a little more. After saying the regular words, I smiled, raised my eyes, and added, "Oh, my God, forgive me." As I performed it, Boris Godunov finds the peace of God when he dies; in the performance that evening before thirty-five hundred Russian music-lovers the opera ended on a high religious note. That is why, I feel, for the first time in the history of the Bolshoi there was sudden inspired applause even as Boris fell rather than after the final curtain had rung down.

A decade ago, I found the greatest friend in the world. I found Jesus Christ. And the thing I want to tell everybody is that Jesus Christ is not just a philosophy to live by. He is that same living Person who was resurrected nearly two thousand years ago.

I know Jesus Christ and I know him in my heart. I know him in person. And Jesus Christ himself has told me that I am his son; that I am saved and that I belong to him because he bought me at the price of his own sacrifice upon the Cross. I have that blessed assurance in my life that I am a son of God, not upon my merits but upon the merit of Jesus Christ, who in his perfection died for my sins. And I can with boldness stand before the throne of God and say, "I am your son, because I stand here upon your merit."

So for me, for the ten years since I found God, my singing career has been a way of carrying His Word. Today, Christ is the morning star of my life. Each day my life is a spiritual battlefield in which I strive to let God be glorified. Yet victory is always the Lord's, for as the Apostle Paul tells us: "My strength is made glorious in weakness. Most gladly therefore will I glory in my infirmities, that the power of Christ may rest upon me." Indeed, God makes us offer up, not only our weaknesses and our gifts to Him, but our very selves. In the end He fills us all with awe and amazement at how He works, never fails, meets our needs, brings us perpetually to Him.

The way I came to know Christ is a long story and, of course, one can never untangle all the threads that lead to it. The various people that you meet, the background you have in your own home, the examples of older Christian friends, and in my case a mother who has loved the Lord as long as I have known her—all these influences enter into it. As we know too, many fine Christian parents sometimes have children who turn out to be non-Christians. It merely indicates that the most a parent can do is point the Way; he cannot give you the Way, because the Way is not a direction but a person and a life which is Jesus Christ. It is only through the mysterious person and presence of Jesus Christ that we are saved; so it has to be a personal spiritual encounter which nobody can perform for us. When I found my Lord and Saviour just ten years ago, it wasn't through a church or a minister. It was because the Lord put his hand upon me Himself, He dealt with me directly, He worked His miracle in my life. Although I originally did not believe in miracles, He used miracles in my life to capture me and prove to me that I was dealing with God Himself. Thus, religion to me is Jesus Christ as a reality and a presence—not just a philosophy to live by. To me there is one Lord of life, and Jesus Christ is His one and only Son. To me any life philosophy that leaves out the living Christ is totally inadequate.

"I am the way, the truth and the life," said Jesus. There is no other way, nor truth nor life. There is no other teaching except Christ's that can transform us and make us instruments of His life and love. To be a Christian, you have to know Christ personally; to be a Christian, you have to discover the reality of God within yourself. Today I thank God for my Bible, for my inspired upbringing, for my worshiping parents, and for His grace that brought me back reborn after I had strayed from the fold. "Watch ye, stand fast in the faith, quit you like men . . . let all things be done with charity." (I Corinthians 16:13)

Often friends and fans ask me which opera is my favorite. As a musician and basso, I have several favorites including *Boris* and *Don Giovanni*. But, as a Christian, I am especially drawn to one —*Faust*. Not only have I sung this the most for the Metropolitan Opera, but this musical drama carries a true Christian message. *Faust* is the story of salvation by faith, salvation without works. In it Margarita, tempted by the devil, has fallen into sin; when at the end she can be saved from death by appealing to Faust and Satan, she turns to tell Faust she abhors him and calls upon God to save her. The opera's mighty climax comes as Margarita falls lifeless to the ground, and Faust stands over her dead body. Mephistopheles cries out that she is damned, but the angel choir responds singing, "She is saved, she is saved." Christ, her Saviour, is risen.

KENNETH D. WELLS

"God and Country should be our watchwords, as we seek to secure the dignity of man, free and unafraid."

* * *

Dr. Kenneth D. Wells is president of Freedoms Foundation at Valley Forge, Pennsylvania, a non-profit, non-sectarian, and non-political organization which presents annual awards to individuals, institutions, organizations, and corporations, who have promoted a better understanding of the American Way of Life during the current year. He has been active as a trustee of the American Humanics Foundation and the National Scholarship Foundation, as a member of the Boy Scouts of America National Court of Honor, Invest in America National Advisory Board, the Institute of Political Studies in Liechtenstein, and the Newcomen Society of North America, and as a Thirty-third Degree Designate of the Ancient Accepted Scottish Rite of Freemasonry.

Among his many awards are The National Association of Foremen Award, The Honor Citation of The Military Order of the Purple Heart, The Gold Medal of Merit, and the Distinguished Service Medal of the Veterans of Foreign Wars of the United States, the National Shrine Citation, the Good Citizenship Medal of the National Society of the Sons of the American Revolution, the Silver Buffalo Award of the Boy Scouts of America, and the Magna Charta Day Award of The Baronial Order of the Magna Charta.

Dr. Wells, who graduated from Northwestern University in 1936, did postgraduate research at the University of Southern California and the California Institute of Technology. He holds honorary degrees from Temple University, Florida Southern College, Trinity College, Texas Christian University, and Salem College.

Dr. and Mrs. Wells, the former Ruth Elizabeth Van Allen, have two children and four foster children. They reside in Valley Forge and are active members of the Valley Forge Methodist Church.

* * *

Speak Up for Freedom

In the heart's journey through life, many people and events seem to help us become the kind of person God intends. Born in an Akron, Ohio, Methodist home, I recall many such people who over the years shed love and light on my emerging life—my father who taught me perseverance; my mother who taught me hard work; my high school coach who taught me good sportsmanship; my wife who taught me compassion; my children who taught me to live today as though tomorrow would never come. A dozen dear friends, hundreds of acquaintances, each has given me a gift, a grace, an insight which has enabled me to keep growing and to keep probing deeper into life.

Out of many inspiring friends and "turning point" experiences, two may be mentioned quickly because of their lasting influence. When I was a child in Akron and attending Sunday school regularly, our white-haired preacher stood up to speak to us one day; he held the Cross in one hand and the Flag in the other. Speaking slowly and soberly, he began, "The old flag has been in many a fix since 1776, but it has never touched the ground. So, with the help of Christ you boys won't ever let it happen, will you?" From that day on, I've tried to make God and country the guiding ideals of my life.

Years later, when I was thirty years old and undergoing a time of danger and despair, the Lord touched me in prayer. In answer to my supplication He turned my life from defeat to victory; in that hour I learned from Him whose name is above all names that nothing counts but the victory of a man over himself. Since that time my only true accomplishment has been in seeking God's will and trying to further His ends, in spite of my obvious defects in mind, heart, and soul. Today, if my work with Freedoms Foundation and if my personal concern for elevating the dignity of free men prove worthy, I believe life can go on with increasing faith and without remorse.

The motto, "Speak up for Freedom," really suggests the whole meaning of my life and the Foundation's program here at Valley Forge. Freedoms Foundation was founded in 1949 by a group of men and women from all walks of life, who believed we need an encouragement organization to stimulate and build an understanding of the moral American philosophy, of our way of life based on a fundamental belief in God, of Constitutional Government designed to serve and not to rule our people, of the unique idea that every single person possesses inalienable personal, political, spiritual, and economic rights. To this end, we have used incentive and recognition ideas essential to voluntary Christian activity in the awards process, with George Washington medals, special classroom teacher medals, special trips as awards for artists, writers, editors, ministers, teachers, and students, special libraries for schools, and many other awards presented to those people and institutions throughout the land who have been selected by the annually convened Distinguished Awards Jury.

Now, with the Communist conspiracy using its traitorous methods, its subversion, its espionage, its propaganda, we have a first obligation not to be fooled. Atheistic socialism is a tired old hoax, but these atheists have a purpose of world dominion. They want the souls, the hearts, the front porches of America. They want to own the podiums, the factories and farms, the kitchen utensils, all the parts of our free life—lock, stock, and barrel. What's on their side? Just one thing—brutal, naked power. This has always been the case with tyrants in the world.

As dedicated citizens and as Christian patriots we're all together in our unyielding determination to give our purses, our prayers, and our personal power to make sure that the candle, which flickered at Valley Forge and did not go out, does not go out now! If we are so determined, we are going to see this tyranny die. Therefore I urge peoples everywhere to study and understand this conspiracy which we are up against and to realize that it has become a virus in the American bloodstream. They have infected us, but America is not going down. We must realize we have a deeply difficult task in adjusting from the older type of shooting war to this new type of Cold War: war by subversion, war by propaganda, war by destruction of moral standards. Indeed, to win we must keep our war power strong, we must keep our will power, faith, and understanding strong and build them stronger every day.

That is why, as president of Freedoms Foundation, I believe God's work is my work. God has few big tasks to be done—just these critical daily details described above—and surely we all can find time and devotion to tackle them before it is too late. At any rate, that is why I work for the greatest of all causes, human freedom, here and now in our tumultuous times.

BILLY GRAHAM

"All have come short of the glory of God."

* * *

Billy Graham, born William Franklin Graham, Jr., in Charlotte, North Carolina, today stands as the foremost evangelist of the world's millions of people. Believers and non-believers have thrilled to his Christ-centered crusades from Chicago to West Berlin and from Glasgow to Melbourne. Additional millions read his syndicated newspaper column, listen to his radio and TV program, "Hour of Decision," buy such best-selling Graham books as My Answer, *and* Peace with God. *He has become an American legend in his own time.*

Born and brought up in a warm Christian environment, Billy was reared in the Presbyterian Church, but is now a member of the Southern Baptist Convention. The supreme experience of his youth occurred in 1934, when during a campaign conducted by the Kentucky evangelist, Mordecai Ham, he was converted to Christ and determined to become a minister. He studied first at the Florida Bible Institute and later at Wheaton College, served as vice-president of Youth for Christ International, and after a long preparation of preaching and prayer conducted his first major American crusade in Los Angeles in 1949. Today, between his worldwide crusades and regular visits with the greatest and humble of the earth, Dr. Graham lives in Montreat, North Carolina, with his wife and five children.

* * *

The Hour of Decision

BACK IN CHARLOTTE, NORTH CAROLINA, IN THE 1920'S, I ENTERED my freshman year in high school and forthwith experienced the supreme thrill of my young life. Babe Ruth, the king of baseball, came to my home town to play an exhibition game. All of us were on the front seats shouting and yelling at the top of our lungs. My father, who had taken us to the game, arranged for me to shake hands with the great Babe. I will never forget the thrill of shaking hands with the fellow who was the idol of all our young hearts.

I didn't wash my hand for about three days. During my last high school years, my keenest ambition was to be a professional baseball player.

When I was sixteen, after finishing a game, I was invited to a church. I was told that a "fighting preacher" was to preach. I was interested, for anything about a scrap or a fight was all I wanted. I forsook my studies and went to church. To my amazement, it was a great evangelistic campaign and five thousand people were gathered.

I sat in the rear of the building, curiously watching all the strange happenings. I wasn't quite sure what would take place next. I had always thought of religion as more or less "sissy stuff," and that a fellow who was going to be an athlete would have no time for such things. It was all right for old men and girls, but not for real "he-men" with red blood in their veins.

A great giant of a man stood and began to preach in such a way as I had never heard a man preach. Halfway through his message he pointed right in my direction and said, "Young man, you are a sinner." I thought he was talking to me, so I ducked behind the person in front of me and hid my face! The idea of his calling me a sinner!

"Why, I'm as good as anybody," I told myself. "I live a good, clean, healthy, moral life. I'm even a member of a church, though I seldom go."

But then he began to quote scripture. "All have sinned, and come short of the glory of God." "There is none righteous, no, not one." For the first time in my life I realized I was a sinner, that my soul was bound for hell, and that I needed a Saviour. But when he gave the invitation, I rushed out into the night and made my way home.

I'll never forget the struggle that followed. All night long I wrestled and fought. The next day I could hardly wait for evening, so I could get back to the service. This night I sat near the front. When the preacher stood this time, he seemed to smile at me. He said in tenderest tones that "God commendeth his love toward us, in that, while we were yet sinners, Christ died for us."

When the invitation was given I made my way to the front with the others. I gave my hand to the preacher and my heart to the Saviour. Immediately joy, peace, and assurance flooded my soul. My sins, which were many, I knew were gone. For the first time I had met the Person who became the Hero of my life, Jesus Christ.

I had sought thrills! I found them in Christ. I had looked for something that would bring pleasure and that would satisfy the deepest longing of my heart! I found it in Christ. "In thy presence is fulness of joy; at thy right hand there are pleasures for evermore."

Christ is the Hero and Idol of my heart. He challenges, thrills, and satisfies. "Wherefore he is able also to save them to the uttermost that come unto God by him, seeing he ever liveth."

JAMES C. PENNEY

"Respect yourself. Respect others. Work hard and continuously at some worthwhile thing."

* * *

James C. Penney, one of the most successful merchants in American history, is at age eighty-eight founder and active board member of the famous stores that bear his name. From a tiny "Golden Rule" store established in Kemmerer, Wyoming, in 1902, Mr. Penney built a chain of more than seventeen hundred stores; last year their gross sales in forty-nine states topped the one-and-a-half billion dollar mark.

More active than ever as a philanthropist, gentleman farmer, and Christian layman, Mr. Penney today serves as a trustee of Allied Youth, the Agricultural Hall of Fame, and International Rotary, and is vice-president of the Laymen's Movement for a Christian World. He once made as many as two hundred speeches a year urging Americans to obey Christ's two fundamental commandments—to love God and to love your neighbor as yourself.

Fifteen colleges and universities have awarded the "Golden Rule Merchant" honorary degrees, including Baylor, Rollins, Boston University, and the University of Wyoming. Mr. Penney is the author of Lines of a Layman, View from the Ninth Decade, *and* Fifty Years with the Golden Rule. *Married and the father of four grown children, he and Mrs. Penney live on New York's Park Avenue where they attend both the Episcopal Church and Christ Church Methodist.*

* * *

Fifty Years with the Golden Rule

FROM MY VANTAGE POINT OF EIGHTY-EIGHT YEARS, I HAVE REACHED one Gibraltar-sure conclusion about life: we cannot perform the high tasks of life without the help of God. We cannot do our duty without faith in Him. We cannot succeed without constant prayer.

My own long life has taught me this painfully, yet perfectly.

Trained by my parents to live by the Golden Rule, I long thought of myself as a religious man. I had confidence in God's goodness, especially as the Penney stores grew in numbers and in profits. Like so many of my fellowmen, I thought it was sufficient to do the right thing, to be self-reliant, hard-working, ambitious. But, in time, I learned one can be too self-reliant.

Through all the years I was building my business, I worked out many intricate financial transactions, supervised merchandise purchasing, production, and distribution, dealt with thousands of men inside and outside the Penney company. In all these matters, my basic feeling was that everything was up to me; I had to make all the right decisions myself. And, of course, as my sense of power increased I felt that with more and more money I could move mountains. I was still, I believed, a religious man, but more and more the spiritual side of thinking and living filled a separate compartment. I still governed myself by the Golden Rule; but, I confess it freely, God had very little hand in my life and business.

Then came the tidal wave we called the Depression—the black years from 1929 to 1932 which engulfed individuals and businesses in every corner of the country. My interests were far flung—*The Christian Herald*, the Florida Memorial Home Community, the National Youth Radio Conference—and when the stock market collapsed, I poured more and more money into these projects until my debts exceeded seven million dollars. Finally, the loss of my entire personal estate of forty million dollars became the most bitter, soul-searing experience of my life. But I learned some valuable lessons, including the fact that money won't insure the success of any project or any life.

In this crisis of my life, I had many inner obstacles to overcome. Constantly in those days I carried a slip of paper on which I'd written (from the ninety-first Psalm): "He shall cover thee with His feathers, and under His wings shall thou trust. His truth shall be thy shield and buckler." It took much time, as well as an entirely new kind of personal discipline, to clarify my thinking—to start thinking more about the power of God and less about the power of money.

One night, for example, at age fifty-six, I was broke, discouraged, ill in a sanitarium in Battle Creek. I felt that I would never see the dawn of another day. I got up and wrote farewell letters to my wife and to my oldest son. I sealed the letters. If I did sleep, it was not a sound sleep. I rose early, went down to the mezzanine floor, and found the dining room was not open. Suddenly, over in one corner of the mezzanine, I heard the singing of Gospel hymns. The song was the old favorite, "God Will Take Care of You." You can imagine how heavy my heart was when I went in. Yet I came out of that room that morning a changed man. Within just a few moments my life was transformed. It was almost as if I had had a new birth. God did take care of me; He did save me. And ever since, I have been trying to fill that obligation.

When finally I got back on firm ground, I had much less in a material sense than I enjoyed before. But I had gained immeasurably in spiritual wealth, for I had learned to turn to God for guidance in all the acts and decisions of my life. All spiritual awakening requires this realization: material arrogance and pride build up a sense of power that separates man more and more from God. Then when some desperate crisis brings this realization, the change appears almost a miracle.

But that miracle is ever within a hand's reach of all of us. That is the wonderful thing about it. We have only to reach out and touch God, to take His hand and ask Him to lead us.

NICK ADAMS

"Of all the Bible's great injunctions, the one I cherish most is 'Be not anxious.'"

* * *

Nick Adams, a New Jersey boy who made good in Hollywood, stars in motion pictures and in television with equal facility. Playing major roles in such films as No Time for Sergeants, Teacher's Pet, *and* Picnic, *he simultaneously attracted national attention in 1960 when he essayed the Johnny Yuma part in the network TV series, "The Rebel." More recently he starred in NBC-TV's weekly newspaper drama, "Saints and Sinners," and the MGM movie,* Twilight of Honor.

Born Nicholas Adamshock in Nanticoke, Pennsylvania, "Nick" attended Snyder High School in Jersey City where he won letters in baseball, basketball, and football. But with the gleam of stage and screen luring him even then, he landed the first acting assignment at fifteen in an off-Broadway production of The Silver Tassels. *After serving three years in the Coast Guard and another five making the rounds in New York and Hollywood, Adams gained his first film part from Mervyn LeRoy in* Mister Roberts. *In addition to his movie roles, he has also appeared on such TV stanzas as "Playhouse 90," "Wagon Train," and "Zane Grey Theatre."*

An accomplished horseman and aspiring writer, he is married to the former child actress, Carol Nugent. With their two children, the Adamses live in the San Fernando Valley where they are ardent members of the Pacoima First Baptist Church.

* * *

The Witness of "Johnny Yuma"

By the year 1961, after a decade of intensive and often futile struggling in New York and Hollywood, I finally "had it made" as an actor. I was the star of a new TV Western, "The Rebel," which had rocketed to the top of the weekly ratings. I had finished my ninth motion picture, *The Interns,* and was starting my tenth for Paramount Pictures, *Hell Is for Heroes,* a war film in which

I played the lead. As my weekly salary topped the five-thousand-dollar mark and as I moved in the glittering Filmland round from Beverly Hills to Malibu to Studio City, I realized that at last I was a "star," a major actor, a success in the field I had selected while still a high school student in Jersey City.

Buoyed by that kind of success and by a lovely wife and two children, I seemed to have everything that a man might desire. Yet, on location that hot July afternoon before the cameras started to roll I felt desperately empty inside. Hungry. Thirsty. Yearning for something which I gradually realized only Christ could fill. Fortunately, also working on the picture was a Baptist minister and special prop builder, Joe De Franco, who had talked to me a great deal about faith and conversion and who was guiding my spiritual development more than I knew. That day, noting my depression and perplexed manner, Joe walked me down the road so that we might be alone. Suddenly, he began to quote John 3:16 in a most unusual manner:

"For God so loved Nick Adams that He gave his only begotten Son that should Nick Adams believe on Him. . . . Go over to that clump of trees, Nick, get down on your knees, confess your sins and ask the Lord's forgiveness. Accept Christ as your personal Saviour. Then if all these other things are taken away, you will be rich, for you will have Christ as your All-in-all."

I did accept Christ that day—on my knees in the Southern California brush country. For the first time in years I felt clean and refreshed within. The radiant change in my mood and appearance was instantly apparent not only to Joe De Franco, but also to my co-workers in the movie, who remarked on my energy and good spirits as we completed the day's filming. Christ had become my All-in-all. Later, when we returned from location after finishing the picture, I joined Joe's Southern Baptist Church in Topanga Canyon.

Today everything I do is because of my faith. Today any success that I have is because of my belief in Jesus Christ and the fact that I read, believe, and follow his words in the Bible. Through prayer and Bible study I am trying to be led in everything that I do, not only in my career but in my home life, my personal life, and in all my relations with others. Thus, I believe my greatest accomplishment to date is the fact that I am a Christian and

I believe in Jesus Christ. I also sincerely believe that for many people who want to believe and to know, Christ is the answer. But for some reason they can't find Him, because it is a difficult thing to believe that someone was the Son of God and came down and died on the cross for us; and by His dying on the cross, He died for all of our sins; and by accepting Him as our personal Saviour it guarantees us eternal life with Jesus Christ in Heaven.

Of all the great injunctions in the Bible, the one I covet most is: "Be not anxious"—do not worry, do not fret, therefore, about tomorrow. Don't worry about this, don't worry about that, but seek ye first the Heavenly Father's Kingdom and His righteousness and everything else will be added unto you. It's a wonderful thing when you do accomplish it. For when you really believe it and practice it, what a difference it makes in your life.

So in my current Hollywood career—whether a TV series is canceled or not, whether my latest movie is a box-office hit or not—I abide by the Biblical promise, "For God so loved the world that he gave his only begotten Son, that whosoever shall believe in Him should not perish, but have eternal life." My whole life is governed by that. Everything I do now, I do for the Lord, and I don't worry about the things that happen here. I know that my home is in Heaven, that this earth is just a temporary dwelling place, that while here I must try to do as much as I can for the Lord and for other people. I know I have been promised salvation and I know I have it.

JOHN D. BRIDGERS

"The most reverent group of human beings I've ever seen is a team of football players before the big game."

* * *

John D. Bridgers, head football coach and athletic director at Baylor University since 1959, is considered one of the nation's top collegiate and professional gridiron mentors. Since his playing days at Auburn University to the early 1940's, he has coached football at Sewanee, Auburn University, Johns Hopkins, and Baylor in Waco, Texas. During the 1957 and 1958 seasons he acted as defensive line coach for the Baltimore team of the National Professional Football League when the "Colts" broke all Baltimore records in defense and led the National Football League in defense against rushing.

At Johns Hopkins University his football eleven won the Mason–Dixon Conference Title in 1956. That same year Coach Bridgers was selected by the student body for the Annual Gilman Award as outstanding faculty member—the first athletic department representative to be so honored. At Baylor, Bridgers' teams play the hard-running, open-passing game of the pros in the tough Southwest Conference. A veteran of World War II and Korean War Service, Bridgers is married to the former Frances Young, and they have a married daughter and two sons. The entire family attends the Seventh and James Baptist Church in Waco.

* * *

Passing, Punting—and Prayer

BELIEVE IT OR NOT, I HAVE NEVER SEEN A MORE REVERENT GROUP of beings in my life than a team of football players just before the big game. The reason for this is that top athletes, no matter how highly skilled or well conditioned, are always looking for that additional help just like the rest of us. Champions need the Christian faith just as much as anyone else. Whether coaching college or professional football, I have tried to build championship teams based on the practice of that very faith. And just as your physical strength languishes unless you exercise, so your faith doesn't amount to much until you start to pay attention to it.

Through the influence of a devout mother I began paying attention to the Christian religion at an early age. She always insisted on the Christian virtues of honesty, fairness, and charity inside the house, and on Sunday morning she always took my brother and me to the Southside Baptist Church in Birmingham, Alabama. I remember one period when I didn't miss church or Sunday school for five straight years! To this day I don't feel right on any Sunday I miss church. In my adult years, too, I found deep fellowship and inspiration in knowing the Rev. Dr. Vernon Richardson, pastor of the University Baptist Church in Baltimore. Today I never fail to encourage all Baylor athletes to attend church and participate in Christian activities.

Yet it was only after following my chosen profession of several years that I learned to apply faith to football coaching. It was in 1956 when I had served for three years as head coach at Johns Hopkins; world-renowned Johns Hopkins, properly stressing scholarship and the preparation for graduate study, grants no athletic scholarships of any kind. Finally that fall, after suffering some pretty disappointing seasons as far as our record was concerned, I decided that the team would pray before and after each game. I made the decision even though I anticipated reasonable difficulties in getting an assorted athletic crew of Protestants, Catholics, and Jews from all parts of the country to pray together!

For our first encounter that year, the small Johns Hopkins' team drove down to Lexington, Virginia, to scrimmage Washington and Lee University. When we took the field to warm up and looked at their bigger squad of sixty or more players, I doubt if any of us felt we had much of a chance against them. But we said our prayers before the game as we had planned, and kicked off. As the game progressed we didn't do badly until near the end of the first quarter when our captain, center and best player, Don Gallagher, suffered a severe knee injury and had to leave the game. His only replacement, Larry Littman, was an unproven newcomer who had not played high school football, and I feared the worst. To my surprise, he became an absolutely different football player in his first varsity game and played so well he sparked the team to a two-touchdown victory.

After the game, as we were preparing to board our bus, I saw Larry Littman standing to one side alone, looking soberly out over the campus toward the Virginia hills. Walking over to him, I remarked, "You played a fine game, Larry. Why are you looking so unhappy?"

"I'm not unhappy, Coach, I was just thinking what a difference the prayer made before our game today. Before, during our scrimmage games, I was always cursing myself and cursing others and, therefore, couldn't do anything right. Today, when I went out on the field I felt that God was with me. It sure makes a difference."

Prayer did make a difference—for Larry and for the team. Because Don Gallagher's knee injury kept him sidelined, Littman became our regular center and averaged fifty-eight minutes of play per game. The Johns Hopkins eleven went on to win the Mason-Dixon Conference Championship, and I have always thought that the prayer we had just before each game helped to bind us together as a team and helped to strengthen us through putting our trust in God. Since then, in all the teams I have coached, including my two years with the professional Baltimore "Colts," and more recently with the Baylor "Bears," we have had prayer before and after each game. We haven't always won, but I do feel it is a very meaningful experience for all the boys who play football. It helps strengthen their deepest convictions even as it brings them closer to God.

In helping young men prepare for highly competitive gridiron clashes, as for the still more fundamental challenges of life itself, I have found that the greatest quality you have to develop is faith or belief. Of course, any coach needs players of outstanding ability, but they also have to believe in themselves and their ability. There are also other Christian virtues necessary if such a group or team effort as championship football is to succeed; among them I would stress dedication, honesty, unselfishness, courage, sacrifice, and, as mentioned, the power of prayer. Whether dealing with college or pro players, certain rules and regulations must be set up and enforced. If you are 100 per cent honest in inforcing them, the boys feel that you are doing what is right and are more than ready to cooperate.

In my own personal philosophy, I accept Jesus Christ as Lord and Saviour. Through his grace I have been able to lead a useful and worthwhile life. Even though as a human being I am subject to temptation and sin, Christ's power and grace have enabled me repeatedly to overcome obstacles and receive forgiveness. For the opportunity to teach young men the principles of both football and Christianity, I am truly thankful.

EDWARD DURELL STONE

"I believe that a splendid physical heritage is part of our moral obligation to future generations."

* * *

Nominated by Time *magazine as the man most likely to succeed Frank Lloyd Wright, Edward Durell Stone already is the most talked-about architect in America. The reason: a multiplication of beautiful buildings from New York to New Delhi. Yet this pioneer modernist was born in an Ozark town he likes to describe as a "hotbed of tranquillity"—Fayetteville, Arkansas. A free spirit and versatile designer who created such milestones as the Museum of Modern Art and Goodyear House, Stone attended the University of Arkansas, won an architectural scholarship to Harvard, and studied at MIT's School of Architecture from 1926 to 1927.*

He began his career in Boston, went to Europe on a scholarship, and then came to New York City where he worked as a designer on parts of the Waldorf-Astoria Hotel and Rockefeller Center. His exquisite feeling for beauty, balanced by his respect for the architectural verities, is exemplified by the United States Embassy in India. His cantilevered-balcony El Panama Hotel became a style-setter for resort hotels from Hawaii to Istanbul. The creativity displayed in the American Pavilion at the 1958 Brussels World's Fair won worldwide applause for the architect and his country.

Mr. Stone is one of the busiest practitioners of his profession today, being at present engaged in a globe-girding array of undertakings that include hospitals, cultural centers, libraries, churches, colleges, and atomic reactor factories, as well as a complete urban development in Akron, Ohio, an international trade mart in New Orleans, and the Huntington Hartford Gallery of Modern Art in New York. A warm and witty Methodist, the architect is proud of the fact that he is building a Unitarian Church in Schenectady, a Trappist Monastery in South Carolina, a National Presbyterian Church in Washington, D.C., a Mosque in Karachi, Pakistan, and the Christian Science Pavilion for the New York World's Fair. He is married to the former writer, Maria Elena Torch.

* * *

An Architect's Religion

I TRY TO IMBUE EVERYTHING I DO DO WITH BEAUTY, BECAUSE I BE-lieve ugliness is sinful.

Yet the personal reaction of some Americans to the idea of Beauty—much less the equation of beauty and virtue—is still one of deep distrust, if not outright revulsion. I don't think I'm stretching things if I suggest that some members of my own sex are torn between associating beauty with effeminancy on one hand, and a seductive Eve lurking outside the bounds of holy matrimony on the other. Many Americans shy away from the word, as though beauty and some of its attributes—refinement, harmony, and grace—were stolen properties . . . and whether stolen from God or the Devil, they're not quite sure. Even if they credit God with original possession they hardly credit the thief, and you get the distinct feeling that if they'd been there they would have approved heartily of Prometheus' sentence. Certainly they don't allow much for other considerations: If God didn't want us to participate in Beauty, why did he fill his world with it, or even an occasional human heart?

Some historians blame the Puritans for this state of affairs. Having been first on the scene, our Puritan forefathers have been nominated as the First Cause and Prime Mover in a number of dubious developments. But I would like to point to the praise that discriminating foreigners have bestowed on the villages that spread throughout the New England countryside. It is doubtful whether anything as pure and as refined and as beautiful as the New England village green, with its stately elms, the white spire of its church, and the quietly elegant houses of the affluent villagers, has existed elsewhere in history. Privately, this graciousness was carried through into the finest details of furniture, china, and silver. As to the commonweal, this environment of beauty, skillfully employing artistic principles, inspired many Americans toward a good way of life—a function of art, as well as religion.

Ugliness, like sin, usually reflects a grossness of mind and a poverty of spirit, quantity for quantity's sake, a robotlike materialism without purpose, a mindless groping after sensationalism, a refusal to consider the good and the true for ourselves and others. Ugliness, to me, implies a denial and destruction of the most valuable qualities of our humanity, those which sometimes create a vision of a higher order . . . a bridge to the angels . . . a glimpse of Perfection. Who can gaze upon Chartres and not suspect that it commemorates something of the Heavenly Spirit?

While it is true that there are some encouraging signs of America developing a concern with beauty and culture, it is nevertheless depressingly accurate to admit that much of our country has been despoiled of its natural beauty and ravaged by ugliness. Look at what greed and exploitation have done to our beaches, our polluted rivers and smog-filled air, our forests and our roads, stripped of trees but not of neon billboards, sprawling junkyards and jerry-built diners, drive-ins and used-car lots. America the Beautiful is becoming America the Ugly!

A bird's-eye view of our country might lead to the observation that Americans can afford everything in life but beauty. And another glance from outer space (where it's not yet exactly livable) would reveal the frightening truth that we have run out of new frontiers in our shrinking land, and cannot go elsewhere to escape the consequences of the crimes we have perpetrated on our environment. The thoughtful consideration, noble effort, and intelligent planning that went into a Yellowstone Park will have to be duplicated in all rural and urban areas, if we are to leave a decent earth for our children.

I believe that a splendid physical heritage is part of our moral obligation to future generations. Furthermore, I consider it just as praiseworthy to share and provide beauty to feed men's souls as it is to give food and shelter to care for their bodies. Otherwise, material providence alone will create something a little less than human. Deprived of aesthetic pleasure, man will turn in his ignorance to pleasures more base and brutal to alleviate his boredom. Take a look around you. Our own society can provide you with vivid examples if you study our slums, certain of our teen-agers, and an occasional tired businessman or two.

Great art, like religion, outlasts the often chaotic and murderous society of its birth. Like religion, it frequently creates an emotion of awe and reverence. I feel this is a valid and not sacrilegious comparison, perhaps because both art and religion embody an inseparable fusion of form and content. Considering how seldom, if ever, society offers us a world of just order, religion and art are probably mankind's principal sources of internal harmony and true beauty; that is, form which springs from content and comes into being from inner necessity.

Artistic order is produced in the sacred and original privacy of a man's soul and, in common with religion and love, intelligently communicates emotion. Neither true religion nor art comes easily to men; both are the results of effort and tension culminating in a moment of equilibrium and vision. Yet both are natural to men and will not be denied. Primitive peoples, in fact, often confuse religion and art and magic. The results frequently include objects of considerable beauty which express a deep commitment to life and exclude cynical superficiality. Higher religions use art to express themselves. Perhaps Da Vinci's definition of the artist's mission explains it: "To make the invisible visible."

Society's order is usually stamped from the outside, as a result of dogmatism and standardization—both fatal prescriptions for the human spirit and the artistic conscience. At the very best they produce a mediocrity that prevents growth and soon atrophies into a dead formalism or an empty vulgarity. Architectural masterpieces, on the other hand, go far beyond the controversial nature of mere attention-getting buildings and produce a feeling of immeasurable dignity and universality.

When I was a young man going into architecture, my brother told me there were two things I should bring to my work: singleness of purpose, and an open mind. By an open mind, he meant that I should try not to fall in love with the first idea that occurred to me. If you love your work and work with energy, dedication follows; because I believe flexibility of idea and open-mindedness are as essential as dedication, I have made it a governing rule for the conduct of both my professional and personal life. In judging both architecture and people, I have tried to see whether the positive attributes do not outweigh the negative ones. No one man can hope to encompass the Inspiration at work in the hearts and minds of other men. So, to the statement of my hero, Frank Lloyd Wright, "Love your work, love your wife, love the truth," I would add, "Love God—that's all there is to life."

MAHALIA JACKSON

"God can make you anything you want to be. He can lift you up, but you have to put everything in His hands."

* * *

Mahalia Jackson, America's great gospel singer, has been making "a joyful noise unto the Lord" for nearly forty years. Born into an indigent Negro family, brought up in the Storyville jazz atmosphere of New Orleans, Miss Jackson has dedicated her vocal genius to the singing of sacred songs. Her position as a priestess of evangelical music is reaffirmed annually whenever she sings in New York's Carnegie Hall, Berlin's Sportspalast, London's Albert Hall, or two hundred other musical auditoriums.

Mahalia (the Biblical name means "Good Woman") joined her father's Baptist Church show at the age of five. A few years later she began to absorb the remarkable technique of such premier blues singers as Bessie Smith and Ma Rainey, but never herself succumbed to what her minister called the "sin of jazz." She left school at age twelve to work full time in the Louisiana cotton fields, then at sixteen in the factories of Chicago. Her first major singing opportunity came with her appointment as soloist in Chicago's Salem Baptist Church. Largely because of her presence there, Chicago has become a center of American gospel singing.

Since 1954 Miss Jackson has starred on both CBS radio and television network programs. Her first single record, "Moving On Up," has sold nearly eight million copies during the past decade. In her only appearance with a jazz group she sang with Duke Ellington's orchestra in "Black, Brown, and Beige," the composer's musical history of the Negro in America. Of a half-dozen performances for United States Presidents, Chicago's Christ-lifted evangelist sang at the 1962 Lincoln Memorial ceremony, commemorating the one hundredth anniversary of President Lincoln's Proclamation of Emancipation.

* * *

A Made-up Mind

I'D LIKE TO TELL EVERYONE THAT GOD'S GOT THE WHOLE WORLD IN His hand. I'd like to tell everyone that God can take nothing and make something out of it. If, for example, I have accomplished anything, it is nothing but the grace of God that has brought me this far: all the way from the backwoods of Louisiana to the great streets of Paris, to Carnegie Hall in New York, Albert Hall in London, the State Opera House in Vienna. God has sent me all over the world just singing the simple songs of the South. That's why I love to sing, "He's Got the Whole World in His Hand."

Anything you want, anything you want to be, anything you want to do, God is able to lift you up. But you have to have one thing —you have to have *a made-up mind.* You don't straddle the fence serving God; we must put our all on the altar and let God abide. In my own life, in the early desperate days in New Orleans and Chicago, I learned to lean on the word of God. I still read the Bible every day and ask God to give me the understanding of His Word. For the Bible says, "Seek Me, learn of Me." This constant inspiration comes only through Divine power and Divine guidance. You can't get that unless you commune with God in prayer, meditation, and reading His Word. That is why I seek Him daily to know Him and His will for me.

To me, the first gospel song happened when the angels sang, "Peace on earth, good will toward men." It has been that way with me ever since I started singing as a child in our New Orleans shack between the railroad tracks and the levee. New Orleans was full of music then—jazz, ragtime, and the blues—and although I don't sing the blues anymore myself, I heard all the marching brass bands, the showboat music on the Mississippi, the great jazz orchestras of King Oliver, Louis Armstrong, and Jelly Roll Morton, and learned to love their powerful beat. But I loved to sing all the more in the choir of our hard-shell Baptist Church, where my papa used to preach after his week's work on the river docks and where I could raise my big voice in "I'm so glad Jesus lifted me." All around me I could hear a real jubilant expression, the feet tapping and the hands clapping. Even today I feel that same bounce when I sing. Like the psalmist said in the Bible, "Make a joyful noise unto the Lord," that's me!

I've been singing now for nearly forty years, and most of that time I've been singing for my supper as well as for the Lord. I've never had a music lesson and I still can't read a note, but I say this from the heart—a gospel song must do something for me as well as for the audience, or I can't sing it. When I'm singing at concerts, sometimes I whisper, sometimes I shout and drive the rhythm real hard. Sometimes when I'm singing inspirational songs like "Just as I Am," or "How great Thou art," I get down on my knees and sing with the folks and keep right on singing afterward in my dressing room until I've expressed all that I feel inside of me.

So, using the gift God gave me, singing the old spiritual songs for people everywhere has been a great personal help for me. Not to become just an entertainer or a star, but to help give people faith—that is the most important thing I can do. Gospel songs are the songs of hope and faith. Thus, I have been lifted up by singing; I have been brought through many trials by singing. Personally, I like to sing before live audiences because I can sing directly to them. I can pick up their vibrations and feel the Spirit of God communicating with me. Sometimes I have been criticized for not using a prepared program for my concerts, but I like to walk out on the stage and let the Holy Spirit guide me. Sometimes when I plan to sing one group of selections, the Spirit tells me to sing something else. Because I know He's got the whole world in His hand, I know there is a reason He wants me to sing certain songs. It is when I feel directly led that I am best able to project God's Spirit into my concerts.

Many people tell me they have been healed through hearing me sing these gospel songs—many tell me they have been saved. Naturally, I'm so grateful for that. You can't reach or uplift people in this way through a mechanical medium such as radio or records or television. Singing directly to a live audience is the only way.

At this time in history so many people are longing for spiritual help. There never was a time when Christians needed to be more Christian than now. They need to feel themselves lifted up in the

Lord. Because there are so many people today really seeking the Holy Spirit in their lives, they would like to know that God uses us. They would like to know the power God has given us. They would like to know God's got the whole world in His hands. And all we have to have is a made-up mind!

So, if the Lord will let me, I'm going to become an evangelist so I can reach many more people. I'm planning now to build a big evangelist temple in Chicago and get up a group of fine gospel singers who have the real beat, to help me express to so many people the happiness and strength that can come from the Lord. I want my temple non-segregated and non-denominational—even though I'm a hard-shell Baptist—and to have our services televised nationally, with or without sponsors, so that people all over the country can hear our singing.

I want to have all kinds of classes connected with the temple to help the many talented singers and musicians, to give them another path of study besides commercial show business where there are so many sinful temptations and frustrations. Some of the young colored people with great talent get hurt badly by discrimination and the doors that are locked to them. It breaks their spirit. It saddens my heart when they come to me and say, "Mahalia, please help us." I say, "I'm trying to, honey. I'm going to. Just give me a little time. I just got my toe in the door after thirty years of trying. It takes time to be delivered by the Lord."

I want to prove to young people that they can take what they've got and go to great heights if they believe in themselves and have faith in God. I say to them, "The Lord took me, and I was nothing, and He put me up. It can happen to you too. If the Lord can bring me this far—take me out of the washtubs and off my knees scrubbing other people's floors—then He can do as much and more for others."

LOWELL THOMAS

"If you make prudence a habit, virtue may be added to you."

* * *

Lowell Thomas, "the most famous Voice in history," is familiar to most Americans through the media of radio, television, newsreels, and films. Now in his thirty-fourth year of network broadcasting, he was for seventeen years the voice of "Movietone News." He has broadcast his network news program every night since September 29, 1930—a world record for broadcasting. Experts estimate that his total radio-TV-movie audience over the years exceeds the one hundred billion mark.

Renowned as reporter, teacher, lecturer, and the author of forty-seven books, Lowell Thomas has led a life of adventure and exploration. His boyhood in the Rocky Mountains helped prepare him for forty-five years of constant travel on the five continents and seven seas of earth. It began in 1917, when he covered the Allied-Axis War in the Holy Land and brought to public attention the spectacular career of Lawrence of Arabia. It continued through World War II when in April, 1945, he flew over Berlin in a P51 Mustang and described the final battle between the Germans and Russians. In 1949, Mr. Thomas and his son, Lowell, Jr., made their near-tragic Himalayan journey to forbidden Tibet.

In addition to doing several television series, including "High Adventure," Lowell Thomas helped develop a new entertainment medium called Cinerama, the forerunner of all the new wide-screen processes. Sixteen colleges and universities have honored him with a Doctor's Degree. President of the Marco Polo Club of New York and a trustee of various educational institutions, he was recently elected honorary president of The Explorers Club—an honor he shares with only three others: Admiral Peary of North Pole fame, and Generals Greely and Brainard, both of whom led important expeditions in the Arctic. Mr. and Mrs. Thomas are members of the Methodist Church in Pawling, New York.

* * *

Exploring the World's Wonder

THE BOOK OF PROVERBS TELLS US, "THE PRUDENT MAN LOOKETH well to his going." During a lifetime of travel and exploration I have come to value very highly the meaning and importance of those words. I have my father to thank that as a boy I was off to a good start. I think that he, too, must have been impressed by the words of the immortal John Milton: "To know that which before us lies in daily life, that is the prime wisdom."

In the midst of the gold camps of the Wild West, he was a Christian teacher and physician who emphasized the importance of education, even to the cultivation of pure and correct speech. I enjoyed an adventurous youth as a gold miner, range rider, and reporter, but I also did postgraduate work at several universities and, with my father's encouragement, became proficient at public speaking. This last accomplishment made possible my career as a lecturer and broadcaster.

I remember a major turning point in my life in 1917. I was in Venice, just having returned from the front lines a few miles away, when I stopped to read a bulletin tacked to a sandbag in front of St. Mark's Cathedral. It announced the appointment of General Edmund Allenby as the new British Commander in Chief in Egypt. Excited by this news, I set off on a memorable trip to the Holy Land. There I was to see the Crusades reenacted in modern warfare, witness the rescue of the Holy City from the Turks, and meet Lawrence of Arabia.

Yet all this wasn't the result of pure chance or simple wish fulfillment on my part. I had known something of Allenby's record in the Boer War and on the Western Front, and reasoned that the appointment of a man of his caliber must mean a new offensive against the Turks in the Near East. A reasonable conjecture had stirred my imagination, and not simply a romantic desire to visit the battlefront in the Holy Land. Subsequent perilous journeys to the primitive far-off corners of the earth increased my appreciation of factual preparation, followed by carefully thought-out decisions. When it comes to crossing a treacherous mountain range, a rash step forward can mean death.

Despite the prudence displayed by some of our great religious figures, many people may ask what such prudence has to do with our Christian faith and morality. They may have forgotten why we honor the judicious wisdom of Solomon or how the renowned Luther, after his brave stand before the Diet of Worms, was discreet enough to grow a beard and pose as a knight. This sensible concealment allowed him to escape persecution and death at the hands of Charles V, just as the prudent flight of the Holy Family into Egypt saved the infant Jesus from the same fate at the hands of the bloodthirsty Herod.

Christ Himself used sagacious figures of speech to drive home his points when preaching to us. The very names of some of His parables that have become common coin emphasize this: The Prodigal Son, The Wise and Foolish Virgins, The Widow's Mite. And how are we to classify His well-judged words—"Render unto Caesar the things that are Caesar's, and unto God the things that are God's"?

In the full sense, prudence is a moral virtue because the intelligence is harnessed to the service of the moral law. But I would even argue for something short of this, something more immediately attainable—namely, a simple moral awareness of what a given decision implies. My contention is that while we must stir consciences, we must also stir enlightened self-interest. There is no more radical evil in American life than the fact that many of us seem devoid of apprehension in the face of irresponsible, immoral acts that are almost sure to get us into trouble.

Consider the fantastic number of Americans in high public positions who have done stupid and evil things that destroyed their careers in full bloom; things any thoughtful ten-year-old could tell them would be considered wrong and scandalous in the public eye. And yet these individuals usually deny that they can see anything wrong and, in their own eyes, seem to be speaking the truth! That is, their intelligence lapses. They have no prudence, no enlightened self-interest.

Remember the Americans involved in the rigged television shows? They were hypocritical certainly, but they were also stupid beyond belief. They thought they could get away with a fraud necessitating the permanent silence of hundreds of people—from contestants and emcees to sponsors and agency men. Disgruntled losers, who knew that they had been deliberately "bumped" and humiliated before a national television audience, had to nurse their grudges in a corner and abjure retaliation. The consciences that were bought had to stay bought. A "no investigation" policy on the part of those in authority had to be taken for granted. Yet a whole group put their minds in their pockets, walked forward into the earthquake, and were astounded when the cataclysm knocked them flat.

This brand of stupidity is as much a disease of our national psyche as amorality. We allow ourselves to be ridden by cults and unintelligence and swept along by powerful movements of unreason. The collapse of good sense can have even more disastrous results than the collapse of good ethics. A hypocrite may have the sense to see the moral law which he violates. But our fundamental problem is that so many Americans seem incapable of violating any standards simply because they haven't the intelligence to see any—even those of enlightened self-interest.

And this is the point at which I would begin my counterattack. Fear of punishment is a potent cure for crime. Enlightened self-interest works through a form of punishment—exposure, loss of a job, ridicule. We have, therefore, a way of influencing those to whom morality means little. The younger generation can be approached more easily on this basis. Tell them to be good, and they may laugh at you and call you a "square." But not even the worst juvenile delinquent wants to be called stupid. He may smirk about having no morals; he will not smirk about having no mind.

Let me put it this way. Our first concern is with conduct, outward acts. How are we to cure our country of scandals, delinquency, and the other social vices that have become only too common? Only a small minority of people will suddenly see the light of morality. Prudence, on the other hand, can be inculcated both easily (since it is a matter of simple good sense) and effectively (since most people have some concern for their own welfare). I would quote William Drummond at them: "He who will not reason is a bigot; he who cannot is a fool; and he who dares not is a slave."

I would begin every effort at moral reform with prudential arguments. Should they succeed, we might then look confidently for a rise in strict morality; for prudence is a virtue and discourages definite vices. Once we learn to think prudently, there is a good chance that we will go on to believe truly and to act morally. Or, as Pascal said in fewer words, "If you make prudence a habit, virtue may be added to you."

GERALD HEARD

"God's kingdom cannot come unless we begin by making our human kingdoms go."

* * *

Author, anthropologist, historian, social psychologist, psychical investigator, Gerald Heard is one of the Western World's preeminent philosophers. As a result of forty years of research and study in the physical sciences, religious experience, and extra-sensory phenomena, he emerges today as a modern seer who champions the unity of life and the synthesis of religion and science. At seventy-three, he lives in Santa Monica, California, and is more active than ever writing and lecturing on his favorite subjects.

Gerald Heard was born in London, and was graduated from Cambridge University where he took honors in history and the philosophy of religion. Before moving to the United States in 1937, he lectured for the Board of Extra-Mural Studies of Oxford University, worked with Sir Horace Plunkett, founder of the Irish Cooperative Movement, and served as science commentator for the British Broadcasting Corporation. A student of the great world faiths, he is an acknowledged interpreter of Vedanta, the essential mystical system of the Hindus.

Among Mr. Heard's forty-three published works are The Creed of Christ, A Preface to Prayer, The Social Substance of Religion, Is God in History?, The Eternal Gospel, *and* Training for the Life of the Spirit. *The bearded British intellectual is probably the only writer ever to have been awarded England's distinguished Henrietta Hertz Prize, for his book,* The Ascent of Humanity, *and the Ellery Queen's Mystery Magazine Contest first prize for the best detective story.*

* * *

Training for the Life of the Spirit

As I SUFFER FROM AN INSATIABLE CURIOSITY, THE UNIVERSE IS MY hobby. In my youth I wanted to become a missionary. My upbringing as the son of an Episcopal clergyman in Bath, England, and my strict training as an evangelical ordinand at home and in church strengthened this intent. Then, at Cambridge University just before World War I, I was deeply inspired by the ministry of that eloquent international missionary, John R. Mott, who was stirring the length and breadth of Christendom with his crusade, "Win the world to Christ." Although my college major was history and although my concept of religion steadily broadened, I became more and more interested in the Christian faith, the nature and function of prayer, and training for the life of the spirit.

That is why my thought, purpose, and (I earnestly hope, to some extent) my practice as a writer and lecturer have revolved around what seems undeniably the core teaching of Jesus—that is, that the one and only truthful criterion by which any religion, faith, or doctrine can be judged is the fruits which that faith and practice produce. So, for fifty years in England and America I have been increasingly concerned to study and practice such rules, under whatever name they go, that produce what St. Paul called the "fruits of the spirit—Love, Joy and Peace."

In our Western Christian tradition faith is the initial step in the three stages that lead through hope to love. Without faith we are hopeless and loveless. But faith today is modern man's chief stumbling block. In the Eastern Hindu-Buddhist tradition, knowledge not faith is the first step. And yet, in any deeper understanding of the eternal Gospel, faith is seen as right knowledge; for faith is not believing something which our intelligence denies. It is the choice of the noblest hypothesis. It is the resolve to put the highest meaning on the facts which we observe.

What then is the noblest hypothesis I have chosen, what are the principal conclusions reached in a lifetime of studying both Western and Eastern religions? The first is that God alone is wholly real, and that beside this Absolute Reality the physical universe becomes only a significant dream. The second is that if we would know God, experience Reality, we must draw our entire being together, recollect our true personality in prayer and meditation, and bring our scattered and dissipated minds into a single pointed focus ("Only the pure in heart shall see God"). The third is that God, the object of devotion, is not some being infinitely distant, not at best a postmortem experience, but a Reality, a Presence that may be known here and now.

God is. That is the primordial fact. It is in order that we may discover this fact for ourselves, by direct experience, that we exist. The final end and purpose of every human being is the unitive knowledge of God's being. And it is only through prayer—ego-eclipsing, soul-awakening prayer—that we experience this higher Reality.

So, day by day God is assembling us, drawing us, pulling us together, giving us, if we will do His will and seek His light, a presence of mind, an awareness of complete significance, a liberating sense of immediate, total meanings. So, day by day as our self-imposed ignorance vanishes and we pursue the path of prayer, renunciation, and love-in-action, we come to see that God has always been present, closer than breathing, nearer than hands or feet. Our lives are nothing but futility unless they become a preparation for Eternity.

MARK O. HATFIELD

"No cause, however noble, can be satisfying without the direction of Christ."

* * *

At the youthful age of forty, Oregon's twenty-ninth Governor, Mark Hatfield, can look back upon these major milestones:

Navy combat service in World War II, climaxed by the United States invasion of Iwo Jima and Okinawa.

Leadership in liberal arts education, marked by his rise from political science instructor to dean of students at Willamette University in Salem, Oregon.

Directed activity as a Christian layman, which has taken him from a small rural parish to moderator of his Salem Baptist Church to Easter Sunrise preacher at the Pasadena Rose Bowl.

A decade of political success as State Representative, State Senator, Secretary of State, and in 1958 and in 1962 Governor of Oregon.

Now serving his second term as Governor, Republican Hatfield's administration has been characterized by fiscal reform, consistent integrity, and the initiation of such bi-partisan programs as a Hoover-style government reorganization commission. An executive committeeman of the National Governor's Conference, he already has served on the platform committee of the Republican National Convention, and as leader of his State's delegation. He also serves on the board of advisors of the Salvation Army, International Christian Leadership, and the Council for the Advancement of Small Colleges. Governor Hatfield is married and the father of two children.

* * *

A Christ-Inspired Life

WHATEVER SLIGHT ACCOMPLISHMENTS MAY BE ATTRIBUTED TO ME to date, I owe to the privilege of being born in the United States, the opportunities of education, the devotion of my parents, and the inspiration of Christ. "Commitment" isn't a word that we hear very often today, and yet I believe it plays a part in every successful life. Coming from a home of strong religious and political convictions, I have been aware since childhood of the need for commitment in personal life and integrity in government. The interest of my father, a railroad blacksmith for thirty-five years, in the affairs of both church and state aroused a similar interest in me. I came to share not only my father's abhorrance of corruption in government, but also his admiration for those leaders who upheld the noblest precepts of our nation. My childhood heroes included nearly as many political leaders as cowboys and athletes.

As for my mother, the guiding commitment of her life was education. Born in rural Tennessee, where the child who finished school was an exception, she was determined to complete high school and college. She did get through high school, but when Grandfather died and Grandmother opened a boardinghouse, her help was needed here. Later, when she married and I came along, everyone thought she had forgotten about college. Not Mother! When she was thirty-two and I was five, she enrolled in Oregon State College and three years later she got her degree. So, commitment to an ideal was a familiar one in our home.

An opportunity to apply these rules came in 1949 when I accepted a teaching position in the political science department at Willamette University. My campus activities involved me in many issues concerning state government, and I soon found myself nominated for the State Legislature. After winning the election and serving two terms in the lower house, I went on to the State Senate. In the meantime, I was appointed dean of students at the University. All of these honors were highly encouraging to me as an aspiring young politician. But with these outward advancements came a disturbing inner awareness of my inadequacy in the area of the spiritual life.

One of my major duties as dean of students was to counsel college men who sought advice regarding academic or personal problems. The tremendous responsibility of this task was overwhelming. I often felt that the spiritual problems they presented to me were not completely answered in my own life and that I had no right to counsel others on matters which I had not worked out personally. If I could offer little real spiritual help to individuals, what did I have to offer the state, the nation, or the world?

Not only did I wonder about my personal inadequacies, but I

also began to think about my purpose in life and my motive for living. This resulted primarily from my contact with a group of students who had asked me to serve as adviser to a Bible study group. These students, by their lives and by the goals for which they were striving, brought to mind some of the things I had heard in church about what Jesus Christ wanted of us. When I compared my self-made ideals with Christ's ideals I found the deepest conflict.

It seemed as though my purpose was self-centered, while the purpose of the students might best be expressed in the words of the apostle Paul: "For we preach not ourselves, but Christ Jesus the Lord; and ourselves your servants for Jesus' sake." Their purpose was to live completely for Jesus Christ. Their motivation was a love for the Son of God. Their enthusiasm for the Bible was not just an academic or scholarly enthusiasm, but a sincere desire to know the hero of the Bible in a more intimate way. This was a real challenge to me.

As I have said, this idea was not completely new to me, as I had always been a member of the church, attending regularly, and giving financial aid. This relationship did not satisfy me, but I gave it little thought because of the press of business. But now, as I saw the impact Christ had made on the lives of these students, I had to re-evaluate my conception of Christianity.

After this, I began to read the Bible in the evenings to see if I could find some of the answers for which I was looking. More and more as the great gospel message began to make sense, I discovered what all can discover if they will only look. All we need to do is put our faith in Christ to make this possible. "As many as received him, to them gave he power to become the sons of God, even to them that believe on his name."

I saw that for thirty-one years I had lived for self, and decided I wanted to live the rest of my life only for Jesus Christ. I asked God to forgive my self-centered life and to make my life His own. I was again assured by the words of Paul that "If any man be in Christ, he is a new creature: old things are passed away; behold; all things are become new."

Following Jesus Christ has been an experience of increasing challenge, adventure, and happiness. How true are His words: "I am come that they might have life, and that they might have it more abundantly." It is not to a life of ease and mediocrity that Christ calls us, but to the disciple-like, Christ-empowered life. No matter what field we are in, we are called to give our complete allegiance to Him. No cause, noble as it may seem, can be satisfying or purposeful without the direction of Christ. I can say with all sincerity that living a committed Christian life is truly satisfying, because it has given me true purpose and direction by serving not myself, but Jesus Christ.

PAUL POPENOE

"Marriage is what you make it."

* * *

Dr. Paul Popenoe is the founder and president emeritus of the American Institute of Family Relations in Los Angeles, California. Since 1930, the Institute has served as a national educational center for the strengthening of marriage and family life. Educated at Occidental College and Stanford University, Dr. Popenoe spent his first professional decade as a newspaper man, agricultural explorer, and editor of the American Journal of Heredity. *After World War II, he served as executive secretary of the American Social Hygiene Association in New York City.*

Married and the father of four sons, he is the author of such books as Modern Marriage, The Conservation of the Family, *and* Marriage Is What You Make It. *"It is interesting to look back," Dr. Popenoe reminisces, "and think how little real information was available for young marrieds a generation ago. In the last thirty-three years, since we began our researches in this great field of love, marriage, and parenthood, we have helped seventy-five thousand couples. Nowadays we are also equipped to aid in child guidance and household management—even the remarriage of the many people who have been divorced. It has been a most worthwhile experience."*

* * *

Faith and the Conservation of the Family

SUCCESSFUL MARRIAGE AND SOUND FAMILY LIFE ARE THE BASIS OF any enduring civilization. For more than a generation the American Institute of Family Relations has not only been the channel through which some of my own deepest religious convictions have found an outlet, but it has served likewise to bring together as co-workers many hundreds of persons who, in striving through the Institute to strengthen the foundations of the modern home, have found that they could collaborate harmoniously, even enthusiastically. Not only have all varieties of Christian faith united effectively in this effort, but since the Institute's outreach is worldwide, we have similarly worked shoulder to shoulder with Jews, Hindus, Moslems, and Buddhists.

All workers at the Institute have discovered that they were engaged in a joint enterprise in which they brought to bear all the resources of religion and modern science in promoting successful marriage and family life. Speaking as a counselor and social scientist in this field, I would say that success in marriage is due to a balance between three factors that are always present to a greater or a lesser degree, so that success of a marriage is, you might say, the resultant of these three factors. The first is the attitude you have toward marriage; second, the wise choice of mate; third, the possession of a certain amount of technical information that you need in any occupation or profession—and certainly marriage is no exception.

Marriage needs research and investigation by those entering upon it. Ideally, of course, we should get our education for it by growing up in a happy marriage where the research is written down before you; you would just pick it up. But with so many marriages unhappy, all of the studies show, and I think it is common sense, that the attitudes one has toward marriage are more important than any other one thing. Unfortunately, nowadays we're building up in our young people attitudes of pessimism, cynicism, and defeatism. Why? Partly because we don't tell anything about the happy marriages.

Nobody puts a seven-column headline in the newspapers to say that Dr. Popenoe and his wife are still getting along nicely after forty-three years of marriage. They put a headline in the paper to say that so-and-so threw his wife off the wharf, or so-and-so locked her husband in the chicken house and threw the key down the well. All this shows only failures in marriage, and generally failures of the most famous and well-known persons. When our young people hear nothing but that kind of education for twenty years, when they see these famous folk with all their advantages fail in marriage, surely they say, "You can't expect us to do any better!" But somewhat cynically they also say, "Let's give it a try, because it only costs three dollars, and I can quit any time I want to!" Obviously, you can't build up success in anything on that kind of faithless basis, and I think that is the main difficulty in American marriages today.

On the other hand, all the studies, as most everyone knows, show that marriages of people who are and who have been active participants in church life from childhood on have a very high degree of marital success. Thus, religion is everywhere found to play a vital part in marriage. To the extent that married couples had no connection with the church or express unfavorable attitudes toward religion, their divorce rate increases sharply. If we can build up now in America what might be called attitudes of determined idealism—a feeling that marriage is the most important thing you'll ever tackle, that you'll exhaust all the resources of religion and science to make it a success, that you'll let nothing but a catastrophe interfere with its fulfillment—if you go into marriage or anything else in life with that frame of mind, you'll succeed.

What's more, you need diversion, recreation, outside activities to keep a well-balanced life in the home. One of the first things we do in counseling a couple in difficulties is to make sure that the wife is getting out of the house and has some chance for recreation, not only with her husband—that's necessary—but for recreation with other women friends, a little individuality and personality outreach, a little self-expression preferably with others, church worship and allied activities, charity work, missions, clubs, societies, sororities, whatever it may be. Every happy wife must feel that she's an individual as well as a wife and mother. Conversely, divorces come about when you start with the wrong attitudes, when you pick the wrong mate, when you have no proper marital information, when there is a lack of a religious outlook, and when neither partner enjoys a balanced recreational program both inside and outside the home.

Like everything else that is worthwhile, you have to work at marriage to make it succeed. Contrary to romantic rumor, neither courtship nor marriage is made in heaven. Too often, a young couple get acquainted, they go around to the movies, parties, and dances; but neither of them ever sees the other in the ordinary or demanding conditions of life. Neither one is at all prepared to find how the other reacts in a situation involving stress, accident, misfortune, or whatever the case may be. So there should be a reasonable length of time, at least a year of acquaintance and six months of engagement, with as much joint activity as possible, before a young couple marries. In that way there is a tremendous protection against unexpected surprises after the wedding.

One of the greatest handicaps to marriage nowadays is the romantic infantilism prevalent in books, movies, and TV—the idea of romance appropriate to an infant who is concerned only with his own sensations and who doesn't care what suffering he causes as long as he gets what he wants out of life. "Romantic love," as pictured by mass media, is affirmed to be a mysterious visitation that comes out of nowhere and that once experienced turns the rest of your life into an effortless ecstasy. If, after marriage, it turns out that there is some effort involved, then it shows you didn't marry the right man after all! Now, I submit you can't build up any kind of a permanent adult enterprise on that basis, and too many marriages are founded on just that theory. No, even if you manage pretty wisely, there will always be problems. I think as long as you are married, you're going continually to foresee new difficulties, adjust to new situations, solve or prevent them by taking wise steps. It's not too difficult to do, as I indicate. You simply have to work together, plan, perform, and study together, share your love and joy together "until death do you part." Of course, you will always have problems in life—there wouldn't be much interest in life if you didn't!

WALTER P. REUTHER

"If we are to bring to bright fulfillment the promise of Christian brotherhod, then we must with the peoples of our world create a moral force equal to the challenge of the H-bomb."

* * *

Walter P. Reuther, vice president of the AFL-CIO, is one of America's leading labor statesmen. Ebullient, eloquent, and dedicated to the labor movement for thirty years, he helped organize the Detroit automobile workers during the early days of the New Deal and today serves as UAW president. He also has emerged as a powerful, yet ethical, force in the councils of varied progressive causes ranging from Americans for Democratic Action to the Democratic Party.

Walter Philip Reuther was born in Wheeling, West Virginia, on September 1, 1907. His interest in the labor movement was stimulated early as his father was president of the Ohio Valley Trades and Labor Assembly. Educated at Detroit's Wayne University, Reuther first worked as an apprentice diemaker at the Wheeling Steel Corporation, later worked for six years at the Ford Motor Company. In 1933 Walter and brother Victor made an extensive trip through eleven European and Asiatic countries to work in the factories and study their labor organizations. In 1935, when the Reuther brothers returned to Detroit, they threw themselves into the tremendous struggle to organize the auto workers.

True to his belief that labor should be an integral part of the American economic system, Walter Reuther has not dealt solely with dollars-and-cents issues. In his view, the health and safety of the American economy are the concern of the laboring man as fully as of the businessman. Thus, in the postwar years Reuther again took the lead in extending the influence of the labor movement within our industrial system. His leadership was recognized formally in 1946, when he became president of the UAW and later succeeded Philip Murray as president of the CIO. Today he also serves as a director of the National Association for the Advancement of Colored People, the Religion and Labor Council of America, and other public service organizations. Wayne University, St. Mary's College, Boston College, the University of West Virginia, the University of Michigan, St. Francis Xavier University, Wilberforce University, and

Georgetown University have awarded him honorary degrees. Mr. Reuther is married, has two young daughters, and lives in a Detroit suburb.

* * *

The Image of Human Brotherhood

I BELIEVE THAT LABOR AND THE CHURCH ARE INSEPARABLY BOUND together because they draw their common inspiration from the great Carpenter of Nazareth. They are both working together in the vineyards of American democracy to apply the principles of Christian morality to the everyday economic and social problems that we face as a free people. The labor movement is important because it is about people, about their needs and their problems; but to me it has a much deeper meaning than just a struggle for economic and social justice. I believe that the labor movement is important because it attempts to give substance and meaning to the Christian concept of human brotherhood.

A number of years ago I went to a dinner given in honor of a Polish-American worker on the occasion of his retirement. I will never forget his words that night. "Brother Reuther," he said, "I want to thank you for all the things that the union did for me. You raised my wages, I live in a better house, I was able to give my children a better education. But," he said, "most important of all, for eighteen years I worked in the foundry before the union came and for eighteen years the foremen and the workers called me, 'dumb Polack.' Now they call me 'brother.' "

This is, I think, the deeper meaning of a movement made up of those who have come together in a common dedication and pursuit of common objectives. In the words of a great spiritual leader, the late Unitarian minister, A. Powell Davies, "O God, how can we love Thee in Thine unseen temple and not love Thee in our fellow man?" I believe that we need more such dedication to apply the principles of Christian brotherhood in everyday life.

This is a world in crisis, where we live in fear of some terrible tomorrow that may bring H-bombs and guided missiles smashing down on our cities. I can't help but believe that this is not just an economic or political or military crisis, but more fundamentally a moral crisis. The human family is in trouble because of man's growing inhumanity to man and because of man's growing immorality to himself, which finds its most frightening expression in the totally destructive weapons of modern warfare.

Our problem today is that man has achieved great power, but he has not learned the simple Christian truth that power without morality is power without purpose. Peace and freedom are in jeopardy because we live in a world of nuclear giants who too often behave like moral pygmies. And we are in trouble because the guided missile has fallen into the hands of misguided men. If we are to make peace secure in our world, if we are to bring to bright fulfillment the promise of Christian brotherhood, then we must with the peoples of our world create a moral force equal to the challenge of the H-bomb. Dr. Davies put it this way: "The world is too dangerous for anything but the truth, and the world is too small for anything but human brotherhood."

Will man demonstrate the moral strength to turn from the weapons of total destruction to the tools of peace, and, with the tools of peace, bring to practical fulfillment man's ancient dream of a world free from sin. from ignorance, disease, and hate? This is the great question.

In America we are blessed, perhaps more than any peoples of the world, with all of the physical and material resources that we need. Can we match our tremendous scientific and technical and production know-how with a comparable human and moral and social know-why? We can, if we realize economic effort is not an end—it is a means to an end—and the end is the enrichment and the fulfillment of human life, not just to give the outer man more gadgets, but to enable the inner man to find outer expression. We will miss the point if we do not make it clear to the Communists that the fundamental difference between their system of coercion and our system of freedom is that all of this material wealth is without purpose except as we dedicate it to moral ends.

Because our moral values are confused, we have demonstrated more concern about the condition of our plumbing than about the adequacy of our schools. Civil rights is not a political problem; it is a moral problem. It is a question of whether, in your relationship to your fellow man, you will live by the principles of Christian brotherhood. Corruption in the labor movement reflects a weakening of the moral fiber of our free society. You can't have a society in which there is overemphasis placed upon the acquisition of material wealth as the measurement of success and not expect corruption in many areas of our national life. I believe that we need desperately to de-emphasize the acquisition of material wealth and to re-emphasize non-material values.

Each of us, as we live our lives, needs to have the moral courage of our convictions—of our inner faith. What the inner man thinks is important becomes real only as the outer man gives expression to the sense of inner conviction. But there are too many fair-weather Christians who will fight for the things they believe in only when it is convenient and comfortable. The measure of our convictions comes when we stand in the hour of storm and stress, when the going is rough, and when to stand outwardly for the faith that the inner man whispers in our ear takes courage and conviction.

Jesus, the great Carpenter, demonstrated that when they were nailing Him to the cross. In His hour of supreme agony, He kept the faith, and He said, "Father, forgive them, for they know not what they do." We need that deep, inner faith in the hour of crisis, in the hour of challenge, in the hour of testing, because that is when it counts. We need to have the understanding that, while the Communists achieve unity by rigid conformity, we in our free society achieve unity in diversity, and that each of us must live within our society respecting the other person's differences, but harmonizing those into a whole within the framework of a system of values based upon the concepts of Christian morality and human brotherhood.

The whole concept of Christianity must be based upon our faith in the belief that love is a more powerful force in the affairs of man than hatred and fear. I believe that man can work and sacrifice and build because he shares common hopes and common loves and common faith. I pray that in this period of human history the Lord will give us the strength, wisdom, and vision, so that we can tap the great spiritual reservoir that lies deep within the human breast, and that we can get people working and building together, not because they share common fears and hatreds but because they share a common love and a common faith. And, if we do that, then I am confident that together with the men and women of good will all over the world, we can fashion a better tomorrow in the image of Christian morality, and we can fashion that better tomorrow in the image of peace, in the image of human freedom, in the image of social justice, and in the image of human brotherhood.

HOWARD E. BUTT, JR.

"When Christ is ministering to men through us . . . life becomes an adventure."

* * *

Howard E. Butt, Jr., vice president of the H. E. Butt Grocery Company in Corpus Christi, Texas, qualified at twenty-seven as one of Texas' outstanding young men. In fact, he won such an award from the Junior Chamber of Commerce in 1954. His executive post with the Butt Company engages him in an expanding business that operates eighty-nine supermarkets in thirty-seven Texas cities. His lay preaching schedule keeps him on the podium before church, business, and educational groups throughout the United States. He also works with a team of laymen who conduct denominational and interdenominational crusades for Christ in various cities.

Mr. Butt, a Southern Baptist, is an executive committeeman of the Baptist World Alliance, a trustee of the Southwestern Baptist Theological Seminary, and a director of the Billy Graham Evangelistic Association. He helped organize the Laymen's Leadership Institute and Christian Men, Inc., both interdenominational laymen's movements, and Laity Lodge, a conference retreat center for laymen in the Texas hill country. A deacon of the Parkdale Baptist Church in Corpus Christi, he is married and the father of three children.

* * *

Agents of Redemption

As a lay minister first and a businessman second, I am but one of that growing army of American commercial and professional people who are letting Christ live through us in daily life. In an age of speed, space, and "Spectator Christianity," there is little enough chance for any of us to act effectively. Yet, despite living in the two worlds of God and mammon, I believe that every businessman—and every homemaker as well—can become a genuine witness, a minister of reconciliation, a servant of God. In my grocery activities and lay witnessing, one chief objective is to encourage laymen within our churches to become real, committed Christians.

A great contemporary heresy can be found lurking in the distinction drawn between clergy and laity. Preachers are not the only men called of God. The clergyman does have a divinely appointed task, but that can never mean that the layman is not called too. The layman's gifts and talents and sphere of vocational activity may be different, but his calling is of God.

The Bible stresses that every Christian is a priest. We are a kingdom of priests unto God. The Biblical and Reformation doctrine of "the priesthood of all believers" does not mean that there are no more priests. The word "layman" originally comes from the Greek word *laos* which actually means "the people of God." We cannot escape it.

The Christian layman is sent into the world in exactly the same way that Jesus Christ was sent—as an agent of redemption.

In my own life, although reared in a Christian home and receiving Christ at an early age, I remained a "Spectator Christian" for many years. It was during college days that I committed myself to Christ in a deeper way. There came a genuine sense of calling to the service of Christ. So it was that I began telling about my experience with Christ and the changes taking place in my life to various church groups and such young people's groups as YMCA, Hi-Y and Tri-Y clubs.

This activity of simply telling what had happened in my life grew until now I spend a considerable amount of my time in lay preaching. The layman has opportunities to speak for Christ that a minister never has; unfortunately, there are many people who think consciously, or subconsciously, that a minister talks about God because that's his vocation. Laymen have an entrée that a minister can never have. People will listen to what we have to say about our experience with Christ, because they figure we have no ax to grind, no professional duty to perform.

A Christian is a man who admits his need for God out of his own weakness, inadequacy, and sin. He believes the good news that Christ provided eternal life through His death and resurrection and, therefore, receives this gift from God. Then his life daily consists in allowing Jesus Christ the Lord to exhibit the power, love, and grace He gives in all the commonplace duties, responsibilities, and relationships of life. I can abundantly bear witness that in my own experience, at deeper and deeper levels, Christ has proved reliable and adequate. I cannot claim to be a good man. I know I am not. I am a sinner. But I am a forgiven sinner, one in whom Jesus Christ dwells by His Spirit.

In a life filled with God, there is a calm continuous outflow of witness. Sometimes it is in the silence of a friendly ear as we take time to listen to others' problems. Sometimes it is an unadorned act of thoughtfulness. Sometimes it is in the openness of admitting our own failures, telling how Christ has worked in them. We often help others most from our own weaknesses, not from our strengths. Christ's grace is perfected in our inadequacies.

Most certainly this life of Christ will be manifest in our personal relations day by day. Christian service then climbs down off the podium. The pulpit can become a coward's corner, as Olford says. And so can the Sunday-school class lectern. A bold, open frankness when confronting men across a coffee cup shows more maturity than is required for the skyrockets of religious oratory. Only Christ gives this—it is a matter of relationship, not nerve, technique, nor a dominant personality. The Holy Spirit's work is characterized by relaxed boldness. This makes easy, natural conversation . . . salty with God.

Sam Shoemaker describes this kind of witness: "They have lost completely all shyness about speaking of these things. Shyness usually means you are pretty shy on religion itself. When your heart gets full of it, so too does your talk. You don't talk dogmatically or self-righteously, but you lard your spiritual experience into your ordinary talk, and people get intrigued."

Recently I heard a missionary from Ceylon describe categories of witness. Imagine an auto accident, complete with tangled steel, shattered glass, and three witnesses:

1. One witness stood on the sidewalk and saw the wreck take place. He was an objective observer.

2. The second witness was in the wreck, wounded but not seriously. He recovered but was badly shaken. His is a firsthand, subjective witness.

3. The third witness was in the wreck and killed by it. He was really a witness; it took his life.

Christ does collide with our human lives. Then men set about to communicate this. We call it witnessing.

1. The Sidewalk Witness. Some of us have seen it happen. We love to talk about other people's conversions. We discuss it objectively but somehow the impact is remote, because we are describing somebody else's wreck.

2. The Wounded Witness. Most of us probably fall in this category. We know it happened because we were there and have the scars to prove it. The wreck was so real that we walk with a Christian limp as a result. We have had enough contact with God to ruin us for anything else. We work hard, dragging ourselves along through life in Christian service.

3. The Exchanged Witness. There are only a few of these. He died in the wreck. And his old life has been buried as a consequence. But out of the crash, a new self was born—in fact, it was like a resurrection. This man demonstrates today what Paul described: "I am crucified with Christ, nevertheless I live; yet not I, but Christ liveth in me." This man is not just witnessing, he seems dead to all this tense religious activity. He is letting Christ witness through him. He lives an exchanged life.

When Christ is ministering to men through us, in his way of calm, shattering honesty, outflowing concern, and transforming power, we can expect anything to happen. And it will. Life becomes an adventure. And so much of our striving human effort seems so piddling. . . . Who really liked tiddlywinks anyway?

WARNER E. SALLMAN

"Dear Lord, we pray that Thy will be our will, and that in all ways Thy will be done."

* * *

The famed Christian artist whose "Head of Christ" is known the world over, Warner Sallman did not attain wide recognition until 1940 when he painted his charcoal sketch of Jesus in oils. Since then approximately one hundred and fifty million color reproductions of this inspired portrait have been sold in more than fifty countries. Born in Chicago in 1892 of Swedish-Finnish parents, he was reared in what he calls "a devout Christian home." As a young lad, he dreamed of becoming a doctor, later he favored the ministry, but finally he became an artist. Today, at age seventy-one, Mr. Sallman is still adding to his voluminous series of paintings showing Christ in various phases of His ministry. The originals hang in a score of museums, churches, and homes as glowing evidence of what God can achieve through a life wholly dedicated to Him.

* * *

The Ministry of Art

Back in 1924 when I was a young man struggling to become a successful artist in Chicago, I attended a series of Bible talks in the Chicago Central YMCA. For weeks before that, I had been vainly trying to make a suitable cover drawing for our *Christian Youth* magazine, but nothing seemed to come through. Day after day I sat at my drawing table, night after night arrived and I had felt no inspiration.

At the "Central Y" I heard one of the most moving preachers of the day—the Rev. Charles R. Goff, later to become minister of Chicago Temple, the Methodist "Skyscraper" Church. He made the Bible come alive for me; his interpretation of the Parables, Beatitudes, and Jesus' profound understanding of men and God made me think of Christ in a new way. Nevertheless, the day before my magazine cover deadline I spent six hours at my drawing table and, having accomplished nothing by midnight, retired thinking that something would surely come the next day. But I couldn't sleep, and I asked God again to give me the inspiration I needed. About two o'clock in the morning a clear, beautiful image of Christ appeared, and I could see in the darkness this vision of the Lord. Feeling immediately that that was the thing I should do, I hastened to my attic studio to make a thumbnail sketch before the face's detail faded from my mind. After I had finished it, I felt peace come into my heart and I returned to my bedroom and slept like a baby. The next morning I got up and made the charcoal drawing, now known as the "Head of Christ."

From what I hear, my "Head of Christ" has certainly had a wide ministry with one hundred and fifty million copies having been sold. I am so grateful that the Lord used my hand to create it. He gave me the vision of it and gave me the ability to do it, but at the time I felt that it just supplied the pressing need for that cover. Since then, through the years of war and depression, I've heard reports that it has been a great comfort and strength and a means of leading to the salvation of many; and others, I know, have been brought back to the Lord and some converted through having seen this painting.

The real story behind the picture begins with a change that took place in my life shortly after my wedding. When I married Ruth Anderson, an attractive and dedicated choir member and organist, back in May, 1916, I was twenty-four years old, was employed as an artist in the field of men's fashions, and was prospering financially. In all, it seemed like a cloudless sky, but storm clouds already were forming below the horizon.

Years before, I had had a tumor in my shoulder. A surgeon had removed it, and it apparently was healed. Then came a major complication in the same area. By the following spring—1917—the pain was acute. I went to several doctors and took various treatments, but the affliction grew worse. Finally, I consulted a specialist who made extensive tests.

"You're pretty sick, my boy," he said kindly. "You have tuberculosis of the lymph glands; I recommend surgery. Otherwise I cannot give you much hope beyond three months."

I prayed for guidance, and I believe God was directly speaking to me when the conviction suddenly came over me: "My wife

Ruth is brave, has a deep faith, and can take it. I'll tell her all."

This I did, not minimizing the "three months to live." Ruth received my words with utmost calm. . . . I gradually realized that she was like a rock—and that through her the Lord would guide us aright.

I do not remember the words we used in our prayer together, but I do know we did *not* ask for a longer life span. We only asked God to guide and bless us and use us. The heart of our prayer was a plea reminiscent of our Saviour's in Gethsemane: "Dear Lord, we pray that Thy will be our will, and that in all ways Thy will be done."

In no manner did we forego medical or surgical help, but we felt that if the latter was to be for me, God would make it known. We continued the medical treatments as before, but no revelation came regarding the proposed surgery.

However, something else did happen: by the alchemy of nature or in the Providence of God, the pain gradually grew less, and there were signs of amelioration of the disease. It took months, but complete healing finally took place. We do not minimize the powerful influence of mind over matter—we implicitly believe the Lord can and does heal.

What better proof can there be than that the predicted three months have stretched into forty-four busy, fruitful, and happy years—with the added blessing of three sons born to our union—and that now, as I near the 72-year mark, I feel almost as vigorous as ever, am well occupied with my work, and have the joy of Ruth's unfailing companionship.

Yet the important part of this experience is not that I was healed, but that I learned an exciting and dynamic principle: when we turn our lives over to God, without reservation, He can and will do remarkable things through us. It was this personal philosophy that made it possible for me to do the "Head of Christ." Although the picture hardly caused a ripple of comment when it first appeared, in 1940 I made an oil painting of the "Head" and, in the years since, its distribution has attained phenomenal proportions. Yet I always think of the portrayal as something God did—through me.

For Ruth and I believe that as disciples of Christ our task is primarily seed-sowing of good deeds, good thoughts, and good purposes. Yet we are human enough to enjoy hearing or knowing of results—often strange and unpredictable—accompanying our labors. For instance, there was a recent incident in Los Angeles. A robber rang the doorbell to an apartment. When the lady opened the door he thrust a revolver in her face and snapped, "This is a holdup. Give me your money and jewelry!"

Just then he looked up and saw behind the woman a large picture on the wall. It was the "Head of Christ." For a moment he seemed to freeze. Slowly he lowered his gun.

"I can't do it, lady," he gasped, "not in front of that picture." And he turned and ran down the stairs.

ROBERT G. LETOURNEAU

"What we need is to see God."

* * *

President of the heavy earth-moving machinery company that bears his name, R. G. LeTourneau is one of an increasing number of American business leaders who devoutly apply Christian principles in their daily lives. He is devoted to his God, to Christianity, to the Christian and Missionary Alliance Church, and to his fellowmen. As he says, "I build a lot of machinery and I love my machinery. But I love the Lord too, so I prove to the Lord that I love Him by leaving my machinery a few days and nights every week to go out and tell folks what the Lord has done for me." Today he lives in Longview, Texas, from where he directs the worldwide operations of Robert G. LeTourneau, Inc.

* * *

The Economy of Heaven

"LET THE REDEEMED OF THE LORD SAY SO." TODAY THAT BIBLICAL injunction is the moral benchmark of my life.

In the Bible, Job says, "I have heard of Thee by the hearing of the ear; but now mine eye seeth Thee." What we need is to see God. It is too bad that many times we wait until trouble swoops down upon us before looking up to God. As I look back upon my life, I know that during times of stress God has always been there, and I have seen Him and seen His hand work in a marvelous way. My experience is simply this: if folks will give God a chance, He will bless their lives.

I believe this Christian life is a school in which God is trying to train us to put first things first. As a young man I believed myself to be a Christian trying to do right, but I was not actively serving the Lord. Of course, I went to church once in a while, put a trifle in the collection, and went home thinking I was in good standing with the Lord. But I have discovered since that God loves us so much He wants us to love Him back a little; He wants us to cooperate with His plan and program. Matthew 6:33 says, "But seek ye first the kingdom of God and His righteousness; and all these things shall be added unto you." This I had not been doing. I was trying to put material things first and God second. I firmly believe that God had to send difficulties into my life to get me to look up into His face and call on Him.

For example, at the age of sixteen I found myself on the verge of moral bankruptcy. I had been brought up in a Christian home and I knew the way of salvation, but the devil was fast getting the upper hand. Just to show you the direction in which I was headed, my chum, with whom I sported continuously, landed in jail shortly after God saved me and snatched me as a brand from the burning. But I became very troubled about my soul and I knew hell would be worse for one who had had the light as I had seen it. One night I responded to the appeal of the evangelist. He said to me, "If your father promised to do a certain thing for you, would you believe him?" And I said, "I certainly would." He said, "Then why don't you believe God?" I couldn't seem to grasp it. I went home and to bed, but had only slept a few minutes when I awoke with the thought on my mind, "I am still on my way to hell! I must do something!" And right then and there I said, "I will believe God. I can't afford to take the chance of going any further without Him." Realizing that the Saviour was mine because I had trusted Him, immediately the joy of salvation burst in upon my soul and I jumped out of bed and ran to tell my mother, thinking that perhaps she might be still awake praying for her wayward boy. And that night, although I had heard about the Saviour all my life, I saw Him, and others saw the change in me.

I went on for another sixteen years or so, living as many Christians do. I knew I was saved and on my way to heaven. I was trying to serve the Lord, but was making a very poor job of it. I wasn't exactly what you would call a backslider, but I came to realize that my life was not counting for Jesus. I was on the verge of spiritual bankruptcy.

I knew that I ought to be witnessing for my Lord, as He had done so much for me. I tried to speak for my Saviour, but I seemed unable to do it. The man working alongside of me in the shop would take the name of my Lord in vain, and I would say nothing. I said to myself, "If someone made fun of my mother or my sister, I would not stand for it, and yet I am allowing the name of my Lord and Saviour who died for me on Calvary to be taken in vain and I make no protest." Then one night I went to the altar again. I said, "Lord, I need victory. I know the love that ought to be in my heart is not there. If you will give me the backbone that I need and fill me with your Spirit so that I can witness for you, I'll do whatever you ask me from this day on." And my Saviour took me at my word. Once again He heard my prayer and I saw Him face to face. I rose from my knees feeling that God had heard and answered. You may call that experience by any name you wish, but I say God heard and answered my prayer.

It was so real to me that I went to the pastor the next morning and I said, "Brother, do you think I should go as a missionary?" For I had two sisters in China at the time and our people believed in missions, believed in getting the Gospel out to those who have never heard. I said, "I suppose I am too old, but I promised God last night I would do what He wanted me to do, and I want to make good that promise." My pastor said, "Let's pray about it." After we had prayed, he said, "You know God needs businessmen too"; and I replied, "All right, I'll try to be God's businessman." I have been trying to carry out this commission ever since and I find it a glorious life to live. I believe if every businessman could realize what an opportunity he has to serve God in business, things would be different, because I believe God has a place for every one of us, whether it be serving Him in business, in the workshop, in the home, behind the sacred desk, or on the foreign field, and we will be happiest if we find that place. How things did begin to go in the business after I made it God's!

I sought to honor the Lord with my substance in a new way and I found that I could not beat Him at giving. I proved the fact: "God will not be any man's debtor." Everything went fine for several years, until one year I failed Him again. Again, it was not a case of backsliding, but I got off on the wrong track. I said, "It will take all my finances to handle the program I have set this year, and next year I'll have a lot of money for the Lord." I was wrong, because God wants the first fruits. It doesn't take much faith to count up what's left and give God a portion of it. God expects us to let Him have the first fruits and to trust Him that the harvest will be sufficient to meet the needs, for without faith we are told it is impossible to please Him. You can guess the result. At the end of that year, and by the way it was right at the beginning of the Depression, I found myself with several hundred thousand dollars of debts to pay and no way to get the money. Many firms who were in better shape than I was went down, never to rise again. But as I struggled along on the verge of financial bankruptcy, not knowing from one day to the next whether the sheriff was going to put the lock on the door or not, once more I met God face to face. I said, "Lord, how can I pledge for missions now when it is all gone and no chance to get the money to pay it?" But the still, small voice said, "Better make the old pledge again and trust me."

At that time we had stalled the material men until we couldn't hold them off much longer. We were running a small factory and the payroll was about five weeks behind. I made a little deal with God that whenever I was able to meet the payroll, I would save out His part. Strange as it may seem under such circumstances, within a few weeks the payroll was coming through on time. What a wonderful God we have! Why don't we believe Him more?

Today I stand as a living witness that the Lord Jesus Christ, who intercedes for me at the right hand of God, is sufficient for body, soul, and spirit; and finances, too!

CATHERINE MARSHALL

"I believe Jesus Christ meant exactly what He said, 'I am come that they might have life, and that they might have it more abundantly.'"

* * *

Catherine Marshall, an eminently successful inspirational writer, was married for twelve years to the Rev. Peter Marshall, chaplain of the U. S. Senate. His tragic death of a heart attack in 1949 only inspired her to greater literary creativity in writing six books in the past decade—all best sellers. The biography of her husband, A Man Called Peter, *has sold over one and a half million copies and in 1955 was made into a magnificent motion picture by 20th Century-Fox.*

Her most recent books are To Live Again, *the story of her life following Dr. Marshall's death, and* Beyond Our Selves, *a Christian self-help book. As a roving editor, Mrs. Marshall writes regularly for* Guideposts *magazine, and currently she also is working on a novel.*

The daughter of a Presbyterian clergyman, John Wood, Catherine was born in Johnson City, Tennessee. She was educated at Klysee, West Virginia, High School and Agnes Scott College, Atlanta, Georgia, where her active interests included writing, debating, and playing both piano and tennis. In 1959, she married Guideposts *editor, Leonard LeSourd, and they now live in Chappaqua, New York.*

* * *

Finding God's Guidance

God can guide us in living in three ways: through the Bible, through direct communication with Him, and through friends and circumstances. After two decades of exploration and experience of God's guidance, I am certain that He wills the abundant life for us when we seek Him in prayer, when we listen with open hearts and minds, when we determine to live lives of compassion and creative love for others. Doing our best to meet God's conditions inevitably gives us renewed faith in accepting His helpful guidance and in claiming the riches of grace. "Ye have not, because ye ask not," cried the Apostle James.

During my teen-age years in our Christian home in West Virginia, I dreamed of going to college. But this was Depression time and the Presbyterian church my father served as minister was suffering financially too. I was accepted at Agnes Scott College in Atlanta, had saved some money from debating prizes, and had promise of a work scholarship—yet we were still several hundred dollars short. When one evening Mother found me sobbing in my bedroom she sat down beside me and said, "I know it's right for you to go to college. Every problem has a solution. So you and I are going to pray about this, and ask God to tell us how to bring this dream to reality."

We knelt beside the old-fashioned, golden oak bed and prayed for God's guidance. Confidence and fresh determination flowed through me, as Mother's faith was contagious. The answer would come—how we did not know. Yet I went ahead and made preparations for Scott College. And soon after, Mother received an offer from the Federal Writers' Project to write the history of the county. Her salary was more than enough for my college expenses. For us that was a first memorable experience in daring to trust God.

I well know how fantastic such guidance may seem to people who have never had any similar experience. Yet the combination of a personal surrender and outside intervention, the juxtaposition of need and supply, all make it difficult to tag such events "mere coincidence." For example, God used the guidance of circumstances in leading Peter Marshall, my first husband, from Scotland to the United States to enter the ministry. Peter wanted to go to China. That door was shut in his face. He then wanted to go into home mission work in Scotland. That door closed too. The way to the United States opened. This last proved to be God's green light. The reverse of this is that when we can get our own way only by riding roughshod over other people's lives and affairs, what we want is probably not right for us. Door-crashing and wire-pulling have little part in God's scheme of things.

Our generation is rediscovering the Bible, which is far out in front as the nation's best seller. Modern translations, making use of newly discovered older manuscripts, have made the Scriptures readable and understandable. There is a sense in which the Scriptures are the fascinating story of the directions God gave men and women; how guidance worked for them when they obeyed the instructions; what happened when they disobeyed. The New Testament contains surprisingly specific guidance for us. Its wisdom has the sure touch of ultimate truth. It is really a primer on the techniques of happy, workable relationships with other people. And that, after all, is the biggest single problem for any of us. We ignore these directions, therefore, to our own sorrow and loss.

Yet the Bible does not contain God's final revelation. God longs to pour wisdom directly into receptive minds capable of receiving it. This is the direct guidance of Mind to mind, of Spirit to spirit, through the medium of an authoritative inner awareness and conviction. For three centuries the Society of Friends has called it "the inner light." When we put our lives into God's hands and ask Him to direct us, amazing results follow.

God also speaks to us through other people. If you have never tried sitting down with one or two trusted friends, sharing your problems and pending decisions, together asking God for His signals, and then pooling your impressions and suggestions—you have missed a releasing and therapeutic experience. When we are not open to the perspective, advice, and common sense of trusted friends, we are probably not relaxed enough to get God's directions in any way. Several heads—provided they are carefully chosen—are always better than one. Moreover, creative ideas often come through in the presence of kindred minds which perhaps would not have come in solitude. The Quakers, long ago, discovered this fact too.

Before the summer of 1944 the possibility of asking a Living Lord a direct question and receiving a specific answer had never once occurred to me. But during that summer a crisis of illness emboldened me to take a leap of faith. I gave God a blank check with my life. Put most simply, this amounted to the willingness to take my marching orders from God for the rest of my life. From the moment of that decision God's guidance became a personal reality. Everyday life lost its boredom and feelings of futility and became a series of exciting adventures.

Actually, life is of one piece. This fact makes it almost impossible for God to direct a man's business life, for example, when the man still insists on running his social contacts or some other part of his life his own way. Many humans fail in early experiments with guidance because they fear the blank check. Deeply ingrained is the idea that God wants to take away our fun. It is at this point that many people refuse to believe or trust the love of God for them. My own observation would prove that what God really wants for each of us is joy, health, productivity in our job, wonderful friends, and fulfilled, integrated personalities.

Abraham Lincoln once said, "I am satisfied that when the Almighty wants me to do, or not to do any particular thing, He finds a way of letting me know it." That's exactly the point. Having experimented with guidance for the last twenty years, I have found that when we really want God to direct our decisions, He will find a way to do so. Since my husband's death in 1949, a series of major decisions were inevitable for me. For many of these, I was poorly qualified, with little basic knowledge or know-how. In at least three instances, the wrong choice would have altered completely the channel and direction of my life. Yet with God's help, in each case I was prevented from making those wrong turnings.

But if we ever wonder whether we are subconsciously mistaking our will for God's will, we can easily test our decision against the other avenues of guidance: the Bible, direct communication through the inner Voice, our friends, or a combination of all of these. But in the end, with our cooperation, He *does* succeed in keeping us on the right path. The stuff of our everyday life lends itself beautifully to this kind of experimentation. A few personal experiences of finding God's wisdom, a wisdom easily recognized as beyond your own, a few proofs of His amazing personal solicitude, and your doubts, too, will melt away. Personally, I believe Jesus Christ meant exactly what he said, "I am come that they might have life, and that they might have it more abundantly."

W. MAXEY JARMAN

"Faithfulness is the most important characteristic that a Christian can have."

* * *

W. Maxey Jarman, Chairman of the Board of the Genesco Corporation, is one of America's outstanding business leaders and dedicated Christian laymen. As the active director of the nation's largest apparel and footwear concern, Mr. Jarman is constantly on the move between his headquarters in Nashville, offices in New York City, and major sales centers throughout the United States.

Born and brought up in Nashville, Tennessee, Mr. Jarman was educated at the Massachusetts Institute of Technology. He is a director of Freedoms Foundation, The Moody Bible Institute, Federal Reserve Bank of Atlanta, and the Mutual Life Insurance Company of New York, as well as vice president of the American Bible Society. He is married and the father of three children.

* * *

Faithful Stewardship

DURING THE WAR BETWEEN THE STATES, ONE OF THE FAMOUS Confederate Cavalry generals was J. E. B. Stuart. Stuart had many communications with his Commander in Chief, General Robert E. Lee, and these communications were always signed, "Yours to count on, Jeb Stuart." It must have made General Lee feel good every time he got one of those messages. He knew that he could count on Jeb Stuart, that he would be faithful to any responsibility that was given him.

Faithfulness is one of the most important characteristics that a Christian can have. God has entrusted to each of us certain responsibilities to look after the things that he has placed in our hands. Paul said, "It is required of a steward that a man be found faithful." Are we faithful and dependable in the things that the Lord has entrusted to each of us individually? Let us ask ourselves the question, "Can I be counted on?"

To me Christian stewardship is a spiritual matter. It is a part of a person's spiritual development and Christian living. My responsibility as a Christian is to the Lord, to be faithful in the use and disposition of the abilities and means that God has entrusted to me. That applies to all talents, opportunities, or possessions, whether they are large or small. I believe stewardship is an act of worship, a privilege, a source of joy and satisfaction to the individual, a channel for great blessings that have been promised by the Lord. Today my personal testimony in life is a testimony to the power of God, not to any merit of my own.

I'm afraid the Lord did not have very promising material in me when I accepted Christ as a boy eleven years old. I was rebellious, stubborn, and self-conscious. As I grew up, my family was in moderately comfortable circumstances, although certainly not wealthy nor luxurious. Somehow, I had an inborn tendency to be economical. As a boy I believed in saving money. My parents, however, early indoctrinated me with the principle of tithing. From the very beginning, I gave to the church 10 per cent of the small allowance I had. There was never any discussion or question in our family about whether we were going to do it or not. It was the same about attending Sunday school and church. When the time came, we went—like sitting down to supper at seven o'clock every night.

My first real job was in the shoe manufacturing business when our company was getting started, back in 1924. We had to begin in a mighty small way. Capital was limited and competition was hard. Because of the Lord's leading and the early training I had, there was never any question about whether I would tithe or not. I tithed my income right from the beginning. The Lord blessed me in every way from the standpoint of business, family, and spiritual development.

Time went on, and as income increased, I began to get some faint glimmer of the fact that money not only has its attractive features but can be a very evil master. Unfortunately I have seen that happen in more than one case—when men allowed the desire for wealth to become the master influence in their lives. Not all of those men were rich men; some were poor men who made their lives bitter because they did not have the money they thought they were entitled to. As the good Book tells us, "They that would be rich fall into many temptations." I began to see that I really needed

God's help to avoid the evils that come along with money and for protection against its lure.

This then was a personal need on my part, to give money away —not only for the good use that it might be put to, but to prevent that money from becoming so important to me that I would want to hang on to any that I got my hands on. The very act of giving up something helps to strengthen a man's spiritual nature. It keeps him from being overcome by the tide of materialism which is so evident in the world today.

From the stage of realizing the need that I had to give and the importance to me of giving, there gradually developed the next stage of being able to give cheerfully. From giving cheerfully, the next development was to give joyfully. The stages of my development might be stated like this—first of all, giving as a habit and a necessary obligation; second, giving proportionately, but still as a matter of obligation; third, giving because of the need for spiritual development; fourth, giving as a privilege and giving cheerfully and joyfully. One way I have been able to do this is through the Jarman Foundation which my father and I established a number of years ago.

The Jarman Foundation has proved to be a very good operation. The value of its holdings has increased very considerably. As it pays no taxes on its income, all the funds are available for God's work. The funds of the foundation are used for foreign mission work, for free distribution of the Bible, for Bible institutes, and for orphanages. Also, according to the foundation, beneficiaries are expected to hold certain fundamental doctrinal beliefs in order to qualify as beneficiaries.

In my own case those beliefs are as follows: The Bible, I believe, is the inspired word of God. I believe Christ was born of a virgin, lived a sinless life, died for my sins, arose from the dead and lives on High today. This Christian faith, of necessity, must be central in my home, church, career, and life work.

By the grace of God alone—not through any merit of my own—I have been brought into a new life in Christ. Trusting in God's love and power during my adult life, I have positive assurance of a glorious eternal life. My religious faith has strengthened my character, caused me not to worry regardless of events, and has enabled me to fill various leadership positions as well as help other people in all walks of life. This has been the effect of my life endeavor as a business man and as a Baptist layman.

The Bible tells us that when we came into this world, we brought nothing with us; and it is certain that when we go out of the world, we will not be able to take anything with us. Alexander the Great is reported to have told his friends before he died to put him in a coffin with his hands outside the coffin to show that he could carry nothing away with him. This pagan was convinced of the truth that we can carry nothing with us. On a recent TV show, Jack Benny's program, Rochester, his man of all work, made the statement about Benny that if he couldn't take it with him, he wasn't going. As much as some of us would like to hold on to some of these things, we know that we are all going, and we can't take it with us.

There's an answer to that—a mighty important answer for every one of us. We can't take it with us, but we can send it on ahead. What does the good Book say about that? "Lay up for yourselves treasures in heaven, where neither moth nor rust can consume and where thieves do not break through and steal, for where your treasure is, there will your heart be also." We can't take it with us, but we can send it on ahead. Even the poor in this world can be rich in Heaven. By cultivating the art of stewardship, by becoming faithful stewards, by liberally, cheerfully contributing to the Lord's work, we are laying up for ourselves treasures in heaven where there are no income taxes, where there is no inflation, where there are no losses, where our treasures have permanent value. You can't take it with you; but send it on ahead, and you will be able to say to God, as Jeb Stuart said to Robert E. Lee, "Lord, you can count on me. I will be a faithful steward."

ELEANOR ROOSEVELT

"O Lord, make me an instrument of Thy peace."

* * *

Universally acclaimed as "The first lady of the world," Mrs. Franklin D. Roosevelt died at seventy-eight not long after being interviewed for this volume. She is included because she lives on in the hearts of millions of admirers and because her influence as diplomat, author, and gentle world leader has been brightened, not dimmed, by death. Gradually, since the passing of her husband, President Roosevelt, in 1945, she had become not only "the most admired woman in the world," but the symbol of all the awakened women everywhere working to achieve a joy-wreathed world of peace.

To the gracious manner born, Eleanor Roosevelt grew up in the Oyster Bay branch of the Roosevelt family, watched her uncle Theodore become Governor of New York, Secretary of the Navy, and finally Republican President of the United States. When she married another Roosevelt—a cousin from the Hyde Park branch—her sheltered life as Mrs. Franklin D. Roosevelt became channeled into the almost identically turbulent course followed by her "Uncle Teddy." During her thirteen crowded years in the White House, she brought to the First Lady role a new dimension of humanitarian activity for the succor of all.

With her uncle's "Square Deal" and her husband's "New Deal" days finally behind her, Mrs. Roosevelt proceeded to broaden her own distinguished career. She became U. S. delegate to the United Nations, chairman of its Human Rights Commission, and one of the authors of the epochal Universal Declaration of Human Rights—an experience she called "one of the most wonderful, important, and worthwhile of my life." She traveled ceaselessly from Lebanon to India to Japan, wrote her column, "My Day," and such books as This I Remember *and* On My Own, *and never withdrew her working support of the Democratic Party. When her great soul passed from earth, she left not only four sons and a daughter and a singular legacy of love-in-action, but also "a name to shine on the entablatures of truth forever."*

* * *

"Faith, Hope, and Charity, These Three"

As Told to Roland Gammon

(The following was based on an interview granted the author by Mrs. Roosevelt in the early summer of 1962.)

GREATNESS IN LIFE MAY LIE IN DIFFERENT FIELDS. TO ME IT IS A proof of life's nobility and prodigal gifts that so many people from so many countries, cultures, and centuries have contributed so much to man's upward progress. And yet, in evaluating what men and what power have had the greatest influence on history we must name the religious as the first and final cause. Indeed, when I was once asked to list the five men who had done the most to shape the world's thinking, I named Christ, Confucius, Mohammed, Buddha, and Plato.

Although denominations mean little to me, I have been a churchgoing Episcopalian all my life. If we pattern our lives on the life of Christ—and sincerely try to follow His creed of compassion and love as expressed in the Sermon on the Mount—we will find that sectarianism means less and less. Jesus was Jewish and yet He founded the Christian religion. To me, the way your personal religion makes you live is the only thing that really matters.

Life is meant to be lived as fully and as helpfully as possible. In addition to prayer and congregational worship, I have found the Holy Bible a remarkably wise and beautiful book and reading a few verses every day a helpful habit. My favorite verses are in First Corinthians, Chapter 13, which starts: "Though I speak with the tongues of men and of angels, and have not charity, I am become as sounding brass or a tinkling cymbal" . . . and which ends so beautifully, "Now abideth faith, hope, charity, these three; but the greatest of these is charity."

Today, religious skeptics frequently charge that Christianity has failed, even as political isolationists carp that the United Nations has failed. I do not think Christianity has failed, because Christianity is something that is accepted or rejected by the individual; even when one accepts it he may not live up to it all the time or even part of the time. Whether you believe as a Protestant, Catholic or Jew, Hindu, Buddhist or Moslem, it is the fruits of your belief as evidenced in your daily life that are of concern to your fellow human beings. If you believe in God, you naturally think that the Supreme Being will judge you both by your acts and by your intentions, taking into account your temptations and sometimes giving you credit for your victories.

So with the churches, so with the United Nations. The UN is only an instrument, a piece of man-made machinery whereby imperfect human beings strive for greater perfection here on earth. Thus, I believe in Christianity and in the United Nations, which I consider to be a working expression of Christianity in the world. That is why when President Harry Truman requested me to be a delegate to the organizing meeting of the United Nations in San Francisco I accepted for one reason: I believed the United Nations to be the greatest hope for a peaceful world. My husband often expressed his bright hopes for the new peace organization, and somehow I felt a personal responsibility.

Since that day in 1945 when I accepted Mr. Truman's invitation, I have had no reason to change my mind. Indeed, I believe more completely in it today than I did in January, 1946, when I met with the delegates in London and was assigned to Committee Three. It was while serving on this committee, concerned with the humanitarian, educational, and cultural problems of mankind, that I began to see the inner workings of the UN. Later, working on the Human Rights Commission in an effort to write a Charter of Human Rights, I learned how the Soviets operate and the need for forceful, patient dealings with them.

Why is this work so personal to me? Well, it seems to me that the only really organized work for peace today is being done through the United Nations. This is the only instrument we have with which to work, the only instrument whose purpose it is to keep peace in the world, the only instrument which can create an atmosphere in which peace may grow. We *must* use all the knowledge we possess—all the avenues for seeking agreement and international understanding—not only for our own good, but for the good of all human beings.

A moral and materialistic struggle now engulfs our planet. We might even call it a bloodless war, which is now going on between Communism and Democracy. The war for Communism, both in an economic way and an ideological way, is led by the Soviet Union; the cause of the free, democratic believing world is led by us. Now, if we are going to lead people we have to understand them: what their conditions are, what they care about and believe in, what their religion is, what their customs and habits are.

In this regard, it is time we Americans took a good look at ourselves and our shortcomings, remembering how we established a land of freedom and democracy, remembering what we believed in when we did it. The only thing that really causes me worry is that I don't think our people are aware we have been challenged; that this great struggle is going on and it is critical whether our way of life and our hard-won freedoms are to survive. Thus, in this continuing struggle it is most essential for Americans to learn to understand people of other lands.

We wonder, for example, why having given so much help, we do not have friends. It is fantastic, really, what we have given—billions of dollars' worth of aid. But what we have failed to do is send the right administrators of this aid—men who understand the people they are giving it to. We are apt to say, "Oh, are you still doing it that old-fashioned way? This is the way we do it in America!" and already we have made our first mistake. No underdeveloped country can make the leap of a thousand years into a highly organized society like ours. All peoples want to do things a little better, see themselves move ahead, apply their moral and spiritual values in their own way. Also, as we get to know them, we are more apt to forgive their trespasses. For instance, I adopted a plan during my UN years of inviting small groups of delegates for a social meeting. It was here I found that much more understanding was possible, that you really could get to know people and what they believed. I must confess there was one exception—the Russians.

When I visited Russia several years ago, I had one persistent, frightening thought: that we might continue to be apathetic and complacent in the face of this gigantic challenge that is the Soviet Union. I can never believe any government preserved by fear can stand permanently against a system based on love, trust, and cooperation among its people. Our system, based on love and trust, removes fear so all are free to think and express their ideas, to work and worship as they choose. In the past, we have never failed to meet any challenge or threat which confronted us. In the future, I am confident we will master this too, but we must use the full resources of our faith in order to prevail.

DANIEL S. C. LIU

"A true public servant must apply Christian principles daily to preserve the honor and integrity of Government."

*   *   *

Under the leadership of Police Chief Daniel S. C. Liu, the Honolulu Police Department has achieved a reputation of being one of the finest in the United States. Chief Liu (pronounced Lee-oo), a descendant of one of the old Chinese families on the island, supervises a force of 845 men, including officers with Japanese, Chinese, Korean, Filipino, Samoan, Hawaiian, and Caucasian backgrounds. He joined the force as a rookie in 1932, and after a steady series of promotions was offered the post of chief in 1948. He declined the offer twice, but after much prayer, he accepted when it was proffered him a third time.

Chief Liu, or "Deacon Dan," as he is called in church circles, is an active member of the Olivet Baptist Church, a regular teacher in the men's Bible class and a leader of the Hawaiian Baptist Convention. He is also chairman of Hawaii's Youth for Christ board, and is a director of the Southern Baptist Foundation of Hawaii. Among his many honors and awards are citations from the U. S. Chamber of Commerce, the Republic of Korea, and the International Association of Chiefs of Police, of which he is now president.

*   *   *

A *Spiritual Duke's Mixture*

I REMEMBER IT WELL, THAT JUNE NIGHT IN 1932. I WAS THE RAWest of rookies with the Honolulu Police Department, and though I was understandably a bit nervous, I was also a pretty cocky kid. I had studied the manual which had been issued me, and I really believed it could be applied to any situation that was likely to arise.

I heard a ruckus in a rooming house on my beat, and going in to investigate I came upon two drunken laborers in a violent fight. I announced in the most official tones I could summon that they were both under arrest for disturbing the peace. In an instant, the two men became united and had made me their common enemy. I was knocked to the floor, and while one of the men beat me on the face with his fists, I caught a glimpse of his cohort coming at me with an iron bar. Somehow, I managed to break away . . . and how I retreated!

It was hours before the feeling of panic left me, and then I began to brood. Because I had retreated from a fight, I felt that I had disgraced my uniform on my very first tour of duty as a policeman, and that I should turn in my badge. Also, by some inexplicable line of reasoning I felt a deep resentment toward whoever had written the patrolman's manual. I had placed my complete faith in this booklet, but suddenly I was aware that it didn't provide all the answers.

Thirty years have come and gone since this incident occurred, and I am happy to report that I have spent them all as a member of the Honolulu Police Department. The instruction manual that is now issued to rookies is a far more detailed book than the one given me, but I know that it cannot be expected to provide solutions to every problem. When I am faced with a really frightening or bewildering problem, I prefer to place my reliance on another book—the Holy Bible.

A sincere, dedicated police officer—and I am personally convinced that the overwhelming majority of policemen in our fifty States fall into this category—needs a special kind of sustainment. The work is far from easy. Oftentimes, it is hazardous. Without the help, the comfort, and the fortification of God, the work would oftentimes prove unbearable; without the inspiration of a sustaining religious faith I know I could not have served my city and country as a police officer.

In 1948, I was promoted to the position of Chief of the force. Before I could bring myself to accept the honor of this appointment, I was torn by inner doubts as to whether I was qualified to handle this job. I had seen too many others attempt it and fail, and yet I realized that no one could hope to succeed unless he were willing to risk the possibility of failure. It was an agonizing decision that I had to make. Twice I turned the offer down. The third time the position was offered me, I spent countless hours in prayer and Bible meditation, and somehow I achieved the inner glow of conviction that God would help see me through. This time I accepted, because everything I had learned in the Baptist Church and every prompting of the Holy Spirit seemed to support an affirmative answer.

My close-cut Christian faith was a long time coming, even though my mother was anxious to give her children a Christian upbringing. As my childhood in Honolulu progressed and as circumstances in our home changed I attended church or Sunday school in a variety of missions—Episcopal, Catholic, Seventh-day Adventist. As a young man, I added to my Christian "Duke's Mixture" by attending the Congregational, Methodist, Lutheran and Adventist churches. It was not until 1939, when the Southern Baptist Convention in evacuating several of their missionaries from the Far East, notably Dr. Victor Koon, established the Olivet Baptist Church in Hawaii, that I found my permanent church home. All through these "exposures" I felt I was being led by God, and I certainly consider it a privilege to witness for Him today.

There are times when a police chief can be the loneliest of men. I think that I am being a perfectly normal human being when I admit that I like to be liked. Everybody does. I cannot imagine anyone really wanting to be unpopular. However, my responsibilities to the people of Honolulu whom I serve . . . and to the Constitution of the United States which I am sworn to uphold . . . do not call for me to win any personal popularity contests. My job is to run an efficient department and to safeguard the peace and tranquillity of my city, as well as to uphold the basic human rights of its local inhabitants and its many, many visitors. In order to do this as I feel it can best be accomplished, I am often forced to make decisions that I know will prove unpopular. Sometimes I find myself morally required to give an order that may alienate me even from my closest friends.

When this happens, I never allow myself to forget God or the lessons of Christian charity, justice, and forgiveness. I remember that the Divine Leader who lived almost two thousand years ago in Galilee also was misunderstood and bitterly resented. I turn to the Bible which I always keep in my desk . . . and I feel the comfort and strength of God's presence, and know that I am not really alone after all.

How often, in my meditations on the Bible, I've thought that if all Americans were to honor the Ten Commandments by actually living them—instead of merely paying them lip service once a week—policemen would no longer be necessary. Should this ever come to be, I will cheerfully become a rookie in the great army of unemployed. But, as this utopian state is still beyond our grasp, I try to follow and to inculcate in my men this philosophy of Civil Service: A public servant before the Cross, recognizing the fact that authority stems from God and that government is ordered of God, is all the more in a position of stewardship and trust. He, therefore, must apply Christian principles to preserve the honor and integrity of government and exercise the courage of his Christian convictions.

HENRY MARGENAU

"The order of the universe is a divine gift."

* * *

Dr. Henry Margenau, Professor of Physics and Natural Philosophy at Yale University, is one of the notable world scientists propounding the compatibility of religion and science. He especially believes that modern nuclear physics with its understanding of non-material force fields, its suggestion of continuous creation, and the principle of uncertainty or, as some say, "freedom" within the atom, tends to undergird the spiritual truths of Christianity.

Educated in the public schools of Germany and at Midland College, the University of Nebraska, and Yale University, Dr. Margenau became an American citizen in 1930. He was appointed as assistant physics professor at Yale in 1931, and has combined atomic research and teaching at the New Haven institution for more than three decades.

Honored by such colleges as Michigan State and Dalhousie University in Halifax, Nova Scotia, Professor Margenau has served as visiting professor at New York University, University of Washington, Heidelberg University, and the University of Tokyo. He is a fellow of the American Academy of Arts and Sciences, served as president of the Philosophy of Science Association from 1950 to 1958. An editor of the American Journal of Science *and a consultant to the National Research Council, he is the author of* Open Vistas, Foundations of Physics, *and* The Nature of Physical Reality. *He is married and the father of three children.*

* * *

Science and the Christian Doctrine

EVER SINCE MY FORMAL SCHOOLING IN BIELEFELD, GERMANY, AND my Protestant training in the Lutheran Church, I have had a deep desire to assist and encourage the amalgamation of religion and science. Subsequent studies as pupil and teacher at such great American universities as Nebraska, Yale, and the Institute for Advanced Study in Princeton, have not only confirmed this fond hope but impressed me that such an amalgamation is today taking place. To me, it is by no means out of the question that a theory of religion, when fully developed, may exhibit the same formal structure as science itself; indeed, nearly fifty years ago the American philosopher William James suggested that a body of religious beliefs is a doctrine capable of pragmatic and scientific verification.

If such a "science" of religion is to be started and supported—if religion is to become more scientific and science more religious—the first question to be answered is what is the empirical place of religious experience? A possible and probably correct answer appears to be the kind of immediate experience which is regarded as distinctly religious. I mean such things as the feeling of gratitude that springs up in man's heart on a joyous day, the peaceful, soul-stirring uplift of worship, the monitoring awareness of a conscience that regulates our lives, the feeling of awe in the face of overwhelming beauty, the guiltful contrition that follows a sinful experience, the sentiments of misery and abandon at the insufficiency of human power before fate, the longing of men for grace and for redemption. To say that these are religious experiences is not to argue that they are exclusively religious; they are also pure facts of interest to the so-called social sciences, and it is far from my intention to suggest that psychology, sociology, anthropology, and psychiatry should not be concerned with them and organize them into their own constructural schemes. All this, however, does not cast out their appreciation and analysis in scientific–religious terms. In developing this new approach, in going beyond the limits of science into a region where science itself can be appraised, I see religion becoming what I should like to call "metascience."

Today, in the popular mind, religion and science are believed to be in conflict. The strife between them has sweeping consequences in human action, in the moral field—consequences which cannot be ignored. For religion, particularly in our Western sphere, has two aspects, one cosmological and one moral. Cosmological religion with its ancient prescientific speculations about the universe covers in part the field of natural science. In its moral phase, religion develops a code of human conduct and tries to commit men to it by an appeal to faith. Now, if science can show that the cosmological claims of religion are wrong, religion's case in the moral field is greatly weakened. This is precisely what has happened in our time. Men believe that science has overpowered religion in the natural realm, and they look to *science* for guidance in the sphere of human action and in the spiritual sphere. The unhappy and possibly tragic feature of this attitude is that it rejects the spiritual gifts which religion brings to men.

There is in fact a need for continual reappraisal of the relation between religion and science, and never was this need greater than it is today, for science has recently undergone a revolution of its fundamental concepts that is unique in history. The complete refutation of old-style materialism in modern physics, the sublimation of mechanics, the reliance placed on abstract ideas, all these are sweeping in their philosophical consequences, and many things that used to be said about the conflict in question are simply no longer true. As we have said, the judgment of science is never final. Science recognized eternal *problems* but no eternal *truths.* It learns, it progresses; yet its job is never done. Nevertheless, as we know, science has its share of dogmatism.

And dogmatism in religion, equally indefensible and equally mistaken, rears itself upon the arrogant conviction that religious truth is laid down once and for all in a static pattern, rigid, lifeless, and inexorable, incapable of progress and improvement. These bone-dry dogmatisms always clash and clatter, and the noise they make through the centuries is usually taken as the sign of conflict between science and religion. These are generalities; let us now face specific aspects of our theme. To me, it has always been a curious and yet significant fact that at the very beginning of the Bible, which Christians regard as divinely inspired, religion is said to grant a charter to science, with an implication that the two shall live in peace. First, you recall, there was chaos, terminated by a divine act of creation. Then followed a period of lawlessness and confusion that ended in the great flood. One interpretation of the turbulent days prior to Noah's Ark, which is elaborated in the Jewish Talmud, emphasized that during this period nature and nature's God did not act in accordance with consistent principles; that there were no natural laws and, hence, no possibility for natural science. Lawfulness, morality, behavior in conformity with reasonable principles, causality, were God's gift to Noah, made in the beautiful covenant of the rainbow. "Jehovah smelled the sweet savor; and Jehovah said in his heart, 'I will not again curse the ground any more for man's sake, for that the imagination of man's heart is evil from his youth; neither will I again smite any more everything living, as I have done. While the earth remaineth, seedtime and harvest, and cold and heat, and summer and winter, and day and night shall not cease.' And God said, 'This is the token of the covenant which I make between Me and you, for perpetual generations, I do set my bow in the clouds and it shall be for a token of a covenant between Me and the earth. And it shall come to pass, when I bring a cloud over the earth, that the bow shall be seen in the cloud, and I will remember my covenant, which is between Me and you and every living creature of all flesh.'"

If I understand this passage correctly, it means to say that the order of the universe is a divine gift. In a sense Judeao-Christian religion here acknowledges the legitimacy of science. Perhaps it still remains for science to make an equally generous reciprocal acknowledgment to religion.

The symbolism of this covenant has remained alive as a vague religious motive in the work of most scientists. The very word "cosmos," meaning ornament of beauty, along with the Greek myth of the harmony of the spheres, discloses a remnant of elemental religion. Expressions of reverent amazement at the regularity of physical nature, at the simplicity of natural laws, at the sweep of the human intellect in its control of nature have sounded through the ages as religious overtones of science. It is heard in the utterances of modern scientists as clearly as it speaks from the eloquent writings of the theologian, Schleiermacher, who paid tribute to the one miracle before which all others lose their meaning, that miracle being the absence of breaches in the lawfulness of nature. Thus, the lawfulness of nature, the orderliness of the knowledge derived therefrom, represent one sufficient basis for claiming general compatibility between nature and science.

What science actually achieves is a correlation of facts with ideas. It needs facts as our body needs food; but within the organism of science facts are processed, combined, organized, and connected by a texture of reason, and it is the whole of the organism, including that texture of reason, of ideas and conjectures, which is science. In a very deep sense, science has its origin in the circumstance that in the deliverances of our senses the facts are not sufficiently well ordered to satisfy our desire for simplicity and consistence. Science is an elaborate answer to the paradox of the bruteness of our experience. To summarize: incoherent facts are unified by science into a consistent whole with the use of reason.

It seems to me that there is also an incoherent rhapsody of unique and troubling religious data which human understanding is called upon to organize into an orderly and satisfying pattern. For my part, I see them residing in those experiences most men acknowledge to be peculiarly religious. Just like the facts of science, they are unconnected, orderless, and insufficient in themselves, requiring a texture of rational organization. And this, I take it, is what formalized religion or theology aims to provide—that its theory is replete with intangible ideas, that in the terminology of its detractors it bristles with the "technicalities of salvation" is small wonder to one who is familiar with the intangibles of science. The success of religion is measured by the degree of rational coherence which it bestows upon these singular religious experiences that assail the sensitive mortal.

Christian doctrine symbolizes the unrelieved and unembellished rawness of our natural reactions to the universality of sin, evil, and misery by its thesis of *original sin*. Guilt and terror strike the soul of man, and he feels unworthy of redemption. Indeed, if one analyzes the oppressive, brute facts of religion, one finds them reflecting, I think, very largely the message in Genesis 3:17 where God speaks to Adam: "cursed is the ground for thy sake; in toil shalt thou eat of it all the days of thy life; thorns also and thistles shall it bring forth to thee; and thou shalt eat the herb of the field, in the sweat of thy face shalt thou eat bread, till thou return unto the ground."

Now pass from there to the words of Jesus in Matthew 11:28: "Come to me all ye that labor and are heavy laden, and I will give you rest." Here is a religious theme of supreme satisfaction, an organizing idea of power and simplicity in terms of which many crude experiences make beautiful sense. To bridge this gap between Genesis 3 and Matthew 11 by a texture of rational connections is one of the important tasks of professional religion. And it is the same task as that performed by science when it converts what Kant calls "the rhapsody of sensations" into orderly rational knowledge.

ELTON TRUEBLOOD

"Men and women, in their fierce and faltering struggle to find the right way, are *not alone.*"

* * *

Dr. Elton Trueblood, religious scholar, lecturer, and one of the best-known Quakers in America, has proved to be a beloved source of inspiration, both in the pulpit and in the classroom. Widely respected as a teacher and writer, Dr. Trueblood is presently a Professor of Philosophy at Earlham College, Richmond, Indiana. For two years in 1954–1955, he served as the Government's Chief of Religious Information and Advisor to the Voice of America.

Elton Trueblood was born in Pleasantville, Iowa, in 1900. After graduating from Penn College, Iowa, he earned his S.T.B. at Harvard University and Ph.D. at Johns Hopkins University. During a long academic career, he has served as professor at Haverford College and Stanford University, and acting professor and chaplain at Harvard. His work as Quaker and Christian won him the Outstanding Christian Service Award in 1952 and the 1960 Churchman of the Year Award. Dr. Trueblood was Chairman of the Friends World Committee for Consultation from 1947 to 1952, and was editor of The Friend *from 1935 to 1946.*

Dr. Trueblood is a member of the board of the Council on Religion in International Affairs and William Penn College. Married and the father of four children, he has been honored by a number of colleges and universities, including Washington and Lee University, Miami University, and the University of Vermont. The Philosophy of Religion, The Yoke of Christ, The Idea of a College, Confronting Christ, The Life We Prize *and* General Philosophy *are among his more than twenty widely read books.*

* * *

The Life We Prize

THE MORAL STRUCTURE OF THE LIFE OF THE WEST DOES NOT STAND alone. It is supported by the basic faith which cuts across many lines, both national and sectarian, by which we are often separated.

Some of the convictions which undergird our present ideal of life in the free world came from ancient Greece, but to a far greater degree they came from Palestine. It is from the Hebrew heritage, with its conviction that all are made in God's image, that we get something which is strong enough to make the democratic ideal credible. As this faith flowered in the life and message of Christ, the notion that each human being is intrinsically valuable was given added support by reference to God's love for each one, no matter how worthless in the eyes of his fellowmen. If every man, regardless of race or knowledge or fortune, is an object of God's care, and one for whom Christ died, then the idea of respect for persons begins to make sense and democracy, or something like it, is the only tenable pattern of life for men. The revolutionary ideas of equality and dignity, and consequent due process, come not of themselves, but from such sources.

In great measure this basic faith is the real inspiration of the life we prize, and this is true even when the source of the inspiration is unrecognized. To understand or to describe our way of life without reference to our religion is an impossible task, yet any reference to it is fraught with great difficulty.

Millions in our culture believe they have outgrown and discarded the faith which originally gave us most of our moral structure. Those who continue to hold, with deep conviction, religious beliefs seem to be tragically divided among themselves. Is not any general statement of faith likely to be rejected by one group on the ground that it is *false* and by all sections of the other group on the ground that it is *inadequate?*

It is true that one of the signs of hope in our troubled time is the increasing number of thoughtful people in the West who are growing increasingly restive under the pagan orthodoxy of their generation. Yet too many of us adhere to the popular position that God exists in some remote manner that involves us in no special responsibilities, that there is no need to belong to a specific church, and that rigorous thought on such matters is unnecessary and somehow not quite intellectually respectable.

Then there is the very good man who is so honest, so eager not to accept anything without adequate evidence, so sensitive to the danger of believing what is comforting merely because it is comforting, that he rejects God—the very concept that makes reasonable his intense effort to be honest. Such a man we can only honor, and trust that he will go on loyally following the evidence wherever it leads. I firmly believe that it leads to the conclusion that men and women, in their fierce and faltering struggle to find the right way, are *not alone.*

I have many reasons for my faith, the most elementary of which is that ours seems, in so many respects, a reasonable universe. Ours seems to be a world of cause and effect, of the non-accidental nature of natural law. It is also a world that has produced life and mind and spirit. It is a world marked by the emergence of sages and heroes and saints, as well as millions of common people trying to do what they *ought.* Now it is essential to the notion of order that there is nothing in the effect that was not already in the cause. If our world is one of order, as we all really believe, then our world must have been, long before mind appeared, the kind of world in which mind was implicit. If God really is and if this is God's world, everything falls into place.

The first and elementary reason for faith in God, then, is the negative one that the notion of something from nothing is absurd. Belief may have its difficulties, as it does, but they are as nothing compared to the intellectual difficulties of unbelief. To believe that the long development in the direction of moral sensitivity, with all the small intermediate steps finally making the cumulative event possible, is the result of chance, in the precise sense of that which is wholly devoid of purpose, is to stretch credulity too far.

Yet, as we go further in faith we soon realize that the strongest reasons for belief are not those of speculation, but those of experience. As a result of His Divine Companionship, we believe in the end, not because we have *inferred* Him, but because we have *known* Him. The most objective evidence for the truth of faith in God is in the lives of men and women throughout the centuries, who, in humility of heart, have claimed to know Him and who have proved their claim by the difference which their experience has made.

Tragically enough, large numbers of people deprive themselves of His Divine Companionship by rejecting the concept of a personal God as illogical and superstitious. To say that God is personal is not to suggest that God has a body or that He has any similarity to human form. To be personal is to be not only conscious but self-conscious, to appreciate value, to entertain purposes, to be aware of ends, to be responsive to the needs and aspirations of other persons. Now the central point is that if God is not personal in such a sense, then God is not the ultimate explanation of that which most requires explanation. What baffles the materialist is the emergence of personal character in a world of chemical reactions. Only one who is supremely personal, as God is, can be the Ground for the emergence of even the finite personality which we see in our fellows and know intimately in ourselves.

As we should suspect if God is indeed truly personal, His most vivid revelation is a personal one. In the person of Christ, God is made understandable to man. In contrast with other great teachers, we find something in Jesus other than genius. He comes, not as a Seeker to tell us what he has deduced, but rather as a Revealer who tells what he knows.

In Christ's short years of public life he seemed to put his chief emphasis on the formation and cultivation of a sacred fellowship, made up of extremely fallible men, but yet a fellowship of such a nature that, rooted in loyalty to him and his kingdom, they could move mountains. To this living fellowship of all who love Christ and see in him the very revelation of God, I seek to belong. The fellowship, which is the true Church, is not limited to any one kind of building or any one kind of organization, but appears wherever men and women gather together in humble dependence upon God as revealed by Christ.

The Light of Christ is not limited to men who have known him in the flesh, or even known about him. "Other sheep have I which are not of this fold," were the words of Jesus. His Light appears, in a measure, in every son and daughter of earth. Who can doubt that a great measure of this Light was seen by Jeremiah or by Socrates and millions more? There is no contradiction between the idea that God has been revealing Himself, in sundry times and sundry places, and the other idea that God has revealed Himself fully in one time and one place. This is a faith which is neither so vague as to be meaningless nor so narrow as to be blasphemous.

The glory of this faith, which both unites and deepens men's lives, lies in its fruits. It introduces us to One who can forgive. Forgiveness transcends alike the frustrating sense of continued guilt and the equally damaging sense that moral considerations are irrelevant. Those who suffer may find abiding peace in the realization that, in their suffering, they are not alone; God, they may reasonably believe, suffers with them, for this is the deepest meaning of the cross. Above all, this faith is a producer of joy. We have many burdens to bear and much injustice to suffer, but if this is really God's world we cannot despair. We are not merely on our own. Even when we lose the way we are not lone wanderers, for He is seeking us far more truly than we are seeking Him.

If the revelation of God in Christ is the true revelation, there is in the world at least one absolute in all our relativity of values. That absolute is the revolutionary love which is so rich in its meaning that the whole of the thirteenth chapter of First Corinthians is required for its definition. The faith based on this love makes impossible the *hatred* of anyone.

We believe love is a moral absolute because it reflects the nature of God. Genuine religion thus differs from philosophy or ethics, however noble and necessary they are. True religion is not man's search for the good life, important as that may be; neither is it our effort to find God, inevitable as that may be. True religion is our response to Him who seeks us. It is not an argument for God, but a response to God's love.

WALLACE E. JOHNSON

"God calls businessmen to His service just as a minister or priest is called to preach."

* * *

Once a self-proclaimed "poor, little old peckerwood boy from Mississippi," Wallace Johnson has become a nationally known mass home-builder and one of the South's outstanding business, civic, and lay religious leaders. As president of Wallace E. Johnson, Inc., he is a champion constructor of low-income housing who has built 1,000 homes a year for twenty years. As president of Holiday Inns of America, Inc., he has the world's largest motel system with 366 inns now open to the American traveling public, with another 70 inns totaling 8,200 rooms presently under construction. A deeply religious, tithing, Bible-reading businessman, it is little wonder that Johnson is sometimes called "the praying millionaire from Memphis."

Born in Attala County, Mississippi in 1901, Johnson was a knock-about carpenter at sixteen and built his first house before he graduated from high school. Shortly after moving to Memphis in 1938, he formed his own home-building firm. He became the first president of the Memphis Home Builders Association, subsequently held top executive posts in the National Association. In addition to his successful home-building business, Holiday Inns' income last year crested the $20,000,000 mark.

A trustee and member of the finance committee of Memphis Union Avenue Baptist Church, Johnson is a member of the Southern Baptist Convention's Home Mission Board, a director of the United Fund and YMCA, and president of the Wallace E. and Alma E. Johnson Foundation. He also serves as chairman of the board of the American Provident Investors Corporation. He is married to the former Alma McCool, who is a full partner in all Johnson enterprises.

* * *

Builder of Men and Homes

Over at our business headquarters in Memphis, Tennessee we have a motto, "Bomah," which I occasionally repeat to startled visitors. I then go on to explain that Bomah means "Builder of Men and Homes." Nearly twenty-five years ago that is what I asked the Lord to let me be. That is what, with His help, I am trying to be today.

From that point in 1939, when as a discouraged supplies salesman earning $37.50 a week I asked God's guidance, things began to change. They continued to change for the better, as long as I prayed and as long as I asked the Lord to let me do the right thing. We builders and boosters of the business world need to depend upon God for our daily wisdom; we need Him just as does the minister or priest who calls upon the divine power to direct his daily actions. Because I believe God calls businessmen to His service (just as a minister is called to preach), I feel He wants me to use my brains to build small, pleasant, modern homes which people of the lower income bracket can buy or rent.

Again, because we have been permitted to build more than 1,000 low-rent houses a year for the last twenty years, I do not hesitate to say God is my partner. Today when someone fondly calls me "the Henry Ford of the Building Business," I accept it sincerely as a compliment to what the God-man partnership can do. In fact, we continue to pray to God for wisdom, even in solving the many little things incidental to the business world. My habit of praying to God for guidance in specific things has been with me for a long time, and even now I keep a daily list of numbers 1, 2, 3, 4, etc.—items to ask God about, praying to Him to show me the way. My own experience has proven to me that God does answer individual prayers, if we will only ask and have faith they will be answered.

The year 1945, for example, was a critical one for America and for myself. My formal prayer on that January 1st, written out on a ruled tablet as is my custom, began by invoking God's blessings on our armed forces abroad and by praying that His spirit would fill our people here at home. I then prayed in the following specific, concrete terms:

"O Lord, help me to be one of the leaders of the nation in the building of men and homes, and help the city officials of Memphis to understand my goal, so they will help us instead of hinder us.

"Help me, O Lord, to be a good Baptist, so that I may help to lead my church to develop a better United States, and teach me how to gain the confidence and win the souls of others to Your teaching. O Lord, help me to understand Thy will, so that I may take my proper place among the businessmen in the United States, and if it be Thy will, give me the proper leadership ability, so that I might help in molding the National Association of Home Builders into an instrument of Thy will.

"God, please, let us build 2,000 units in 1945, and if it be in accordance with Thy divine purpose, let us accumulate enough money in that time to carry on our business.

"O Lord, help us to build a good house, an inexpensive house for both white and Negro citizens in our community that has never been available to them before, and, God, please, oh, please help us to convince the bankers and businessmen of our community that these are safe investments, so that we can go on and on and on. Amen."

This specific prayer has been fundamental to my relationship with God and to my progress as a pioneer low-cost builder. (In 1945, incidentally, we did build 3,000 homes and apartments and ended the year with nearly $450,000 in the bank.) In that same spirit of constructing trim, attractive homes for thousands of slum-ridden white and Negro families, I haven't hesitated to ask God's help in getting the things the projects needed—a critical gas line, an increased lumber supply, a $200,000 loan. Yes, indeed, when there is good to be done for others, God answers our incidental day-to-day prayers!

I revere the home because I was brought up in a good Christian one down in Mississippi's piney woods. I had picked my first bale of cotton before I was eight, joined the church when I was eleven, and contracted to build a $9,000 house for our local railroad agent before I got out of high school. Although my mother, who traced her ancestry back to the famous New England preacher, Jonathan Edwards, often read from the Bible to us, there was no pleading or praying over me when I joined the church. I just felt the divine call—as I did later to build houses for the millions—and there was little ol' Wally Johnson walking down the aisle all by himself to give his heart to Christ.

You might say providing well-built homes is my practical way of living my religion. A good home often makes a bad man good and a good man better. When you take a sorry sort of fellow out of the slums and put him in a house he can be proud of, he is apt to leave off his boozing, gambling habits and start to make something of himself. Over the years, I've watched what a good home can do for people—get them settled down, working in their own homes and gardens, starting to go to church and learning to love the Lord.

In these troubled times, when I lie down at night and turn the light off, I'm asleep by the time the room gets dark. I know I won't let the Lord down, and I know He won't let me down. What I've done so far is just the beginning. I've put a lot of people in good homes, homes that are going to inspire them to be better Christians. But I've just gotten started. There are still thousands of acres of slums across this country that ought to be replaced with decent housing. And if all the people who've been backing me keep their faith in me—I'm just going to keep going on and on.

If I just accomplish one thing, I will be well satisfied. If I can just convince all my brother builders all over the country that they can not only make money for themselves but can help their community by building low-rent homes, then I have done a whole lot for humanity.

PAUL DE KRUIF

"This I believe: to come to grips with God, to bow down before His will, to constantly seek His guidance, we should all try to make our own prayer."

* * *

Paul de Kruif, a roving editor for The Reader's Digest *since 1940, pioneered the popular medical treatise for magazines and books. His early reporting on medical topics for such magazines as* The Saturday Evening Post, The Ladies' Home Journal, *and* Country Gentleman *resulted in his widely read books,* Microbe Hunters, Men Against Death, *and* The Fight for Life. *In 1925 he collaborated with Sinclair Lewis on the best-selling novel,* Arrowsmith.

Paul de Kruif was born in 1890 in Zeeland, Michigan, a town which he boasts is "still the nation's largest city without a cinema or saloon." A Ph.D. graduate in bacteriology and virology at the University of Michigan, he served with the Sanitation Corps, U. S. Army, in World War I, became a research associate at the Rockefeller Institute in New York City, and in 1922 published Our Medicine Men, *a spoof at the pompous pretensions of a part of the medical profession. Here he first introduced the term, "mutation," now widely used in microbiology.*

A champion of the general practitioner or family doctor as still "the heart and soul of medicine," Mr. de Kruif helped organize the National Foundation for Infantile Paralysis, served as consultant to the Chicago Health Department, and is an honorary member of the Michigan State and Ottawa County Medical Societies. His autobiography, The Sweeping Wind, *was published in 1962.*

* * *

Research for Prayer

NOW THAT I AM APPROACHING MY SEVENTY-THIRD YEAR ON EARTH, I feel I can confess that for my first fifty years I could not pray. Why? Simply because science could not prove to me there was any God to pray to. Then a man—for me he will remain miraculous—began to heal me of my worship of my own reason. Half-ashamed, I made a first stuttering attempt to pray.

Now, this has grown into a formal, yet simple, little prayer. Though the whole of it is brief enough, shorter bits of it can be detached for a quick block against this or that temptation. For me that makes it especially useful. Often (not always) God answers. How do I know? By an instant feeling of what it's right to do, in a comfort of my conscience.

I can't give the full name of the man who played doctor to my sick soul; his first name was Earl. Humility, inherent in his religion, demands his anonymity. This was what I admired intensely in Earl, without having it myself. He radiated reliability. As I myself did, he made promises easily, but what distinguished Earl was that he kept them. All of them. As I got to know him better, Earl revealed a quality that is far from common. He had compassion. Few realize that compassion is sympathy translated into action. Earl had it. Not for disasters or emergencies, but steady. I mean not just the kind of pity that is sorrow and sympathy for suffering human beings. Earl's was sympathy and sorrow exploding into action to spare them and to save them.

Earl was only one of a strange army of over one hundred thousand of ex-doomed. He was an Alcoholics Anonymous, one of the very earliest—now thirteen years postgraduate from the gutter.

"What's your secret weapon?" I asked Earl one day. "Only prayer," he answered. "We've got to ask a Higher Power to help us. We begin the comeback only when we know we can't help ourselves." Earl explained that went for all of them, the whole miraculous hundred thousand of them. If they didn't pray—as some were too proud to—if they hadn't compassion to save other alcoholic downfallen—as some were too busy or too lazy to do—they were almost sure to slip back to destruction.

"You mean—you pray—to God?" I asked. This name I had used often, but only in profanity. Earl answered that he besought help from a higher Power—not himself. Surely this prayer must be a mighty one, to save wretches from the gutter after medical science had failed. On the contrary, Earl's prayer turned out to be plain, even humdrum.

Praying, he simply said: "Help me to do the right thing in this situation—Thy will, not mine be done." That was all—and every day, and in the dark of night, this was his sole defense against relapse into alcoholic doom.

For me, this was life's turning point. Though not alcoholic, I, too, lived in constant, deadly peril. As my own little God—all my grown-up life I'd struggled for the kind of character that Earl had superlatively. My brain—all the God I had—could distinguish bad from good. Yet, too often, I did the bad.

Now secretly I began to pray, telling nobody, not a living soul. For the first time in my grown-up life I said "God" in a whisper, and not cursing. In trying to make a prayer, I turned professional. The writing man in me told me Earl's prayer lacked rhythm (as if that mattered!).

"God, help me this day to do what's right." There, that's got rhythm. Then I added—and it was the toughest thing I've ever had to say—*"Thy will, not mine, be done."* That marked the beginning of a rugged battle against the big-I-guy in me that had so long misruled me. Whispering it to myself over and over day and night, it didn't help me much—except for this: I didn't try to define what God is, or to picture Him to myself; now I knew there is a God, I just bowed down.

For months I chewed at an answer. It was simple: I wanted God's help to be a better man, not a truly good man, only a bit better. Now came what seemed an answer. I quit trying to figure out, myself, how to be better. I kept stupidly, obstinately, asking God. His answer? It made me begin to drag out and dredge up and face my fundamental defects—I'd ducked this, lifelong.

What was one stymie in my fight to be better? Vanity. Having had some success as a writer, people patted me on the back and told me how good I was in there. I glowed, and believed them. "Help me, now, to fight vain thoughts." When praised, I began saying that to myself. I began to ignore the hoorahs. In the night I began to give a hard look at my hypocrisy. Outwardly respectable, inwardly plagued by bad thoughts. "Help me to think only what all may know." This was really a tough one, but I kept asking it.

Always these whispered cries for help were followed by—"Thy will, not mine, be done." And it was strange how this gave power to these bits of prayer. One of my worst roadblocks in trying to be better was passing the buck to others, for what really were my own mistakes.

"You are an alleged success," I told myself, "but how have you gotten ahead in life?" From the darkness came an answer, and not pretty. By hard work, but sometimes aided by a technique less admirable. I had been praised as a somewhat foolish, but big-hearted Otis. In the dark I reviewed the times this generosity was for my own advantage. "Help me to give without thought of return." This now was added to the slowly growing prayer.

So four years went by, and I began to feel different. Not mentally, but deep below my thinking brain. And, praise God, conscience seemed a little stronger in me. At this part of the prayer I'd been working longest, "help me this day to do what's right." Yet here was the toughest of this discipline of self-examination. Was my conscience really strong? No—its muscles were flabby. What in this gravest matter, to ask of God? This year came a simple answer—"Help me to learn better what it's right to do."

A few years ago, I dared at last to join these fragments together, to set them down in a kind of order and with a rhythm that might make them easier to remember. I looked at the prayer, read it over and over. And this was eerie. It was as if I had not written it. I knew I had not written it. I felt cut down to size. I felt what my given name actually means. I felt—little.

Little enough to throw away what's past, to begin life over, to begin the exercise of everyday, not merely emergency, compassion —before recommending the practice of compassion to others. What is this little prayer? Only a rule of life that can't possibly be lived up to but can be struggled up toward.

I do not recommend anybody to follow this rule or even to try to remember it. This I believe: to come to grips with God, to bow down before His will, to be constantly reminded of the need of His guidance, we should all try to make our own prayer. Here is mine:

> God, help me this day to do what's right—
>   Thy will, not mine, be done
> —help me to learn better what it's right to do;
>   and then do it, no matter what the pain
> —help me now to fight vain thoughts; and to think
>   only what all may know
> —help me always to blame myself; and to give
>   without thought of return
> Dear God—make strong my faith in Thee—Thy
>   will, not mine, be done.

ROY ROGERS

"There is nothing in the world more important than understanding the power of God."

* * *

Cowboy star Roy Rogers and his beautiful wife, Dale Evans, are a husband–wife team known from coast to coast of our own country. Through their "Wild West" films they are also known in many other countries the world over. During the past fifteen years Roy and Dale have appeared together in nearly one hundred feature films, TV and radio shows, special telecasts and "live" rodeos. Although they first acquired fame as the stars of cowboy thrillers, perhaps their finest "silent" influence has been as charter members of the Hollywood Christian Group, an organization of motion picture personalities dedicated to applying Christian principles in their lives and work.

* * *

Christians in Hollywood

ALL THE TRIALS, TEMPTATIONS AND STRUGGLES THAT DALE AND I have experienced since becoming Christians have only exercised and increased our faith. I've had to study God's Word and I've had to pray. I've had to give myself completely into His hands. Yet, through Christ, I have had such a wonderfully abundant life I am always glad to tell people about it. The only trouble is that there is so much to tell I never know where to start.

In recent years, God has made our lives amazingly rich and rewarding. It has been an especially wonderful thing to be able to apply the teachings of the Lord Jesus even in the entertainment industry. Here, as many of our fans know, we have such terrific opportunities to witness for the Lord in our work when we go on tour, when we do benefits, and when we appear in movies or television.

The Lord Jesus Christ saved me nearly fifteen years ago, when with Dale's help I started to go to church again. The Holy Spirit came into my heart and brought such a change as to transform my life. To me today, Jesus is life itself; today I can only be grateful for the opportunities He gives me for service. One group Dale and I love to work with is the Hollywood Christian Group. Along with Connie Haines, Jane Russell, Collen Townsend, Tim and Velma Spencer, Dale and I were among the original members of this fine organization. For many years the Hollywood Christian Group has been a particular blessing in our lives.

A typical example of the Group's uplifting effect has been its influence on my "cowboy" career. For instance almost six years ago, I introduced something entirely new into the show Dale and I were doing down in Houston, Texas—the annual Fat Stock Show and Rodeo. I didn't even tell Dale ahead of time what I was going to do. Not that I was hiding anything from her; I guess it was just something I had to do by myself.

At the end of one of my songs, I held up my hand to show that I wanted to say something. Then I just held onto the hand mike and opened up. I didn't have a prepared speech; just the thoughts I wanted to express. They went something like this:

"I've been getting a lot of mail from kids—boys especially—who ask me if I don't think it's pretty sissy for them to go to Sunday school. I want to say right here and now that it isn't sissy at all. In fact, I think that going to Sunday school is one of the best things any child can do.

"When your parents tell you to brush your teeth, they know what they are saying. When they tell you to eat your spinach and drink your orange juice, what they're trying to do is get your bodies ready to stay strong and healthy when you're older. And when they tell you to go to Sunday school, they're trying to help you grow strong in spirit. The things you learn in Sunday school will give you the strength you'll need against difficulties and temptations of all kinds when you grow up. So go to Sunday school regularly, and learn all you can about the Bible and Christ's teaching—you'll always be glad that you did."

Now this was quite a statement for a cowboy to come out with, right in the middle of a rootin', tootin' arena show. Dale told me later that when I first began to speak, she could hardly believe her ears. But she said she was glad I spoke up that way—and so was I. I felt it was the blessing of God's spirit that I could do it and I meant every word, especially to the children who have always been my big boosters in this business.

Since our first Hollywood Group meeting many years ago, we have seen more than one thousand people make a definite decision for Christ. Many have become full-time Christian workers. Actually, eternity alone will reveal how many people have been moved by the Hollywood Christian Group here in the film capital. That is why Dale and I always reserve time in our busy schedule for this work. Today there is nothing in the world more important to us than giving our Christian witness to the power of the Lord.

We don't intend for our group to take the place of church worship. We feel it is more of a mission, where men and women can come for spiritual help. Once we interest a person in God, we strongly encourage him to go out and select a church in which to serve. We channel all such new friends into the churches, because otherwise many never would find their way there. Thus, because we have accepted Christ as Saviour, it does our hearts good to get up and tell people all around the country what He has done in our lives.

Today, I can say along with Dale the Christian testimony we have made our creed:

"We believe John 3:16: 'For God so loved the world, that he gave his only begotten Son, that whosoever believeth in him should not perish, but have everlasting life.' We have both accepted the Lord Jesus Christ as our personal Saviour. We love Him, try to follow Him in our daily lives, and are bringing our children up under His guidance. To us, Jesus Christ is truly 'The light of the world.'"

SAMUEL M. SHOEMAKER

"The will of God must become every man's North Star."

* * *

The Rev. Dr. Samuel M. Shoemaker, named by Newsweek *as one of the ten greatest preachers in the United States, served for nearly forty years as rector of just two churches—Calvary Episcopal in New York City, and Calvary Episcopal in Pittsburgh. Yet, through the spoken, printed, and broadcast word, he has succeeded in making faith a vital experience in the lives of countless people throughout America and the world. Until his retirement from the Pittsburgh church last year, his weekly sermons were mailed throughout the United States and to twelve foreign countries. His "Faith That Works" radio program was broadcast every Sunday night for years over station KDKA, and in 1957, 1958, and 1960 he was the speaker on the nationally broadcast "The Episcopal Hour." He now broadcasts regularly over WBAL in Baltimore.*

Canon Shoemaker believes a personal active faith must be part of our daily lives at home and in business. He launched his now famous "Pittsburgh Experiment" in an attempt to "make God as important as steel," in the great industrial city. He has written twenty-five books, including Realizing Religion, How You Can Help Other People, *and* With the Holy Spirit and with Fire. *In 1961, Episcopal Bishop Austin Pardue appointed him Honorary Canon of the Diocese of Pittsburgh.*

"Dr. Sam," as his friends call him, had much to do with the founding of Alcoholics Anonymous, and the Faith at Work *magazine and movement. A board member of World Neighbors, Inc., and a graduate of Princeton University, he is the recipient of honorary awards from such diverse groups as the Veterans of Foreign Wars, the All American Conference to Combat Communism, and The United Mental Health Services. Married and the father of two daughters, it has been said of "Sam" Shoemaker by Canon Bryan Green, "He has done more than any other living minister to help forward the work of evangelism within the Protestant Episcopal Church of America."*

* * *

A Spiritual Anniversary

FORTY-FIVE YEARS AGO IN OLD PEKING, CHINA, WHERE I HAD GONE to teach Chinese lads in a YMCA mission school, the "Princeton work in Peking," began my first experience of trying to get faith across to an individual. It was the last year of World War I, and following my graduation from Princeton, I went to China on a short-term teaching assignment. I had heard the famous preacher, Dr. W. E. Orchard, say, "Foreign missions are the one Christian flag flying at the moment."

Besides teaching in the business school, I was given a class of young business men who were inquirers into the Christian faith. We gathered in my room round a stove on cold autumn evenings. The first time we had about twenty, the next time about fourteen, and the third about seven. I was becoming aware that something was the matter with that inquirers' class! I suspected that it was not only my dense ignorance about how to teach, but something else that got in the way. For I had been brought up in a responsible, conservative church-going Episcopalian family. My early associations with religion were happy and valuable as was my attendance at one of our great church schools in New England. These associations were enough to dispose me toward a decision to enter the ministry.

But it is one thing to be interested in religion and even to conduct services or to feel called to the ministry; it may be quite another thing to be able to communicate your faith to individual people.

There was one very intelligent and promising young man in the group of inquirers who seemed more interested than the rest in Christianity. Now a gentleman had just come to Peking who told wonderful stories of helping people to find Christ. I thought to myself, "I'll ask him to get hold of my inquirer!" So I went round to ask if he would not see this man and try to win him for Christ. Without the least hesitation, he said to me, "Why don't you win him yourself?" I replied that I was an Episcopalian, and we did not go in much for this sort of thing—I'd rather have someone who knew better what he was doing deal with him. I should not like to jump in on such delicate work as this, any more than I should begin to operate on a man for appendicitis with a penknife. But he was by no means convinced. He said to me, "Now what do you think is the real reason?"

I countered by asking what he thought the real reason was. And quick as a flash he said, "Might be sin. Resentment kept me from doing this kind of work for a whole year." He then reminded me of the Four Absolutes, which the late Dr. Robert E. Speer called the essence of the Sermon on the Mount: absolute honesty, absolute purity, absolute unselfishness, and absolute love. We all know that no human being ever reaches any of these, but I find that when people seek the absolute, they get at least the relative; when they seek the relative, they may get almost nothing at all.

I went home that Saturday afternoon with what Studdert Kennedy called "a pain in my mind." That evening I got ready my material for a class at the Chinese English Cathedral next morning, and knelt down to say my prayers. Somehow everything jammed! I kept saying words, but they didn't seem to get as high as the ceiling, let alone any higher. I knew then and there that I was up against my Waterloo. Either I would or would not "let go" so far as I understood God and his will. For, while I was decided about the ministry, and was then a teacher in China on short term, I knew I had not faced the issue of the mission field for life. A couple of years was fascinating, but a lifetime out there? That was something else. It seemed to me I heard Somebody saying to me, "You want to do My work in *your* way." I knew that I could not even pray, let alone give God a chance to use me to win someone else, until I "let go."

So I went over and looked in the mirror and shook my finger at myself and said, "You've got to come across or you've got to go home—you are out here under false pretenses now." And then, with much more of will than of emotion, I knelt down beside my desk, and one by one let go of the things I knew were standing between me and God and between me and other people. The crux of it was the willingness to stay in China all my life if God should will it. As in the case of Abraham and the sacrifice of Isaac, the willingness was the important thing. I felt no great emotion, but I did have the feeling that my life had slipped into place where it belonged. Lying in bed that cold, crisp January night, I received what I feel was the first clear guidance I ever received in the words, "There is no work of Mine to do for him who is not wholly Mine."

Next morning I awakened with an uneasy feeling that somehow that day I must go and talk to my young Chinese businessman friend about Christ. That afternoon I got in a ricksha in the West City where I was living, and drove over about three miles to the East City where he lived. At his house, I paced up and down outside his door, and almost prayed he would not be home; for if he was at home, I was going to have to try to win him for Christ, and I did not know what to say! I don't know what would have happened to him or to me if he had not been at home, but he was; and when I rapped, he said, "Come in!" My heart sank. As I crossed the threshold, I asked God what on earth I was to say; and it came to me as clearly as I am telling it to you, "Tell him what happened to you last night."

He asked me to sit down; and in a pair of creaky, wicker chairs we began to talk. I told him I thought he had been interested in my class, but not satisfied with it. I told him I thought the fault was mine. Then I told him what I have just been telling you. He only said, "I wish that could happen to me." I said, "It can. Be honest with God about your needs and ask Him to come in and take over your life." We talked about our sins, and we talked about Jesus Christ and His love and power. That day he made his decision and found Christ.

As I look back, I see that there were four elements that went into this initial spiritual decision:

1. The break with conscious wrong. Someone said truly that we "take hold of God by the handle of our sins." He comes to us, like a doctor, at the point of our need. If we've got a temper, we must surrender it. If we resent someone, we must surrender the resentment. To be sure, these surface sins will later uncover some that may lie much deeper; and we must surrender at deeper levels. But let us begin by trying to be honest with God about the things in us that stand between us and Him or between us and other people, by being very specific.

2. Daily time for personal devotions. If the new life is to grow and continue, it must be fed like a fire needing fuel. Set apart a regular time each day before the day's business begins. I soon had a prayer list of a lot of people I was trying to win for Christ and

prayed for them daily. The Bible opened up as a book of experience. I'll never forget how much it helped me to look up every reference I could find to St. Peter, and discover in nearly every one of them weaknesses like my own; yet Christ called him a "rock" and greatly used him.

3. The necessity to put life's major decisions in God's hands. You can be a merely professional minister; what kind of ministry does God want you to have? He wants to mold, not only the spirit, but the locus of one's life. Marriage needs to be considered from the angle of God's will, not from human desire alone. Every young person needs to realize these things and act upon them. The will of God must become every man's North Star, to which he is continually adjusting the compass of his life.

4. The need to learn how to witness. Most Christians are tongue-tied and unconvincing, and most Communists are articulate and persuasive—this is the most serious human factor of our day. Keep quiet about the trivia of your religion; talk about the great elements in it—God, sin, conversion, divine grace, prayer—and people will listen to you if you mix your experience with your convictions. Many have beliefs, few have power. If all of us believed the things we say and sing, sought to live them daily, and talked about them in natural ways, we should win others to Christ.

Such an experience is not a passport to perfection. One meets many of the same problems and situations after an experience like this as before. Christian conversion is a process, in which growth and new decisions will be necessary. I am a little wary of people who glibly call themselves "surrendered, born-again Christians." Even a true conversion is only a beginning. Just as one's promise in marriage before the altar is but the beginning of a relationship with one whom we love, so conversion is but the beginning of a relationship with God through Christ. We spend a lifetime working it out together. I know how important this beginning is. Before a child can grow, it must be born. Before we can begin to grow spiritually we must be born again. Growth is gradual, birth is sudden. My Church believes in the necessity of Christian decision, and the heart of our Confirmation service is the bishop's question, "Do you promise to follow Jesus Christ as your Lord and Saviour?" and the answer, "I do."

I speak in this very personal way, also, because our Lord told us to confess Him before men, to witness to Him. The great thing in a witness is, of course, Jesus Christ Himself. All Christian preaching is a witness to Him, to His Divinity, to the "mighty acts" of redemption, and to His power to give men the answer to their lives. Three times over in the Book of Acts is recorded the story of St. Paul's conversion to Christ, twice in the first person singular. Unless that personal conversion had happened, he would never have had any Christian theology to write about. He was wise enough to mix his general witness to the Deity and Atonement and Resurrection of Christ with his personal witness as to what Christ did for him. This has always been part of Christian witness, and always will be.

God grant that our lives may all be footnotes to His great command, "Verily, verily, I say unto thee, Except one be born anew, he cannot see the kingdom of God."

WILLIAM C. JONES

"The only security you'll have in this life is the knowledge that God loves you."

* * *

President of the W. C. Jones Publishing Company in Los Angeles, William Jones is a world traveler, Christian businessman and internationally known lay speaker. During the past few years he has made thirty trips to the Orient and more than twenty journeys to Russia. In Moscow, he visits with the Baptist Church and films various medical projects being done in that city.

Born in 1913, W. C. Jones rose from a background of poverty to become the proprietor of several small newspapers and now owns a technical publications firm. He is a member of Billy Graham's Personal Board of Directors, International Christian Leadership, and the Faith City Mission Board of Amarillo, Texas. For the past six years Mr. Jones has been host of ICL's annual Presidential Prayer Breakfast in Washington, D.C., attended by the President, the Cabinet, business and religious leaders, and a majority of our Senators and Congressmen. He has also sponsored scores of similar banquets throughout the world, all with a central Christian emphasis. Mr. Jones is married and the father of five children.

* * *

In Search of Reality

I HAVE SPONSORED APPROXIMATELY TWO HUNDRED AND FIFTY BANquets throughout the world, stressing one simple message—"What Christ did to my life." The quest for life's answers ended the night I accepted Jesus Christ. Conclusive evidence that Christ is the answer to life will never be certain unless He changes your life.

I was brought up in a poor family and thought money would be the answer to life. By the time I was nineteen I owned a newspaper; by the time I was twenty-two, I owned five of them. And yet there was a vacuum within me. I saw people drinking and going to horse races. They seemed to be having a better time and getting more out of life than I was; so I followed them. By the time I was twenty-eight, I had drunk away my friends and gambled away my business. The nicest thing you could say about me was that I was a hopeless drunk.

I started again, and when financial success came a second time, I began giving money to the church. I began with twenty-five dollars a week in 1941, and by 1950 I was giving eight hundred dollars a week. But simply giving money wasn't the answer. Christ wants more than that.

I learned the hard way, that you have to identify yourself with something, or someone. If you don't take Christ and make Him the Lord and Master of your life, you'll take something else and make it lord and master of your life. In my life, first it was money and prestige, and then drink. Giving money to the church didn't prevent me from getting drunk about every other night. I was so hungry for reality that even if it was in a bar, I wanted it.

In 1952 my wife and I were about to be divorced. The love in our home had gone dead. My insecurity and confusion forced me to face up to the fact that my money couldn't buy everything. I would have given anything I had just to be able to get back that love. In a way, I was very lucky. As the Bible indicates, you must have a need before you can find Christ. If your life is self-sufficient, God can't do a thing for you.

It was during this desperate low in my life that I met a man who really knew Christ. Only two weeks after meeting this man I knew I wanted what he had in his life. He asked me if I would like to accept Christ. I said yes. The night that my wife and I knelt and asked Christ to come into our hearts, a miracle happened. My desire for liquor left, never to return. Christ took over our lives and everything changed. Our home was brought together; it was a brand-new start, something we could share equally, a whole new life beginning together. We fell in love again. And the love we found was so much better than anything we had ever known!

In fact, God poured so much love into our home that we had to adopt five children to share it with. I don't think I knew what the love of God meant until I found the answer in those five children. You see, my children can grieve me and disappoint me, and do all manner of things to upset me; but they are powerless to change the fact that I love them. In this way I found Christ to be the final reality. The only security you'll have in this life is the knowledge that God loves you. I'd give up, if I didn't know that God loved me. I know I don't even have the power to change the fact that God loves me. And when you find such reality, there is no place else you can go. This is the source of assurance that gives you objectivity in dealing with life.

I've had five of my best friends, at various times, try to steal my business from me. What should I do—be like them, or remain faithful to this identification with Christ? If you remain faithful to Christ, you have to pay the price. Few people, I find, desire to identify themselves with Christ because it means they will have to live differently in front of their neighbors, friends, and business associates. It's a responsibility to identify yourself with Christ.

I was at a meeting the other day and the question was asked, "How do you, in traveling around the world, witness about Christ when you don't even know a foreign language?" I have yet to meet a witness for Christ who required a language to portray the fact. People aren't listening to you; they're watching your life. This is the reality that Christ brings into your life. The life that Christ has promised us comes as a natural result of dedication and obedience to Him, and making decisions that will be pleasing in His sight. Then, He Himself instills His very nature within you, that your life might be His witness.

Since becoming a Christian eleven years ago, I have tried to eliminate all practices in my business that weren't pleasing to God. I don't ask God to bless my business; I ask Him to bless the ingredients that go into the business. I pray for the wisdom to do work at a lower rate than my competitors, the conscientiousness to do it better, and the dependability to keep my delivery commitments. During this period, our business has put approximately 90 per cent of its net earnings into Christian missionary and evangelical enterprises.

I found that when Christ became the reality in my life, my taste and desire for many things disappeared. Our family lives on a fraction of our income, because the desire for things that money can buy has been replaced by a greater desire. Similarly, in Russia, I have seen what Christians there have to give up to attain the reality of Christ. When they accept Christ, all their educational privileges are at an end. They lose their jobs and become security risks. They are looked upon as traitors. Yet their faith remains and so does the joy in their hearts. They are a constant source of inspiration and a testimony to the sustaining power of Christ. Nearly one million Russians go to the Baptist churches in the Soviet Union, and last year they baptised fifteen thousand new members.

My ministry in Russia and Japan is enhanced because I am host to the annual Presidential Prayer Breakfast in Washington, D.C. I believe that God always honors an effort that glorifies Jesus Christ and allows the Holy Spirit to take over and lead. Our value consists of our relationship to Him. God asks for one thing: you be faithful to Me. Keep Me in the front of your life, and I will lead you into works that I have ordained.

The greatest obstacle to the Christian life is the constant urge to create our own good works and follow a path of our own choosing. We must remain obedient and susceptible to the call of God to work in the path that He has already ordained for us. The ultimate of happiness that any one of us is going to find in this life will come from the assurance of our usability to God.

PAUL TILLICH

"Faith as ultimate concern is an act of the total personality and involves body, soul, and spirit."

* * *

In stature and significance, Dr. Paul Tillich stands almost alone among contemporary Protestant theologians and religious philosophers. A theologian of Lutheran background who taught for twenty years at the Union Theological Seminary in New York, his influence extends far beyond his church. He has been called the favorite Protestant thinker among Catholic theologians in this country, and his work is highly valued among Jewish intellectuals.

Paul Tillich was born in Brandenburg, Germany, in 1886, the son of a Lutheran minister. Matriculating in the theological schools of Berlin, Tübingen, and Halle, he received his doctorate of philosophy in Breslau in 1911. From 1919 to 1933, while serving as professor of religion at various German universities, Dr. Tillich endeavored to bring religion into relation with politics, art, philosophy, depth psychology, and modern sociology. The professor's categorical opposition to Nazism in 1933 resulted in his immediate dismissal from the University of Frankfurt am Main when Hitler seized power.

Late in 1933 Reinhold Niebuhr's invitation to come to the Union Theological Seminary was accepted by Tillich, who moved with his wife and two children to New York and later became an American citizen. His association with Union Seminary lasted until his retirement in 1954. Dr. Tillich was then appointed University Professor at Harvard where he continues the lecturing and teaching he has always found a source of "the greatest anxiety and the greatest happiness." Among the books which have made Paul Tillich a powerful intellectual force in contemporary religious thought are The Interpretation of History, The Shaking of the Foundations, Systematic Theology, The Courage to Be, The New Being, The Dynamics of Faith, *and* Christianity and the Encounter of World Religions.

* * *

Courage and a Dynamic Faith

Today the term "faith" is more productive of disease than of health. It confuses, misleads, creates alternately skepticism and fanaticism, intellectual resistance and emotional surrender, rejection of genuine religion and subjection to substitutes. Indeed, one is tempted to suggest that the word "faith" should be dropped completely. But there is as yet no substitute expressing the reality to which the term "faith" points.

Faith is the state of being ultimately concerned. Man is concerned about many things. When a particular concern claims ultimacy, it demands the total surrender of him who accepts this claim, and it promises total fulfillment even if all other claims have to be subjected to it or rejected in its name.

If a national group makes the life and growth of the nation its ultimate concern, it demands that all other concerns, economic well-being, health and life, family, aesthetic and cognitive truth, justice and humanity be sacrificed. The extreme nationalisms of our century are laboratories for the study of what ultimate concern means in all aspects of human existence. Everything is centered in the only god, the nation—a god who certainly proves to be a demon, but who shows clearly the unconditional character of an ultimate concern.

In our highly competitive Western culture the ultimate concern of many people is with "success" and with social standing and economic power. This god too demands unconditional surrender to its laws even if the price is the sacrifice of genuine human relations, personal conviction, and creative eros. When fulfilled, the promise of these misplaced faiths proves to be empty.

An opposite—and more than an example—is the faith manifest in the religion of the Old Testament. The content of this concern is the God of justice, who, because he represents justice for everybody and every nation, is called the universal God, the God of the universe. He is the ultimate concern of every pious Jew, and therefore in his name the great commandment is given: "You shall love the Lord your God with all your heart, and with all your soul, and with all your might." (Deut. 6:5) This is what ultimate concern means and from these words the term "ultimate concern" is derived.

Faith as ultimate concern is an act of the total personality and involves body, soul, and spirit. It happens in the center of the personal life and includes all its elements, conscious and unconscious, rational and non-rational, emotion and will. Otherwise faith does not occur and compulsions take its place. For faith is a matter of freedom. Freedom is nothing more than the possibility of centered personal acts. In this respect freedom and faith are identical.

What is the source of this all-embracing and all-transcending concern? Man is driven toward faith by his awareness of the infinite to which he belongs, but which he does not own like a possession. This is in abstract terms what concretely appears as the "restlessness of the heart" within the flux of life.

Faith is uncertain in so far as the infinite to which it is related is received by a finite being. Only certain is the ultimacy as ultimacy, the infinite passion as infinite passion. This is a reality given to the self with his own nature. It is the self in its self-transcending quality. But there is not certainty of this kind about the content of our ultimate concern, be it nation, success, a god, or the God of the Bible. Their acceptance as matters of ultimate concern is a risk and therefore an act of courage.

Every faith has a concrete element in itself. It is concerned about something or somebody. But this something or this somebody may prove to be not ultimate at all. That is the difference between true and idolatrous faith. In true faith, the ultimate concern is a concern about the truly ultimate; while in idolatrous faith preliminary finite realities are elevated to the rank of ultimacy. Thus faith can be a failure in its concrete expression, although it is not a failure in the experience of the unconditional itself. A god disappears; divinity remains. Faith risks the vanishing of the concrete god in whom it believes.

If faith is understood as being ultimately concerned, doubt is a necessary element in it and must be accepted with the courage of faith. There is only one point which is a matter not of risk, but of immediate certainty and herein lies the greatness and the pain of being human; namely, one's standing between one's finitude and one's potential infinity.

Where there is faith there is tension between participation and separation, between the faithful one and his ultimate concern. Without some participation in the object of one's ultimate concern, it is not possible to be concerned about it. But faith would cease to be faith without separation—the opposite element. He who has faith is separated from the object of his faith. Otherwise he would possess it. It would be a matter of immediate certainty and not of faith. The "in-spite-of element" of faith would be lacking. But the human situation, its finitude and estrangement, prevents man's participation in the ultimate without both the separation and the promise of faith.

Out of the element of participation follows the certainty of faith; out of the element of separation follows the doubt in faith. And each is essential for the nature of faith. Sometimes certainty conquers doubt, but it cannot eliminate doubt. The conquered of today may become the conqueror of tomorrow. Sometimes doubt conquers faith, but it still contains faith. Otherwise it would be indifference. Since the life of faith is life in the state of ultimate concern and no human being can exist completely without such a concern, we can say: Neither faith nor doubt can be eliminated from man as man.

Even in those described as firm in their faith—even in those called saints—the element of doubt, though conquered, is not lacking. In saints it appears, according to holy legend, as temptation which increases in power with the increase of saintliness. In those who rest on their unshakable faith, pharisaism and fanaticism are the unmistakable symptoms of doubt which has been repressed. Doubt cannot be overcome by repression, only by courage. Courage does not deny that there is doubt, but it takes the doubt into itself as an expression of its own finitude and affirms the content of the ultimate concern. Courage does not need the safety of an unquestionable conviction. It includes the risk without which no creative life is possible.

There may be an idolatrous element in one's faith, including Christianity. We must be alert lest human interpretation of the content of our faith, from the Biblical writers to creedal formulations, receive ultimacy. The fight against the idolatrous implication of this kind of static faith was waged by Protestantism. In the interests of a dynamic faith, the Protestant Principle points out that liturgical, doctrinal, and ethical expressions of faith are not beyond doubt and ultimate in themselves; rather their function is to point to the ultimate which is beyond all of them. Such criticism and doubt show that the community of faith stands "under the Cross," the divine judgment over man's religious life.

Obsolete tradition, wishful thinking, and the attempt to mold the ultimate to one's own purposes, confusion of the bearer of the ultimate with the ultimate itself may all inject an idolatrous factor in one's faith. A protest against such confusion is found in the Fourth Gospel, which has Jesus say: "He who believes in me does not believe in me but in Him who has sent me." Nevertheless, the Christian can have the courage to affirm his faith in Jesus as the Christ. He is aware of the possibility and even the inevitability of idolatrous deviations, but also of the fact that in the picture of the Christ itself the criterion against its idolatrous abuse is given—the Cross.

Out of this criterion comes the message, which is the very heart of Christianity and makes possible the courage to affirm faith in the Christ, namely, that in spite of all forces of separation between God and man this is overcome from the side of God. This alone makes the courage of faith possible.

If faith is understood as the state of being ultimately concerned, love and action are also implied in faith and cannot be separated from it. The concern of faith is identical with the desire of love: reunion with that to which one belongs and from which one is estranged. In the great commandment of the Old Testament, confirmed by Jesus, the object of ultimate concern, and the object of unconditional love, is God. From this is derived the love of what is God's, represented by both the neighbor and oneself.

If faith is understood as what it centrally is, ultimate concern, it cannot be undercut by modern science or any kind of philosophy. The central phenomenon in man's personal life, it is manifest and hidden at the same time. It is religious and transcends religion, it is universal and concrete, it is infinitely variable and always the same. Faith is an essential possibility of man, and therefore its existence is necessary and universal. As an ultimate concern, it cannot be discredited by its superstitions or authoritarian distortions within and outside churches, sects, and movements. Faith stands upon itself and justifies itself against those who attack it, because they can attack it only in the name of another faith. It is the triumph of the dynamics of faith that any denial of faith is itself an expression of faith, of an ultimate concern.

EARL WILSON

"To think that we accomplish everything on our own—without God's help—is naïve."

* * *

Earl Wilson, a refugee from the Ohio farm country, has won himself the newspaper role of America's top humor columnist. Today the ex-hog-slopping, cow-milking farm boy writes a sophisticated, syndicated column, "It Happened Last Night," which appears daily in the New York Post *and one hundred and fifty other national papers. But despite his glamorous city life and journalistic preoccupation with movie stars and page-one personalities, his reputation rests largely on his old-fashioned virtues—gentlemanliness, faith, kindness, loyalty, laughter, and an apt ability to treat other human beings as friends.*

"He has more datelines than any other columnist," boasts his Hall Syndicate, and any one year will find him writing from such scattered vantage points as Rome, Paris, Cairo, Mexico City, Honolulu, San Francisco, and now and then from Rockford, Ohio, his home town. "I leave town so often," Wilson says, "because I've found some of the best folks in America live outside New York. I want to find out what they're laughing about, and report it to my readers." Not restricting himself to covering glamour news, he also has written "scoop" stories on TB cures, Salk vaccine, and the Rev. Billy Graham. Nothing tickles Wilson more than when someone tells him, "I read you as religiously as I used to read O. O. McIntyre."

Before becoming a New York columnist, Wilson covered small-town beats for the Piqua Daily Call, Tiffin Tribune, *and the* Akron Beacon-Journal. *After a copyreader stint on the* Washington Post, *he migrated to New York in the middle 1930's where he landed a rewrite assignment on the* New York Post. *Mrs. Wilson, "the B.W." or "Beautiful Wife" of column mention, is the former Rosemary Lyons of East St. Louis. They have a son, Earl L. Wilson, now a student at Bucknell University.*

* * *

Glamour, Grammar—and God

After a generation of covering Broadway—and occasionally Hollywood, Paris, Rome, and Las Vegas—I've discovered that many of the rich and famous are pretty religious. As an ex-Rockford (Ohio) Sunday-school teacher, I sometimes become Old Parson Wilson and preach a sermon in my syndicated column. The sermons draw by far the heaviest mail from all one hundred and fifty cities where the column is published.

I spent my first eighteen years growing up in an average home. We lived on a farm, or in small towns, and my mother saw to it that I attended the Methodist Church every Sunday and eventually "got converted" and became a Sunday-school teacher, as she was. I learned to milk the cows, to finish my homework before bedtime, and to avoid cheating and stealing and lying and hypocrisy—at least part of the time!

A couple of Methodist preachers whom I admired made an impression on me. One was a semi-cripple whose patience and energy won everybody's respect. We didn't talk much about God at home. My mother, in fact, thought that some of our relatives were too strict, too "sanctimonious." But as a teacher of a class of boys my age, she would drive our baseball team to a nearby town for a game and help umpire, if necessary.

The idea was that we would try to be honest and do right—and always be respectable people.

Today, when everything is Cheatsville and corruption is fashionable, I find it harder and harder to set the Christian example I want. When I was a little lad—and I was once, with the darlingest dimples and the cuddliest curls—I met the Devil only in sermons. Now that I'm older, I know that Satan walks the streets with you and me; indeed, the Devil's Disciples are all around us.

Now this year of Our Lord 1963 (and how ironic to invoke Deity in an age of blasphemy), it is chic to cheat. Today I'm afraid we often take the Devil to lunch, buy him a cocktail and invite him home for dinner, and introduce him to the children. Satan is a devil of a fellow. He's the "fixer," the crooked lawyer, the graft-taking income-tax agent; or the Devil could be the classroom cheat, or even the slimy pickup girl in bars. He's the marijuana puffer, the bribe-hungry cop, the young woman living off old men, and young men living off old women. He's the pornography peddler who calls it art and the simpering simpletons of the fashion world who encourage the deviationists.

Time has taught me that I'm not the brightest boy around. I'm a plodding workhorse, but because I'm slow, I may see some things the Derby winners miss because they go too fast. And I notice that our acceptance of phonies, of charming crooks, of curvaceous courtesans, on the ground that they're "such interesting characters," has contributed to the general amoral condition of America. I blushingly confess that I've been as guilty as anybody. Often I have lent a glint of glamour to some usurer or international larcenist or transcontinental trollop—but I'm going to try to write about worthier types.

Despite everything that's wrong, despite this crazy world of gimme and greed, I'm still an optimist, still a believer (I move around on occasional Sundays from Christ Church Methodist to New York Universalist to St. Patrick's Cathedral!). And quite often I interview VIP's with a deeply spiritual story to tell. Like our attractive 1945–1947 Minister to Denmark, Ruth Bryan Owen Rohde, whose hobby was answering prayers. The daughter of the late William Jennings Bryan, she tried to help everyone who ever approached her for help—on the street, in a cab, by phone, or letter. "I figured out when I was sixteen," she told me, "that when people prayed they were usually cornered or in desperate need of something. I try to be an answerer, not an asker." Her philosophy of trying to do the right thing for others has been a guide to me.

Then, too, sometimes a columnist does a good deed—accidentally. Several years ago, when the Wilsons were in Rio de Janeiro on a trip, I wrote a little chunk about one Oscar Ornstein.

"Hardly anybody at home knows him," I thought, tapping it out. "But he deserves it." I told how Ornstein—entertainment director of the Copacabana Palace Hotel—talks on two phones and is "a typical New Yorker." But that he was born in "Hamburg, Germany."

I could have merely said Germany. But perhaps because of my fondness for the delicacy allegedly invented there, I wrote "Hamburg." A stoutish man of fifty-two with a German accent soon came to my office—and was trembling. Leo Eis, drummer and saxophonist of 601 West 156th Street, who heads a Bavarian orchestra, had hunted Oscar Ornstein for twenty-three years.

"I give him up," he said. "Oscar thought I was dead in the gas chamber. The same as my friends, my mother, father, and two sisters. Killed by Hitler! But"—and his eyes shone—"when I read Hamburg, Germany . . . there can't be too many Oscar Ornsteins from Hamburg. I right away telephoned Rio de Janeiro. And it's him—my 'baby brother' seven years younger, about forty-five now! They say I need a short name for a band, so I take my mother's. But my passport"—and he held it out—"says 'formerly Ornstein.' "

On the call to Rio, he and Oscar "were both crying on the phone" and amazed too that they hadn't met, for Leo was in South America until seven years ago when he came to New York, and Oscar, who'd gone to Rio from Austria, comes here often to book acts.

"Not until you wrote that little thing!" Leo said. "What does Oscar look like now? And he's successful?"

"Everybody important in Rio knows Oscar," I assured him.

"Ah, he always was a smart boy." Leo nodded. "I am expecting a cable saying what day next week Oscar will be here. The last time I see him was 1934 in Berlin at the restaurant I am playing in—long before the war."

Of course they did meet in a happy reunion. Oscar cabled me, too, and signed it "Eternally your debtor." It has made the South American trip seem worthwhile.

On another occasion, I wrote a column which resulted in a Negro girl whom I'd never seen going to college. The following is what I wrote at the time in "It Happened Last Night."

Ten weeks ago I found in my mail a hand-written letter on pale blue stationery from a city in Indiana. "I am the eldest Negro girl in a family of five children," it began. "I want more than anything to be able to graduate from college. No one in my family ever has. . . ." Janet (as I'll call her) was nineteen. She'd been trying to work full time, and go to night classes while helping take care of the small children. Did I know of someone who'd help her go to college full time?

"After I graduate and start working, I'd pay them back, honest,

I would," she said. "Please, Mr. Wilson, help me." Maybe you think columnists don't read such mail. I reread that phrase, "honest, I would," many times. Greatly touched, I quoted her letter. Quick response from you readers showed me we could help her. I advised Janet to apply for admission.

A month later, while the B.W. and I were in Europe, came the flash! Janet had been accepted at Howard University in Washington, D.C. She'd quit her job, was scrounging for a wardrobe, buying her bus ticket. . . . And was I embarrassed! We had no scholarship fund. But we couldn't turn back then. The B.W. and I airmailed her a loan to get her started—and soon Janet was writing me excitedly about college. The B.W. and I feel good about helping her. I suppose we have a secret belief it'll help us get past the velvet rope at St. Peter's portal. In any event, the happy result of the column and the contributions—Janet graduated from college and is now employed as a Social Welfare worker in New York.

My faith has been heartened too by many "name" personalities I've met and interviewed—Jane Russell, Eddie Albert, Joe E. Brown, Lillian Roth, Bob Hope—Christian stars who are really trying to live their religion. Every time I ask such people about religion, I learn something more about God, prayer, the struggle to achieve the good life. In that struggle, all of us need help. As Eddie Albert said to me, "To think that we accomplish everything on our own—without God's help—is naïve."

BROOKS HAYS

"Government says 'Justice'; religion says, 'love.' "

* * *

Brooks Hays, prominent in United States statecraft, politics, and church life for two generations, today ranks as a special assistant to President Kennedy. Now sixty-five, and an original Arkansas Traveler, he was elected to the United States House of Representatives from that State eight times between 1942 and 1958.

Young Hays, who was educated in Arkansas public schools and graduated from the University of Arkansas, entered politics under his father's aegis in 1922 shortly after graduation from law school. That same year he was elected secretary of the State Democratic Convention, the youngest man ever to hold that position. Although he twice ran unsuccessfully for Governor, he was elected National Democratic Committeeman in 1932 and to the United States Congress in 1942.

A long-time crusader for extension of educational and economic opportunities for southern Negroes, Mr. Hays became the Congressional authority on farm tenancy problems, helped to develop the Arkansas Plan to extend full civil rights to minority groups, and twice served as civil rights specialist on the Democratic Convention Platform Committee. It was this interest in building bridges of understanding between the races that led him to arrange the Newport meeting of President Eisenhower and Governor Orval Faubus at the time of the Little Rock school desegregation crisis in 1957.

Mr. Hays served two terms as president of the Southern Baptist Convention. One of the Convention's most distinguished laymen and speech-makers, he is regarded as a top American storyteller. He also serves on the board of directors of the Boy Scouts of America, Religion in American Life, and the National Conference of Christians and Jews. Before assuming his present White House post, Mr. Hays was a member of the U. S. Delegation to the United Nations in 1955, and served on the House Foreign Affairs Committee, and the Select Committee on Space Exploration and Astronautics. He also held the posts of Director of the Tennessee Valley Authority under President Eisenhower and Assistant Secretary of State for Congressional Relations under President Kennedy.

* * *

This World: a Christian's Workshop

IN MY YOUTH IN RUSSELLVILLE, ARKANSAS, I AVOIDED CONFUSION about God's attitude toward the world by assuming that when a minister said I should "despise the world," he meant I should despise "worldliness." The Bible, read in our Baptist Sunday school, told me that God "loved the world," so I concluded I must love it too. I thrilled to the beautiful old hymn, "This is my Father's world," and to the forceful statement of my beloved minister, "It was deliberately in the mind of God not to reveal very much of the other world because he did not propose to detract from the critical importance of *this* earthly existence." Thus, I believe if our Christian doctrines regarding God, the world, and man are to be taken seriously, it is apparent that this world is a Christian workshop.

Early in my political career, I determined that I would not identify my candidacy with "a righteous cause." This is not to say that in the light of moral values, political campaigns do not often present clear choices; in many cases the "right" is distinguishable as favoring one side over the other. What I would stress is the fact that invoking Divine approbation in order to win at the polls is not in our tradition and should be repudiated, as I believe it generally will be. (I recall seeing in a recent political advertisement the words, "Vote Christian," above a candidate's name. He was overwhelmingly defeated!)

Religious inspiration has had its chief significance for me in my individual determination of grave political judgments and policy decisions. My long political course has been full of frustration, yet I believe that God has made strength and counsel available to me in these major decisions. I haven't sought to win assurance of success through prayer, but rather to find, in resort to spiritual resources, the answer to the question that stirs the heart of more public men than the people know, namely, "What is right?" Christian witnessing can then take on new meaning every day.

The most meaningful experience of my professional life followed one of a series of defeats early in my political career. Before I was thirty-two, I had twice been defeated for the Arkansas Governorship, and in a special contest for a Congressional seat I attempted to retrieve something from these two intensive campaigns. As I had angered the political leaders in my district, it was now a critical race for me. In one county of the district with a registration of only 1,632, the county "bosses" reported 1,850 votes for my opponent (who was the beneficiary rather than the perpetrator of the scheme), and 616 for me. A fraud had obviously been practiced, and it became the subject of a long, tedious lawsuit. When, at last, the judge, a sincere, honest man who wanted to correct a palpable wrong, had to dismiss my case because of higher court rulings, I struggled against human reactions that would impair my faith. But my deeply grounded faith in God and in my fellowman survived that bitter experience; indeed, it was that faith that pulled me through.

There have been many other situations in which I felt the need of falling back upon the resources of faith. One of them came soon after I was elected to Congress when highly controversial legislation was introduced which stirred rabid interest in my district. Although a number of close friends called to urge me to support the pending bill, I finally decided I should vote against it; protests from several campaign supporters made me realize that I might have to pay with defeat for my convictions. Because I wanted to remain in Congress, it was extremely difficult for me to vote against what I knew to be the prevailing opinion in my district. But I was unconvinced by the arguments, and voted "no." Again I had help in prayer. Sitting by an old friend in the House Chamber, who remained silent when the roll was called because he knew of the conflicts troubling me, I asked God to help me—to give me that inner peace that comes from doing what one knows he should do. As in the election crisis, I received the assurance that an answered prayer provides. I walked from the Capitol with the same calmness and peace that had come in the earlier experience. From these two experiences I had had my most convincing proof that the eternal God is indeed our certain refuge and underneath us are the everlasting arms.

So, I believe it is that government and religion are interrelated, though the symbols and phrases are different. Government says "justice"; religion says "mercy." Government says "union," for we must think in structural terms; religion says "unity," for spiritual force must supply the quality that gives strength and cohesiveness to our legal institutions. Government says "power"; religion says "responsibility," for power must be used with a sense of dedication. Government says "order"; religion says "discipline," and only the inner disciplines that spring from a life of faith can sustain external order. Finally, Government says "tolerance," but religion says, "love."

FATHER JAMES KELLER

"It is better to light one candle than to curse the darkness."

* * *

Father James Keller, a Roman Catholic priest, author and lecturer, lives under the conviction that men and women endowed with spiritual truth and a sense of personal responsibility can help change the world. To that end, in 1945, he began the Christopher Movement which now reaches more than a million persons in all parts of the world. The basic idea of the movement, which has no memberships, branches, or dues, is to stimulate dedicated persons to positive action in strengthening the fields of government, education, labor-management, and the creative side of literature and entertainment.

Educated at the Maryknoll Seminary and Catholic University in Washington, D.C., and ordained a priest in 1925, Father Keller champions the doctrine of Christ-like love which undergirds effective belief in the majesty of God and the dignity of man. In his many talks and writings he often quotes the Apostle Paul: "Be not overcome by evil, but overcome evil by good." (Romans 12:21) His syndicated column, "Three Minutes a Day," appears daily in 104 newspapers, while "The Christopher Program" is carried regularly by 306 TV stations and 2,720 radio stations. Among Father Keller's widely read books are, You Can Change the World, Government Is Your Business, *and* Three Minutes a Day.

* * *

Overcoming Evil by Good

We must try to change the world for the better. Despite certain notable achievements in science, medicine, industry, education, and the arts, this is the bloodiest century in history. Atheism, corruption, materialism, greed, brutality, and subversion are corroding the foundations of society.

There is no reason for despair, however. The Lord will always provide all the grace and help we need to measure up to our full potential and better the spiritual and temporal condition of mankind. All He asks is our cooperation. It was for this reason at the end of World War II that I started the Christopher Movement as an attempt to stir lay persons in every walk of life to do their bit with God's help to right the world's wrongs.

There is nothing new or original about the Christopher idea. It is as old as the hills—the hills of Galilee. Its chief purpose is to inspire millions of men and women to fulfill the role God expects each of us to play in sanctifying the *whole* of life, not just part of it or none at all. In the universal mission of Christ every person has an important mission to fulfill. Every follower of the Lord is expected to make a zealous continuing effort to do what he can to apply the principles of the Gospel to the whole world, the whole of life, and the whole man, body, mind, and soul.

Thus, the aim of the Christophers is to keep reminding you that you are "a man with a mission." You are needed in God's plan to renew the face of the earth. The rebuilding of the world starts with you as much as it does with anyone. Cultivate the expansive "God, myself, and everybody else" attitude rather than just a narrow "God and myself" outlook. As God sends some of his blessings to others through you, don't deprive them of what is rightfully theirs.

Let love of all people be the hallmark of everything you think, say, and do. "By this shall all men know that you are My disciples if you have love one for another." (John 13:35) Carry the love, truth, justice, and decency of Christ out of the sanctuary of your home and church into the marketplace of the world. The need is desperate. Be able to say with St. Paul: "The love of Christ impels us." (2 Cor. 5:14) Since God's loving solicitude includes every phase of human life and activity, take an apostolic interest in the whole of life. Remember that darkness is the absence of light, evil the absence of good, hatred the absence of love. Strive to restore what is missing, and *everybody* will *benefit*. So, while you can encourage others to exert an influence for good, the only person in the world you can force is yourself. You as one individual can do much by prayer, word, and deed to apply the law and order of heaven to the running of things here on earth. "I can do all things in Him Who strengthens me." (Phil. 4:13)

The name "Christopher" comes from the Greek word "Christophoros" meaning "Christbearer." It reminds you that whether you are a housewife, bus driver, student, policeman, nurse, or lawyer, you can carry the love and truth of Christ into the marketplace. You personally can be a Christopher or Christbearer. To focus attention on personal responsibility, the Christophers have no organization, no chapters, no memberships, no meetings, no emblems. All we do is strive to enkindle in human hearts an apostolic sense of mission, purpose, and direction. The motto of the Christophers, "Better to light one candle than to curse the darkness," is a reminder that God blesses the slightest positive effort to right what is wrong. The smallest flame you light is a step in the right direction. It is far better than any amount of negative faultfinding for "there is nothing so sterile as complaining," as Cardinal Suhard has said.

The battle for the minds and souls of men is being waged as never before. It is difficult, if not virtually impossible for men to fulfill the divine purpose for their existence if the climate in which they live glorifies what is base, false, and tawdry, and stifles what is good, true, and beautiful. The more you realize that you, too, are "a man with a mission," the more ardently you will desire to be a co-worker with Christ. A recent newspaper article referred to a conscientious public official as a "dedicated man with a sense mission." The word "mission" comes from the Latin verb *mittere* meaning as a "definite task or errand, usually calling for performance in a combat area or enemy territory." You personally have a "mission" in life. God has "sent" you into the world to fulfill some role, however small or difficult, in applying the law and order of heaven to every aspect of human life. So, I believe we all have a share in the same mission Christ gave to His apostles: "As the Father has sent Me, I also send you." (John 20:22)

DANA McLEAN GREELEY

"Religions are many, but religion is one."

* * *

Born and bred to liberal Christianity and a world view, the Rev. Dr. Dana McLean Greeley serves as the first president of the Unitarian Universalist Association. He was elected in May, 1961, at the time of the formal merger of the Universalist Church of America and the American Unitarian Association. Today he is giving the unified, swiftly expanding cause of liberal religion a crusading zeal it has lacked for decades.

Dana Greeley was born in Boston and educated at Harvard College and Harvard Divinity School. His father, a prominent New England architect, served both as president of the Unitarian Laymen's League and moderator of the American Unitarian Association, and young Greeley began his ecclesiastical career as president of the Young People's Religious Union. Before assuming the pulpit of Boston's famed Arlington Street Church in 1935, he held pastorates in Lincoln, Massachusetts, and Concord, New Hampshire.

Dr. Greeley, who is a leader in civic as well as religious affairs, was president of the American Unitarian Association before merger with the Universalists. He also is a past president of the Massachusetts Council of Churches and the New England Citizens' Crime Commission and serves on the board of United World Federalists, the Planned Parenthood Federation, and the Institute on Religion in an Age of Science. His books include Toward Larger Living *and* A Message to Atheists. *Dr. Greeley is married, and his daughter, Faith, is the wife of a Unitarian minister, the Rev. Carl R. Scovel.*

* * *

One Sublime Idea

IF, AS MY PARENTS TOLD ME, I WAS BORN AT ELEVEN O'CLOCK ON A Sunday morning, that may help explain why the church and preaching have been primary interests of mine since school days. And if one knows that my father was a one-time president of the Unitarian Laymen's League and moderator of the American Unitarian Association, and my mother a director of the Women's General Alliance, then it follows that *liberal religion* runs strongly in my veins, although I have always insisted that our free faith is a quest rather than a bequest. Add to that the fact that I was a Boston boy, nurtured on literary transcendentalism and William Ellery Channing's "one sublime idea" of the dignity of man, and it will not seem incongruous that I made the Unitarian ministry my lifework.

With this kind of prejudicial background and with Harvard Divinity School and Boston's pioneering Arlington Street Church as educational training to age fifty, I am fond of saying that today it is our job to make all religion more liberal and all liberalism more religious. Thus some of my emphases in the new Unitarian Universalist Association have been on a more vigorous world churches program, more significant social relations projects, and a more inclusive witness in word and deed for brotherhood's sake. Indeed, if I had but one sermon to preach, it would be on the dignity of man. But I would preach another one in rapid succession on the universality of religion and the necessity for recognizing the rightful fellowship of all faiths and the interdependence of peoples everywhere.

Today, because Unitarians and Universalists admire the scientific spirit, stress ethical concern and believe in one world and the indivisibility of truth, most of us no longer accept the God of the Garden of Eden or of Greek mythology or of St. Thomas Aquinas's "prime matter" and "substantial form." But again, because we consider all of life, indeed the whole creation sacred, we pursue the new search for God with all our intelligence and intuition, with all awe and reverence, and with an unprecedented modern mixture of theology and science. That is why it is very hard to be a religious liberal today: to lift your powers of comprehension to a level worthy of the universe that produced them, even while you strive to make your daily conduct conform to the highest profession of life and ethics. We were not born to be curious and then to be deceived, but to achieve a moral wisdom as valid as the mathematics of Whitehead, the music of Beethoven, and the love of St. Francis.

In a familiar passage from the New Testament we find the Apostle Paul exhorting the Ephesians to unity. He had been converted to the cause of Christ, and that cause seemed to him to be the most commanding in all the world. And so Paul wrote in his letter, "With all lowliness and meekness, with long-suffering, forbearing one another in love, endeavor to keep the unity of the spirit in the bond of peace." He might have put it in modern parlance by suggesting that Christianity and bigotry are antithetical to each other. John Greenleaf Whittier, the great American Unitarian–Quaker poet, had the same idea when he wrote a hymn that is still much beloved: "Thy grace impart! In time to be shall one great temple rise to thee, thy Church our broad humanity. A sweeter song shall then be heard, confessing in a world's accord, the inward Christ, the living word." Both men believed in unity; and both men's lives constituted a prayer for that unity.

For twenty-three, for me wonderful and meaningful years, I served as pastor of Boston's Arlington Street Church. One of my great predecessors there, Dr. Samuel A. Eliot, was a proponent of such unity. "More and more men realize," he said, "that the things that divide them into hostile sects are transient and insignificant beside the deep faiths of the heart that unite them. More and more they come to see that our theological systems are but broken lights of the eternal, that the universal elements in religion are the only permanent elements, and that the river of spiritual truth cannot be made to flow in any regular and undeviating channel." The reformations of history have been rebellions against the narrowness of sectarianism, and the greatest leaders of Christianity and of all religions have always been those whose convictions and whose love have overleaped the limitations of the creeds and the sacraments. It is heartening today to see the emphasis that is being placed upon so-called ecumenicity, which means universalism or worldwide fellowship in religion.

Paul asserted on another occasion, "There is one body and one spirit, even as ye are called in one hope of your calling. One Lord, one faith, one baptism, one God and Father of all who is above all and through all, and in you all." It is a great passage, and it is pregnant with meaning for us in our generation. The unity that he sought, within the churches and among the churches, was a Christian unity, just as ecumenicity in the twentieth century, commendable as it is, is a vision that still has reference *only* to Christians. I want to go a step further and affirm that "religions are many, but religion is one." Jesus of Nazareth could have been the greatest of all the prophets, and the most religious man in history, even if there had been no one like Paul after him to change the name and the nature of the faith that he professed, and to promote it as a new movement throughout the Roman Empire. For the truth of his teachings and the beauty of the Sermon on the Mount were derived not from the fact that they constituted the enunciation of essential religion. Those teachings would have been just as truthful and that sermon just as beautiful if Jesus had never lived, and they had been delivered by Moses at the foot of Mount Sinai or by Socrates in the marketplace in Athens.

Religions are many. As soon as man began to stand erect on his two hind legs, and to look up at the stars, and to contemplate even in the most elementary fashion the mystery of the universe, he commenced to be religious. Long ago in the Punjab in India, immigrant tribes of Aryan stock composed the Vedas, which are like the psalms of ancient Israel; and out of the poetry and the philosophy of these Vedas Hinduism sprang, with its rich and manifold expressions of faith. To the north in the sixth century, in the valley of the Ganges where two tribes dwelt in close proximity to each other, the rajah of one tribe married the two daughters of the rajah of the other tribe, and the son of one of these girls was Gautama, afterward called the Buddha. When he became a man he renounced his princely life, and hundreds of millions of people from then to now have tried to follow his noble eightfold path to Nirvana or Heaven.

If we journey from eastern Asia west to Iran, we may recall the inspiration and leadership of Zoroaster, who was a man of many visions and who emphasized in Persian fashion the struggle between light and darkness. Zoroastrianism teaches that Ahura Mazdah created the sky, then the water, then the earth, then plants and animals and mankind, and the whole creation took a year of 365 days. Next to Judaism, this is the oldest ethical monotheism in the world, and it has much in common with Judaism. As late after Jesus as Buddha had been before Jesus, Mohammed was born in Mecca in the sterile land of Arabia, and in what seemed sterile times besides; and he grew up to proclaim Allah as the one true God and to be revered as his prophet; and as the

Bible is the book of the Jews and Christians, so the Koran was written as the book of Islam. Today four hundred and fifty million people believe in Catholicism as a religion, and most of them think that it is the only religion. But there is Christian Science with its emphasis upon faith and the spiritual power of healing; there is Mormonism, whose founder Joseph Smith must have been as extraordinary a person as Mary Baker Eddy herself; and there are the Baptists with their genius for freedom, and the moral law of the Jews, and the simplicity of the Quakers, and the enthusiasm of Jehovah's Witnesses. Religions are many, but religion is one.

I think I might contend that Jesus of Nazareth and Socrates could have been very close friends and had more in common with each other than Jesus and the tentmaker of Tarsus who made his name so famous. I think I could argue that the great Hindu pacifist of our century, Mahatma Gandhi, and Count Leo Tolstoi of Russia and Albert Einstein, an Americanized Jew, were of one mind and one heart. They were not separated by geography, or by three different religious heritages. They were united as children of one Creative Spirit, all with a universal outlook, a deep faith in brotherhood, and a hunger and thirst after righteousness and peace.

Perhaps the greatest object of the liberal church today is to revive real religion in the hearts of men, not creedalism, nor a popular facile faith, nor orthodoxy, nor neo-orthodoxy, but real religion; to recover a sense of the universality of religion and of the unity of mankind, and to follow the implications of this unity. In 1932 the governments of Canada and the United States ceded lands in Alberta and Montana—some of the most inspiringly beautiful acreage in the world—to form the Waterton–Glacier International Peace Park. It may not be as easy as that to obliterate the boundaries of most national, racial, class, and even religious divisions, but it needs to be done. May our religion more and more reflect the common faith and heritage and destiny of all mankind.

BUD COLLYER

"Make demands on God. His love is boundless and never fails."

* * *

For twenty-five years Bud Collyer has been a prominent performer in radio and television. Today he is the star and master of ceremonies of the TV show, "To Tell the Truth," on the Columbia Broadcasting System. A former president of AFTRA, the national actors and announcers' union, Mr. Collyer makes his home in Greenwich, Connecticut, where he teaches Sunday school in the First Presbyterian Church. He is married and has three children.

* * *

Keeping a Christ-focused Life

A MAN'S LIFE IS MADE UP OF MANY PHILOSOPHIES, NOT JUST ONE. But it is true that there is a central focus in every life. It is like a musical strain which runs through a composition and is repeated over and over. In my life that focus is Jesus Christ. Christ *is* my life.

Maybe you wonder what that really means. Here's what it means to me. Christ came to prove to all and sundry that we can live the kind of life God expects and that this life can be lived simply. Christ is the man part of God. . . . He is God as man. He lived the perfect life. And yet He used only man efforts and man powers to do this. This is what I think we tend to lose sight of: the fact that when He lived his earthly life, He didn't use any miraculous powers that are not open to you and to me.

Here's another angle I think people often miss. I always refer to the miracles myself as the "so-called miracles." Because I simply don't believe they *were* miracles. I believe they were a perfectly normal function and use of the power of God in each one of us. Each of us is born with this in our heart. We can use it if we will. But we must have faith. We must just know it in our hearts.

Any Christ-focused life must involve prayer. This isn't a case of tossing a prayer upstairs and then saying, "Now, I wonder if that will be answered." You have to believe in your heart and life that it will be. That's the power in the prayer—your belief in it. When you believe, then, to you is opened such power as you never dreamed of, and there isn't an atomic bomb in the world that can take it away.

I think probably part of our problem in this country is that we're not as fearless in the use of propaganda for the right things as other nations are in using it for the wrong. Just as the word "love" and the whole emotion of love has become a thing to read about in the tabloids or to be ridiculed as a kidding, laughing word when actually love is a word of great strength. If the force of love could be reduced to the truth that it is and turned loose in the world as people are trying to turn the atom bomb loose, then you'd have a wonderful world and a lasting peace. But people shy away from it. It seems too easy. I sometimes try a little change on words when I preach and talk about that phrase, "The peace of God that passeth all understanding." I bring the other word, p-i-e-c-e, in. You own a little piece of God which passes to you all the understanding you'll ever need. But somehow we won't release this. We take it for granted. We don't set it to work in the world.

The best way I know to get a life focused on God is to put it to the test. How do you do this? First, make a demand upon God. He won't be offended. He'll be pleased. Throughout the Bible, we're invited to do this. In Malachi we find, "Prove Me now herewith, saith the Lord of hosts, if I will not pour you out a blessing, that there shall not be room enough to receive it." In Hebrews: "Let us therefore come *boldly* unto the throne of grace, that we may obtain mercy, and find grace to help in time of need." In Matthew: "Ask, and it shall be given you; seek, and ye shall find; knock, and it shall be opened unto you." These are great invitations to make a demand upon God.

We tear along through life and bounce ourselves off people and never give ourselves a chance to absorb anything from them. One of the greatest sources of learning in the world is our daily contact with other people, which is of course the simplest side of Christian living. I'm a great believer that friendship should be readily given, and once readily given, easily used. I think you should make a demand upon a friend. However small it may seem at the time, make a demand. It's like a muscle. If you don't exercise it, it atrophies. Ask for a favor; I don't care what it is. If something is tiring you, or you're in a great big rush, call up someone who says he is your friend, and say, "Would you do this for me?" And then urge him to make demands upon you, because this is the only way the Christian heart can beat. You make demands upon your heart all the time; it wouldn't function very well if we didn't. But the heart God gives you, the heart of love, is one that's boundless and endless and never fails. But it's just got to be used.

So think about making a demand upon a friend and a higher demand upon God. Start doing it today. You'll find it works "so-called" miracles. It will start those Christian heart muscles working as never before. These arteries won't break down, they'll be stronger than ever. They will become a tie that binds our hearts in Christian love. You'll see.

ROLF ALEXANDER

"Consciousness is the 'Kingdom of Heaven,' and when that is attained, 'all other things shall be added unto you.' "

*   *   *

Dr. Rolf Alexander, the New Zealand physician who became one of the world's great creative thinkers, died last year in Miami, Florida, while this book was in preparation. At the time of his death, he had just finished a series of recordings on the "Third Force"—Alexander's name for nature's invisible power—the same power which human beings use when they think or pray, and which can influence health and happiness or affect events at a distance.

As dramatic proof of the non-spatial nature of mind, Dr. Alexander first demonstrated his famous Cloud Dispersal Experiment near Toronto, Canada, in 1954, when before fifty government and press witnesses he dissolved a cloud target in ten minutes, by purely mental processes. Later, critics suggested that this oft-repeated, carefully controlled demonstration of mental power foretold the approach of the new Psychological Age as world-shaking in its implications as the first atomic blast at Alamogordo, New Mexico, in 1945.

During his eventful seventy years, Dr. Alexander's medical and parapsychological studies took him from Down Under to Europe and Asia, and finally to America. He was the author of Creative Realism, The Doctor Alone Can't Cure You, The Power of the Mind, *and* The Mind in Healing. *A Universalist in his religious outlook, Dr. Alexander had an unforgettable influence on all with whom he came in contact, and there are thousands throughout the world who have been helped by his books.*

*   *   *

Creative Realism

You ask me what faith is? Question the birds that fill the azalea thickets with their music, or ask the questing bees who sip nectar from the perfumed blossoms, or go to the yak for an answer as he stands upon yonder lofty peak, chewing his cud and meditating upon the majesty and glory of Creation.

If these creatures could speak in words, they would tell you that faith is an inner certainty, born of the understanding that each living thing is one with the whole of Creation, and the knowledge that the mighty Creator of all who brought them into being for a creative purpose and provided for their needs of yesterday and today will not forsake them tomorrow, unless they forsake the Creator and refuse to play their appointed part. So, according to a great Tibetan philosopher, "To enter the Kingdom we must be born again, but before we can be reborn we must die. In order to die we must live. In order to live we must awaken to life, and in order to awaken we must realize that we are asleep."

My whole life experience and the fruits of fifty years of metaphysical study confirm this fact for me that the great purpose behind nature's long upward climb is the evolution of consciousness, and that nature has brought forth man as the instrument of this consciousness. My upbringing as an orthodox Christian in New Zealand, my education as an M.D. in Europe, my witnessing of "miraculous cures" at Lourdes, France, my study of Yoga in India and Tibet, my investigation of the ancient Polynesian magic system practiced by the Maori Indians of my homeland pointed toward the conclusion that all truth merged into one larger truth —the existence of mind as the only known reality and of an ocean of mind, like a great oversoul, enveloping the planet Earth and all its creatures as a special field.

This mental field, which forms the mind of nature, is the source of all human reality, the wholeness of which each mind is but a part. Each of us, in turn, expresses this consciousness through the cooperative activity of some ten thousand million brain cells; nature expresses *her* consciousness through the cooperative action of some three thousand million human beings. Thus, each of us is, in a sense, a single brain cell through which the consciousness of mother nature is striving to express itself.

Search as we will, we can never find the reality we all hunger for in the conditioned illusions of our subconscious, nor in our intellects which are oriented to these illusions. We may only find reality by becoming conscious of it—through direct experience. To experience reality directly, we must return to developing the instrument of conscious perception abandoned by us in childhood—the true personality or soul. The story of the Prodigal Son, beautifully told in both Christian and Buddhist scriptures, illustrates this truth. No matter how long we have "eaten husks among the swine," after squandering our birthright we can still return to our "Father's House" in consciousness. Nor will this return be a mere retracing of the steps, but we shall bring back with us the experiences and the intellectual gains, hard won through our bitter wanderings. Could all humanity become just occasionally conscious of the reality of the great mind of nature by which we are all linked in a common brotherhood, the effect would be to bring about a spiritual mutation in conscious evolution as dramatic as the one that isolated our ancestors from their brothers, the great apes.

Today, as in every age and culture, countless millions of people believe in the healing power of prayer backed by faith to restore their bodies to health and to lift their minds to higher consciousness. The young science of parapsychology has gathered much evidence that indicates the existence in nature of a whole realm of metaphysical law that is beyond our experience in the physical laboratory. It would seem that when the human mind is released from its stresses and tensions into the condition called faith, it expands outward as it were, to unite with a greater aspect of mind: one Overmind or Oversoul, which then becomes in effect an extension of the individual's mind and responsive to the triggering of the individual's sincere desires.

Personally, in support of this hypothesis of a master field of mind interpenetrating space, I have devised a measurable, controllable and repeatable experiment, known as the *Cloud Experiment* and performed by myself more than five hundred times before responsible witnesses in Britain and the United States. A calm clear day is chosen for the experiment when there are medium-sized cumulus clouds present. A group of clouds is chosen by an independent observer and one cloud from this group is selected by another observer as the "target." Photographs are taken at half-minute intervals of the entire group of clouds. Then, by mental means alone, especially the concentration of consciousness, the "target cloud" is made to dissolve and disappear while the adjacent clouds (which serve as controls) remain substantially unchanged. Obviously, there can be no collusion between a man on the ground and a group of clouds five miles up in the sky, so the experiment demonstrates that under the right conditions an individual mind *can* achieve an extension of itself in space.

Through the development of self-awareness, the integration of consciousness, the freeing of the higher mind from its subconscious domination, we may attain the highest objective of which a human being is capable—a truly conscious mind. Thus, the means of our salvation rests in the development of our true personalities or divine souls. Consciousness is the "Kingdom of Heaven," and when that is attained, "all other things shall be added unto you." Let us then make this our purpose as human beings, for this purpose is also the purpose of the mighty Power which formed our souls in the first place.

CONRAD N. HILTON

"Ever since I was a boy I had dreamed of doing something some day, however small, for the country I loved. Prayer showed me the way."

* * *

Conrad N. Hilton, the hero of one of America's great success stories, today is the number one hotelman of the world. Born on December 25, 1887, he grew up on the New Mexico frontier, later went into business with his Norwegian-born father, one of the State's pioneer traders. From 1912 to 1913 he served in the New Mexico House of Representatives and then returned home to organize the New Mexico State Bank. When this country entered World War I, Conrad Hilton interrupted his banking career to serve in France as a second lieutenant.

The eventual creator of the world's leading hotel organization saw his opportunity in Texas when he returned from the Service. He bought his first hotel, The Mobley, in a Texas cowtown named Cisco. After buying and building hotels throughout Texas, Mr. Hilton went on to obtain hotels in major cities in the United States. Purchase of the majority interest in the Waldorf-Astoria in 1949 marked a milestone in the history of the hotel industry. This was climaxed in 1954 when Hilton Hotels acquired the famous Statler chain. Today Hilton dispenses American hospitality in sixty hotels around the world.

Raised in the Roman Catholic faith by his mother, Mr. Hilton has built the Hilton Mount Carmel School and Convent in Socorro, New Mexico, as a memorial to her. As the host of the Presidential Prayer Breakfast for a number of years and the recipient of the Annual Brotherhood Award of the National Conference of Christians and Jews, Conrad Hilton has worked toward a great dream—that of uniting the free world into one human family, brothers of one Father.

* * *

America on Its Knees

THIRTEEN MILES OUTSIDE OF ALBUQUERQUE, THE ANCIENT ISLETA Indian pueblo rises moundlike on a plain of gray sand. Many years ago, as a child, I used to visit there with my mother. She had a special fondness for the pueblo and the old church with the painting that fascinated me when we first saw it together. The holy picture had been pierced by an arrow when Pueblo Indians fled attacking marauders and sought safety in the church. My mother explained to me how the peaceful Pueblo Indians had sensed the strength and refuge within those walls, even before they fully understood the way of the one God whose religion they had adopted. They had sought and been granted protection in His Church.

My mother's words stayed with me. Many times afterward when I did not fully understand His Way, I knew I could still seek His Protection. They used to call New Mexico "that Godforsaken Territory" in the 1880's. Iowa-born, my mother knew nothing about the New Mexico frontier before she journeyed there to marry my father, but she was sure of one thing. No spot on earth could be "Godforsaken." She was a woman of abiding faith, and she passed on this faith to all of her eight children. Courteous, reserved, hard-working, yet occasionally given to sunlit laughter, my mother had one answer, one cure, for everything—prayer!

For her, prayer was a normal part of life, every day, precisely as necessary and life-giving as food or air. When I was a child in tears over the death of my beloved horse Chiquita, when I was a disappointed youth whose dream of a Dartmouth education was smashed by the panic of 1907, and still later when I was a man and the Great Depression destroyed the success of my life's work, my mother's advice was always—"Go to church and pray, Connie; it's the best investment you'll ever make."

There are many such spiritual investments in my own experience with prayer. For example, on the occasion of my first major speech in 1950, before the National Conference of Christians and Jews at the Waldorf-Astoria, I was a nervous wreck. But I managed to say what I strongly felt about "The Battle for Freedom":

"What is this freedom? What right have we to it? This is why: because we possess an intrinsic human dignity, an inner majesty, which gives us an appetite, a passion for freedom. Man possesses human dignity because he is made in the image and likeness of God. This image is found personally in every man; each one possesses it entirely and undividedly. . . .

"Peace is more than the absence of war. . . . It is life with honor, life with the dignity of the children of God. . . . In this struggle for freedom, at home and abroad, our greatest weapon, both a sword and a shield, will be our love of, and faith in, God. To open the hearts and minds of men to this truth will require a mighty river of faith and effort. Each one of us is a drop to swell that river and augment its force."

I sat down, perspiring with nervousness, and convinced that I would never make another speech, that I lacked the skill and persuasion to make my point. I was stunned by the reaction to my speech. Thousands of congratulatory letters poured in, from General George Marshall to a young corporal in the U. S. Army, from salesmen and Gold Star mothers, all thanking me for expressing their love of God and country!

One of those letters proved as important as any letter I have ever received in my life. It read:

I have read your talk in the *Herald Tribune* and I think it was wonderful. Especially that our faith in God was our only hope. You are very right, and I think if everyone would fall down and pray we would have real peace.

Sincerely yours,
Daniel Paolucci

P.S. I am a boy of 12. May I please have an answer?

I sent Daniel a conventional thank-you note, but I couldn't get that P.S. out of my mind: "May I please have an answer?" I reread the *Herald Tribune* clipping concerning my speech and suddenly I knew that I had left out something that had been in Daniel's letter. Although I had trusted in the power of prayer all my life, I had not mentioned prayer in my talk!

I was thinking about that letter on a train going to Chicago when I first saw a mental image of Uncle Sam on his knees, praying. Praying for what? Certainly not: "That God be on my side." Through two ghastly wars, both sides made that prayer and it didn't obtain much peace even for the victor. Obviously that hadn't worked. Daniel himself must have learned how foolish it would be to explain to his algebra teacher how *he'd* like mathematics to work.

"That I be on God's side." That would be Uncle Sam's peace prayer. The first thing that caught my eye when I got off that train was a cartoon of a harassed Uncle Sam sitting before a desk littered with papers and problems. From the wall an infinitely compassionate portrait of Abraham Lincoln spoke: "Have you tried prayer, Sam?" To me that was confirmation of my vision.

In the meantime, with the encouragement of Dr. Norman Vincent Peale and my devoted friend, the late Fulton Oursler, I had been working on a prayer. On July 4, 1952, I published in a number of magazines a full-color pictorial presentation of "America on Its Knees," the earnest portrait, painted by a former secretary, and the prayer. It read in part:

Our Father In Heaven:

We pray that You save us from ourselves.

The world that You have made for us, to live in peace, we have made into an armed camp. We live in fear of war to come. . . .

We have turned from You to go our selfish way. We have broken Your commandments and denied Your truth.

We have left your altars to serve the false gods of money and pleasure and power. Forgive us and help us.

Help us to do Your will as it is done in Heaven and to be worthy of Your promise of peace on earth.

Fill us with new faith, new strength, and new courage, that we may win the battle for peace.

Be swift to save us, dear God, before the darkness falls.

Almost immediately the letters and requests for copies started to pour in. From every state in the Union, from almost every country in the world, from the young, and the old, from the rich and the poor came requests for over three hundred thousand reprints, and messages that sometimes brought tears to my eyes.

Less than a year later I was on my feet again at the speakers' table, and this time I had the great honor and privilege to play host at the first annual Presidential Prayer Breakfast in Washington, D.C. The President of the United States, the Chief Justice of the Supreme Court, Senators, Congressmen, and diplomats all bowed their heads together in prayer. The Mayflower ballroom in which they gathered was dominated by an enlargement of "America on Its Knees." To be host to such a gathering and to see my vision of Uncle Sam in such a setting . . . it all seemed like a miracle.

Ever since I was a boy I had dreamed of doing something some day, however small, for the country I loved. Prayer showed me the way. To me, then, prayer is the hub that holds the wheel of life together. Without our contact with God we are nothing. With it we are "a little lower than the angels, crowned with glory and honor."

RALSTON YOUNG

"Christ can open up your heart and your mind to horizons you never dream exist when you are pent in by bitterness and despair."

* * *

Grand Central's famous "Redcap 42" is now sixty-five years old and slightly stooped from the weight of thousands of bags he has carried through the years. Yet Ralston Young is surprisingly slender and young-looking, as though his work load has somehow been lightened by his faith. The reason: for nearly forty years he has been lifting people's bags and burdens as the "Good Samaritan of Grand Central Station."

Mr. Young came to New York City from Panama, where he was born and raised. Working in the Brooklyn shipyards in World War I, he earned enough money to bring his wife, mother, and younger brother and sisters from the Canal Zone; but when the war ended and the shipyards closed, he was once again out of a job. It was in 1924 that he started his work as a Redcap at Grand Central Station.

Over the years Ralston Young has become known to thousands of Grand Central travelers as the Redcap who is always willing to help—not only with their bags—but with kindness and prayer as well. Three times a week he holds noontime prayer meetings in an empty coach on Track 13, which are attended by both Manhattan executives and casual passengers passing through the city. A former member and evangelical speaker of St. Philip's Episcopal Church in New York City, he was the recipient of the 1962 New York Bible Society Award. Ralston Young has been the laudable subject of articles in many national magazines, including Coronet, The Reader's Digest, Guideposts, *and* Faith at Work. *He lives with his wife, Sadie, in Vauxhall, New Jersey, where they are members of the St. Stephens Episcopal Church.*

* * *

God's Work in Grand Central Station

MAYBE YOU COULD SAY THIS IS THE STORY OF HOW TO GET TO JAPAN by way of Grand Central Station—without even buying a ticket. Of course it took me a good many years along the way, and I don't think I'm going to put the airlines out of business by telling you how it happened. It also offers fresh proof of how our Christian faith is growing around the world.

Back in 1959, I opened a letter from a friend of mine describing his latest trip to Japan. He is a representative of Democracy in Action. Keeping Christ in the center of its thoughts, this non-profit group does worldwide research in an effort to promote creative leadership in business.

My friend wrote that he had mentioned my name to a Mr. Matoa Susuki, the President of a large manufacturing plant. Mr. Susuki, who is concerned about the absence of a meaningful faith among the young people of Japan, asks the men and women he employs to try daily prayer—in their own words and their own way—as an active ingredient in their lives. Although a Buddhist, he felt that my work in trying to bring Christ's love to passengers in Grand Central Station was an example of value to people in his own plants. He told his twenty-five hundred employees about me.

It makes me feel awkward to repeat such a story and I'm not practicing false humility when I say that I know Mr. Susuki could have found millions of people more worthy to be used in such a cause. But I'm telling you the story because I had so little to do with it. It's an example of the way Christ can open up your heart and your mind to horizons you never dream exist when you are pent in by bitterness and despair. Melvin Evans, my friend in Japan, wrote that the Japanese he talked to said they were followers of the Buddhist or Shinto religions, but they never thought of religion as having any relationship to life itself. It was something for holidays or marriage ceremonies. They wanted to know what it meant to be a Christian. Do Christians apply prayer to everything they do? How does being a Christian change living from day to day? A man like Mr. Susuki, for instance, was learning about Christianity and actually trying to put Christ into his daily life.

Thirty years ago I was asking the same questions. Before that I was sunk in my own empty, self-centered world. I was learning that unhappiness and prejudice cannot fill the human heart. If anyone had told me that someday I would be involved in a small way in the spread of Christianity in Japan I would have sneered in cynicism and utter disbelief.

I came to New York City with visions of a good job and a nice place to live for my widowed mother, my younger brother, and two sisters. But the only work I could find was lugging bags, just for tips. Redcaps received no salary in those days, and as we had no hand carts, we would load ourselves down with bags in hope of getting a dime instead of the usual nickel. You might take home fifty cents after a long day and fall into bed—hungry and exhausted. I was ashamed of the work I was doing and never told anyone away from the station what my job was.

But the Depression was on and you were lucky to have anything. You had to hang on. Any complaint from a passenger and you were fired. So when you heard, "Here, boy! Pick up those bags . . . step lively, boy!" you picked up the bags, stepped lively, and kept silent. Grand Central Station is a big place but it was a small, mean world to me. I was "smart" enough to keep my eyes on the floor—on the passengers' shoes. Expensive shoes usually meant a bigger tip. If the shoes were cheap and the bags big, I'd pretend not to hear. When I couldn't escape, I'd boil inside.

Prejudice, my own, hemmed me in behind another wall and made my world as narrow as any prison cell. It seemed to me a plain simple fact: Redcaps who worked hard and got little were Negroes; the people who hurried from taxicabs into Pullman cars, the snappers and command-givers were whites. It was as simple as that. White against black.

Then I met Miss Sarah Cooper. She was poor—like the rest of us—and growing old and sickly. Yet everytime I met her she seemed so happy. She smiled a great deal and she was one of the kindest people I have ever known. Why was this little woman with all her troubles so happy, I wondered? I knew Miss Sarah Cooper went to church regularly, but that was someplace I hadn't been in twenty years. I told myself that the church was where the pious hypocrites went on Sundays, after cheating their neighbors from Monday to Saturday.

I was too proud to ask Miss Cooper outright about the source of her happiness. So I began by looking for an argument. How, I asked, did she feel about the people who abused her? She said she felt sorry for such people! Miss Cooper said that someone who felt the need to abuse others must be very empty inside and needed help.

Shocked, I asked her why she would want to help anyone who hated her.

"Because the one who has the most faults is the one who needs help most. . . . The only one I know who is free of imperfections," she added, "is God."

Her response broke through my shell of resentment and disturbed me. Reluctantly, I admitted to myself that I was impressed by the depth of her thoughts. Where, I wondered, did she get such ideas?

One Sunday I hesitantly entered her church, St. Philip's Episcopal, in New York, and found the answer. The Rev. Shelton Hale Bishop spoke of the boundless love of Jesus Christ who suffers for and with all men, even those, like myself, who rejected Him. I knew at last the secret of Miss Cooper's peace and happiness, and it dissolved my wretched, arrogant, little self-centered world. Freed of the blindness of hate, I looked into my own heart with shame: if others, black or white, felt the way I did, the world was indeed an ugly place.

But now I knew that Christ loved in all times and places. The thought that God was everywhere you were, including Grand Central Station, electrified me. I stopped judging people by the cost of their shoes and began to reach for their bags because they needed my help. At first, I didn't know how to go beyond that, but Miss Cooper and my minister encouraged me not to let my shyness stand in my way. You have to stick your neck out if you want to bring Christ's love to others.

One day a tipsy passenger threw me his bags and demanded to know where he could get a drink. Surprised by my own boldness, I answered, "Please don't. You soon will meet friends—perhaps your family." I expected the worst. Instead, he stared at me, curiously, and then said, "Okay! You talk so I won't want a drink."

I started to talk about sports and kept it up until his gate opened. He seemed to enjoy it. We were talking together—as men. As we walked to the train together, he turned and thanked me. "I'm sorry I was nasty," he said.

Once I would have ducked a passenger like that with too much to drink, and I would never have gotten to know the good that was in him. Prejudice comes from not knowing other people, from not letting God's love join you together. But I do believe that God's love is working in our country today, knocking down the walls of hate that men have built up between them. You can feel the difference just in the last few years. All people are slowly opening out their hearts and minds to the spirit of God, and that spirit extends beyond the farthest horizon, uniting all men in brotherhood and in the love of Jesus Christ.

ROLAND GAMMON

"God is. God cares. God can be known."

* * *

Roland Gammon, the author–editor of this book, is a religious writer, lecturer, and communications consultant who lives in New York City. For fifteen years he was a working journalist on such national magazines as Life, Pageant, *and* See, *and today he writes for* McCall's, Good Housekeeping, Redbook, This Week, Parade, American Weekly, *and* Christian Herald. *He is the co-author (with Henry James Forman) of the best-selling volume on the world's great religions,* Truth Is One.

A native of Maine and a Phi Beta Kappa graduate of Colby College, Mr. Gammon is a member of the Overseas Press Club, Society of Magazine Writers, Religious Newswriters Association, The Laymen's Movement, International Christian Leadership, and The American Veterans Committee. He served with the U. S. Army Air Forces in the Middle East and Asia during World War II. A member and trustee of the Universalist Church of New York, he is a past president of the National Association of Universalist Men and presently serves as a national program committeeman for the Unitarian Universalist Association.

In line with his international activities, Mr. Gammon also is vice president of Communicorp, Inc., a New York public relations firm.

* * *

Exploration into God

WHEN ALEXANDER THE GREAT BECAME MASTER OF THE CIVILIZED world in the fifth century B.C., he led his triumphant armies across the Ganges down into the plains of India. Hearing in Old Delhi of an Indian prince who had renounced his wealth to seek the Lord, Alexander determined to meet him and learn the secret of his illuminated life. Finally, the emperor's couriers found Siddhartha Gautama and his disciples in a Deer Park near Benares where it was arranged for Alexander to see him.

When the Greek leader and entourage entered, the orange-robed Buddha was seated in meditation. Without formality, Alexander asked: "Tell me, Enlightened One, where is your god?" There was no reply, and again Alexander asked the question. Still the sage did not answer. Finally, the imperious conqueror raised his voice, "I command you, O Tathagata, where is your god?"

Softly, without opening his eyes, the Buddha replied: "God is in silence."

Many centuries later on the opposite side of the world, a young French girl named Bernadette Soubirous saw a glowing vision of the Virgin Mary in a rocky grotto near Lourdes. Leading a religious tour there in 1957, I overheard one of my party exclaim to a frail peasant woman outside the cathedral, "But why would the Holy Virgin want to appear to an untutored farm girl instead of to a recognized religious or political leader?"

"Ah, *mon ami*," the little lady said, "you do not understand. The Holy Virgin did not *appear* to Bernadette. It is just the opposite. Bernadette was able to *see* her."

My own religious quest has taken me from my birthplace in Caribou, Maine, to New York and New Delhi, to Chengtu and Rome and Jerusalem, to the shrines and holy places of the world's great faiths. More important, it has made me a pilgrim in search of my own soul. I am convinced that life is a divine miracle; that the universe is a living, luminous, limitless Being whose purpose is the development of higher consciousness and happier life; that everything of which we are aware—from atom to rosebud to leaping antelope to exploding nebulae—emerges from and is part of what Einstein calls one vast "unified field," and that the one activating field necessary to explain all other physical, biological, psychological, and electromagnetic fields is the *spiritual* field; that we see and hear and know God in exact proportion as our senses are cleansed, our minds enlightened, and our personalities unified; that in unselfish service, all-inclusive love, and Christlike dedication to God's will we issue at last into life eternal.

Heaven lies all about us, but we see it not. The Kingdom of God shines within us, but clouds of ignorance and indifference obscure the inner light. We live and move and have being in a world Soul or cosmic Consciousness, which envelops and interpenetrates the planet and its creatures like an invisible ocean; but like fish swimming in the earth's visible oceans, we can only ask: "Where is the sea?"

Thus for all of us, life should become an exploration into God. It should lead us to the discovery that there is an ideal Existence outside of time that parallels existence within time. ("God within, God without, beyond compare," sang Angelus Silesius, "a being wholly here and wholly there.") It should enable us to prove on our own pulses that body and soul are not two substances but one and that they are but two different ways of becoming aware of the Self. It should stir us to pass from holy matter to holy spirit, confident that the world is spiritualized in man and confident that man, the co-creator with God, is building here a pantheon of bread, beauty, and brotherhood wherein the divine order will triumph.

The Hindu seer Shankara tells us: "He who believes, perceives." Jesus of Nazareth, the perfect embodiment of that Christ which pervades and perfects man and nature, told his Apostles: "Only the pure in heart shall see God." The Protestant mystic, William Law, once wrote: "Although God is everywhere present, He is only present to thee in the deepest and most central part of thy soul. This depth is the unity, the eternity—I had almost said the infinity of thy soul—for it is so infinite that nothing can satisfy or give it rest but the infinity of God." So, for each one of us today the same God lives and He lives in us; the same pathway of silence, of service, of ceaseless and selfless love leads to His presence; the same Incarnating Christ—called by whatever name, Logos, Tao, Nirvana, Atman, Elan Vital—still recovers and redeems the living cosmos within the energizing, organizing layers of his unifying Love.

Thus, little by little we come to *see* and to *understand* and to *love*. God is. God cares. God can be known. In my own case, this steep ascent to heaven began in a happy childhood, inspired by a poetical mother and a hard-working father, nurtured in a love-filled home, and victory-sweet school days, confirmed in the ever challenging Universalist Church, and an ever widening editorial career. Gradually, through innumerable falterings and failures, I began to see the earth's "10,000 things" in their infinite Oneness. Gradually, through innumerable joys and loves and sunlit openings, I began to understand life as a sacred trust with the individual soul sustaining it, moral law governing it, and an immanent and transcendent Love lifting it upward. Gradually, through work and worship, study, service, prayer, adventure, and the insights of both victory and defeat, I began to love God not only as the absolute creator, lawgiver, preserver of the Void's far turning galaxies and the Atom's sun-bursting vortex, but as life's infinitely tender Father–Mother who knocks at the gate of every lonely heart and quickens the spirit of every child who seeks Him. Gradually—and through God's grace it shall continue—I began to love the whole creation and everyone in it with an all-encompassing love, even while learning ever so faintly to

> Hear through the roar of mortal things
> The God's immortal whisperings;
> See the world wonder rise and fall;
> And know that Beauty made it all.